Glyphs and Gallows

The Rock Art of Clo-oose and the Wreck of the *John Bright*

Glyphs and Gallows

The Rock Art of Clo-oose and the Wreck of the *John Bright*

Peter Johnson

Heritage House

Copyright © 1999 by Peter Johnson

CANADIAN CATALOGUING IN PUBLICATION DATA

Johnson, Peter Wilton
Glyphs and gallows

Includes bibliographical references and index.
ISBN 1-895811-94-5

1. West Coast Trail (B.C.)—History.
2. Nootka Indians—History.
3. Petroglyphs—British Columbia—Clo-oose.
I. Title.

FC3844.4.J64 1999   971.1'2 C99-910743-7   F1089.V3J64 1999

First edition 1999

All rights reserved. No part of this publication may be reproduced, stored in a retrieval system, or transmitted in any form or by any means— electronic, mechanical, audio recording, or otherwise—without the written permission of the publisher or, in the case of photocopying, a licence from CANCOPY, Toronto, Canada.

Heritage House wishes to acknowledge the financial support of the Government of Canada and Heritage Canada through the Book Publishing Industry Development Program, the British Columbia Arts Council, and the staff of the British Columbia Archives and Records Service (BCARS).

Design, layout, and maps by Darlene Nickull
Edited by Joanne Richardson

HERITAGE HOUSE PUBLISHING COMPANY LTD.
#108 - 17665 66 A Avenue, Surrey, B.C. V3S 2A7

Printed in Canada

Canadä

For Melanie, Stephanie, and Alain

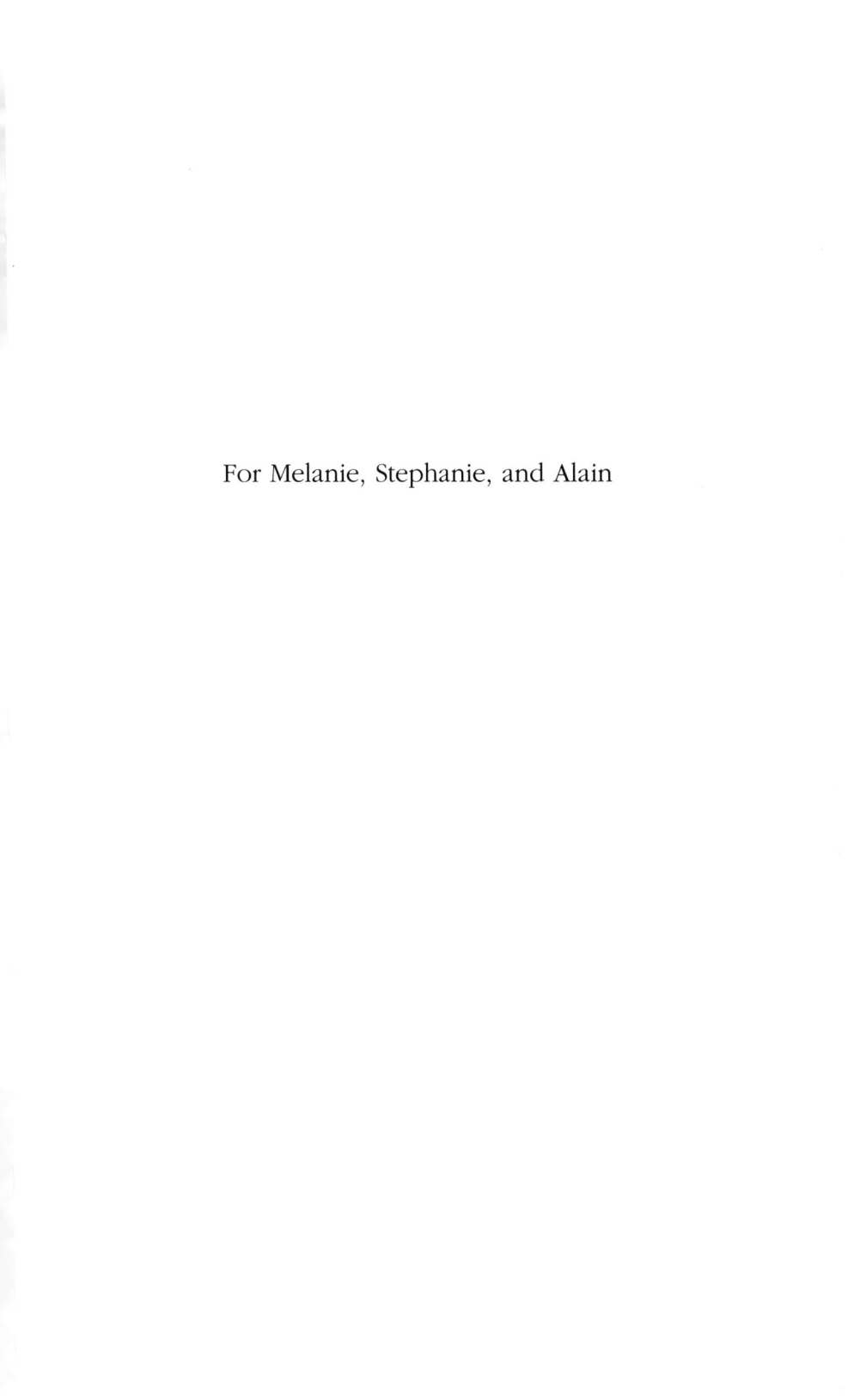

Acknowledgments

Beth Hill was my mentor. She first showed me the power and the beauty of the petroglyphs. Her enthusiasm was infectious. She met several of my high-school classes and encouraged me, when I visited her home in Victoria, to go beyond a rough draft of the *John Bright* story. Thanks also to my good friend and colleague John Gellard, whose keen eye and unflinching spirit made the long slogs into Clo-oose adventures in themselves. Many of the photographs are his. Jennifer Mohan of the British Columbia Provincial Archives in Victoria went well beyond the call of duty to assist my efforts. Liza Verity and David Taylor of the National Maritime Museum, Greenwich, and Mary-Anne MacDougall of the Vancouver Public Library, did the same. Thanks also to David Stone and David Griffiths of the Underwater Society of British Columbia for much needed information. Thanks, too, to my neighbour Ilze Elliston for the use of her collection of coastal history books. Canada Coast Guard Communications Officer Micheline Brodeur enabled me to return to Clo-oose and see Matlahaw Point, while coxwains and crew Geoff Lindsay, Cliff Evans, Don Amos, Jeff Osterman, Ian McKenzie, and helicopter pilot Glenn Diachuk, brought it off. Rick Baker and Connie Strub of Blue Pacific Yacht Charters kept my sailor's hands well worn. The work of Wilson Duff was inspirational. Thanks to Darlene Nickull, designer at Heritage House, for her enthusiasm. Thanks also to Rodger Touchie, my publisher, who kept telling me to have fun, and to Joanne Richardson, my editor, who made me pay for it.

Table of Contents

Introduction   7
Chapter 1: Echoes of Myth: The Glyphs of Clo-oose   9
Chapter 2: The Sound of "Nu-tka" and the Fight for Trade, 1774-1875   19
Chapter 3: Pilgrimage   42
Chapter 4: Victoria, 1869: Afraid to Know Itself   55
Chapter 5: Dead Reckoning   72
Chapter 6: The Admiralty on the Northwest Coast: 1812-1869   81
Chapter 7: The Riddle of the Glyphs: A Tryst With Nature   104
Chapter 8: The Wreck of the John Bright   119
Chapter 9: Frocked and Righteous Men: A Terrible Crime and Its Punishment   142
Chapter 10: The Motive for Metaphor   172
Epilogue: Revelation and Desecration   201
Appendix   217
Endnotes   225
Selected Bibliography   243
Index   249

While researching events related to this story in the British Columbia Provincial Archives, I happened upon a 30-page handwritten letter sent to a retired publisher/politician by a troubled missionary who had spent most of his career amongst the Nuu-chah-nulth of the west coast of Vancouver Island. That letter, dated March 7, 1904, would once and for all change my perspective on the *John Bright* affair and some of its key personalities—long seen more as heroes than as villains.

Throughout this story my personal journal is in italics while the historical narrative is in regular type.

P. W. Johnson

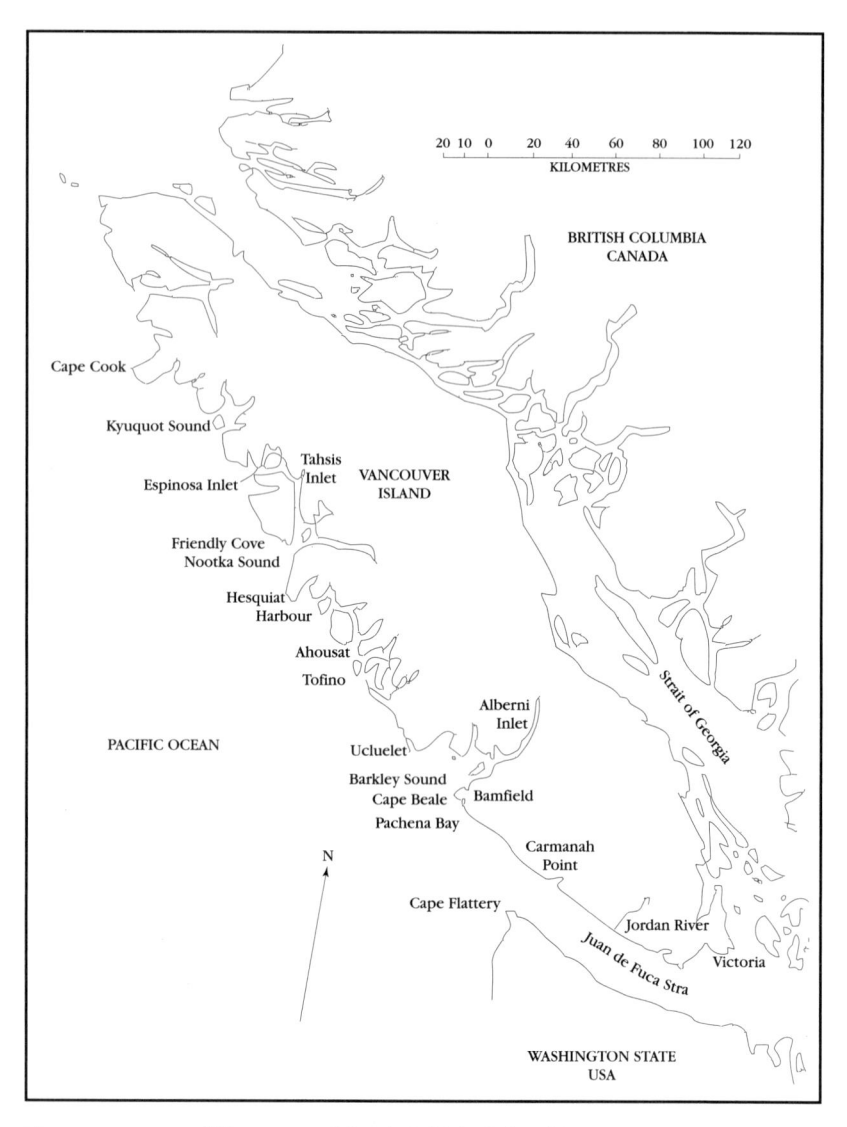

The west coast of Vancouver Island, British Columbia

Introduction

At the core of *Glyphs and Gallows* lie shipwrecks, headless bodies, corrupt sea captains, misguided journalists, hangings, and nineteenth-century racism. And while the cast of characters may ensure us of some colourful content, they are not in themselves the story.

This is a story in three parts. First, this is a story about Aboriginal rock art, and it begins with my search for a unique set of petroglyphs that exist on a remote, uninhabited part of the Northwest Coast. Petroglyphs, or glyphs, as they are commonly known, were part of the art produced by various Native cultures that lived on this raincoast, stretching from the Columbia River Basin to the very outermost edge of the Aleutian Islands. For centuries, thousands of curiously cryptic images were graven upon sandstone shelves and other exposed bedrock bordering this northern sea. The glyphs recorded much of the culture and spirituality of these ancient coastal peoples and, not surprisingly, marked some of the events that were to bring about their demise. One such event, the arrival of the European coastal traders, did not escape being recorded. In a sense, this story started the day I read about an exceptional set of sailing-ship glyphs that was imprinted on the coastline rocks near the now abandoned outer-coast village of Clo-oose.

Second, this is the story of the clash between the colonial empire of Britain and those Aboriginal peoples on the Northwest Coast whose land, life, and cultural traditions were taken from them. British colonialism in the mid-nineteenth century remained unabashedly expansionist in spite of the rude awakening the American Revolution had brought decades earlier. Twenty years of Napoleonic wars (1793-1815), and a subsidiary confrontation with the United States (1812-1815), made life tough for all classes in Britain. Too often, Britannia's sea-lanes were closed, and overseas supplies of wheat and other foodstuffs were threatened. The ill-conceived Corn Laws (1815) made the poor poorer, and as Britain's industrial revolution took hold, the unspoiled villages of rural England were left to the birds. Whole populations migrated to the cores of unsanitary cities, where wretchedness fed only the growing moods of discontent. Those who fought their desperate plight soon felt the stern hand of government repression in the cotton factory towns of the midlands and in the massacres of Peterloo (1819). Soon the downtrodden looked for any means of escape.

The droves of working poor who made it to Upper Canada and Lower Canada saw the ownership of land as a real possibility as long as they looked west. From a more elevated perspective, the members of the English upper class, many of whom disdained a life in the Church of England or the army, also saw the New World as a source of opportunity, adventure, and potential wealth. Rapidly, the enterprise of ambitious immigrants spread across North America. By the 1860s, in the remote colony of British Columbia, just north of the fast-growing Oregon Territory, a cultural clash between the region's Aboriginals and merchant adventurers was inevitable. The glyphs of Clo-oose can only be understood if one considers the ramifications of conflicting values and the imperfect evolution of colonial government. Equally relevant is the role of the Royal Navy in the Pacific.

Third, this is the story of my quest to discover the glyphs themselves. This story centres on the West Coast Trail but begins and ends near the Native village of Hesquiat on the northern outer coast of Vancouver Island, where an English trading barque was wrecked in the spring of 1869. The events surrounding that shipwreck typified the hardened attitudes of the Native and European cultures of the day.

Research 130 years after the disaster has yielded insights not only into the ensuing call for justice in the colonial capital of Victoria, but also into the evolving nature of both social history and our understanding of Aboriginal art itself. In this context, we must explore the nature of petroglyphs, understand the origins of their iconography, and raise overdue questions about their meaning. *Glyphs and Gallows* attempts to interweave two pertinent aspects of the cultural origins of British Columbia — its coastal history and its long tradition of petroglyph art.

Peter Johnson, July 1999

CHAPTER 1
Echoes of Myth: The Glyphs of Clo-oose

Here are our signatures: geese, fish, eskimo faces, girl-guide cookies, ink drawings, tree-plantings, summer storms, and winter emanations.

Miriam Waddington[1]

I was drawn to them first by their abstraction and then by their age. I sought them, and lingered among them for many years, because they were filled with mystery. Many were human or animal in form, yet I knew that their artists had no intention of limiting them according to such Western notions of singularity. They are more compelling than the silent Stone Circles that I had seen years before while hiking on the open grasslands of Alberta and portaging between the marshy, lowland lakes of northwestern Ontario. They are related, I would learn, to the rock art of the Columbia Plateau and of the Amur River region of Khabarovsk, Siberia.[2] They had the same presence as the Megalithic Menhirs and Dolmens — the long rocks and rock tables of Brittany; and they held the same fascination as did the strange stones of Avebury, the stone Tikis of Polynesia, and the Moai of Easter Island. Best of all, they were right here, beneath my feet.

Petroglyphs are found all along this thousand-mile coast that stretches from Oregon to Alaska. There are literally hundreds of them, with that many more again, still moss-covered, waiting to be rediscovered. These cryptic rock-art engravings are highly significant renderings of the myths, dream wishes, events, and privileges belonging to the Indigenous peoples who arrived in this harsh and lovely land some 2,000 years before the Europeans. These silent stone images are of small faces (many with "halos" of radiating lines); whales; strange sea creatures; squatting men shown

Degnan Bay is near Gabriola Passage, separating Gabriola Island and Valdes Island in the Gulf Islands. This tidal passage has strong currents and has been a fine salmon-fishing area for seals, whales, and humans. The internal structural lines are common to such glyphs on the inner coast and are believed to represent a human skeleton. If so, then this glyph has its origins in shamanistic rites.

frontally, arms uplifted as in a dance; horses; men on horses; deer; raven; simple concentric circles; symbols of genitalia; wonderful curvilinear lines; family groups; and much, much, more. They were graven upon beach boulders and shoreline rock shelves by artisans who held a special status within Aboriginal tribal groups. Their forms and meaning, and their relationship to other Aboriginal art forms, are yet to be fully appreciated. Stone sculptures, masks, ceremonies, songs, and stories offer only a glimpse into a complex way of life that differed vastly from our own.

My first encounter with petroglyphs was magical because I came to them by sea. The gods were with me that fine August day some years ago, as the last remnants of a rainy, boisterous southeasterly drove me steadily north, up Trincomali Channel under reefed main and small cruising spinnaker. I had put into Degnan Bay, Gabriola Island, to await slack water in a channel leading to the Strait of Georgia. I had just sailed up from Victoria and intended to overnight about midway through the islands before tackling the windy gulf the next morning.

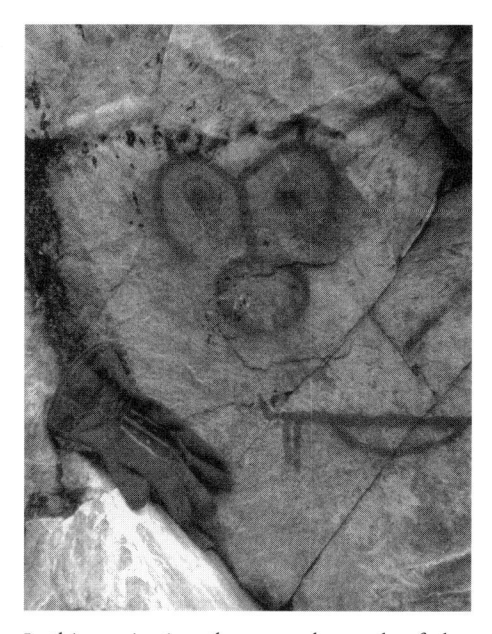

Is this projection the pursed mouth of the "Dzonokwa," the female supernatural ogress who dwelt far in the woods and ate children? Or is it a rendering of a Kwakwaka'wakw "Xwe'xwe," whose large eyes and huge lolling tongue were marks of high rank? Could it be a labret? Among the Tlingit, a carved bone was inserted inside the lower lip of a woman after her first period. The size of the labret was an indication of status. Whatever the case, this petroglyph is very much about power.

The Gulf Islands lie between the mainland coast of British Columbia and Vancouver Island, a rugged land mass that protects a myriad of inner waterways from the open fetch of the Pacific Ocean. This sailors' mecca of pristine waters and accessible shoreline has provided me with what now seem endless summers of safe anchorages and interesting harbours. In order to make the evening's anchorage, I needed to cross Gabriola Passage at slack water.

Slack water occurs four times within 24 hours. It coincides with the changing tides: a low and a high during the day and the same during the night. At the turn of the tide, ocean undulations cease, and the surge of water through constricted channels hangs momentarily, like a breath at the top of a yawn, before beginning its relentless reverse flow. To navigate a narrow pass at any other time in a calm wind is to invite being swept away. I would wait for slack water at Degnan Bay.

A local fisher, who treated the small government wharf at Degnan Bay as his own, wouldn't let me raft up to an old seiner for my half-hour wait, so I anchored in the bay and went for a row. Serendipity! I saw it first on a sandstone shelf, just inches above the rising water. It was a large glyph of a killer whale,[3] at least it was interpreted as such by locals because of its huge dorsal fin. It was located near the end of the bay, where a small, flooding, freshwater stream met the ocean. Behind the

This glyph, pecked onto a beach boulder on the northern end of Gabriola Island, faces the open Strait of Georgia. On an adjacent boulder, a ceremonial bowl has been carved out of a natural depression in the rock.

glyph was a steep bank that looked layered. It was full of shell fragments and may, in the distant past, have been a midden. At the moment of high tide — slack water — the glyph would be entirely covered.

I was captivated and lingered in this secluded bay in the late afternoon sun. Suddenly, I was with those who had abraded the glyph in centuries past. Did they put ochre in the deep-grooved outlines, intending it to wash out to the pass at high slack and warn the Salmon People of the danger of the killer whale? Or was it a warning to the Salmon People, from their ancient cousins, the Coast Salish, that they were soon to be caught? I photographed and drew the glyph, wondering how many millennia it had resided here. Slack water passed. I would stay the night and walk over to Silva Bay and see my friends, Phyllis and Ted Reeve, at Page's Marina. They would know about the glyph.

Of course they knew. The Reeves had been at Silva Bay for twelve years. Ted had been a physician in Vancouver, Phyllis a university librarian. They had retired to Silva Bay to operate a delightfully quaint marina and a small shop that Phyllis filled with books of local lore. In addition, this warm, gentle couple had turned their house into a gallery for island artists. In a lifetime of sailing and teaching the humanities, I must have brought hundreds of my high-school students here on June trips, where they joined those from places ranging from Carolina to Calgary, England to Illinois.

Phyllis knew that the abraded lines of the whale gylph had been deepened by Frank Degnan at the turn of the century and that the X-ray *style and oval eye were significant. I bought the Bentley book[4] and the Hill book,[5] went back to my stout little vessel, the* Molly Golver, *and began to read. The die had been cast.*

Later that fall I assigned an excerpt from the journals of Samuel Hearne to a senior Humanities class. The discussion was lively and full of questions about the power of shamans in Aboriginal culture. I thought of the whale glyph at Degnan Bay and called Beth Hill. A field trip was definitely necessary. Beth and Ray Hill had, in 1974, written a remarkable, comprehensive book on petroglyphs on the Northwest Coast. She was delighted by my call and met us all on Gabriola Island. She showed us the Dancing Shaman and a haetlik, or sea monster, at sites that were more compelling than medieval cathedrals. I was hooked.

By bicycle, often by boat, I spent my ensuing summers exploring the south coast of British Columbia, with copies of old theses and long-out-of-print books. I would follow the vague directions and offhand comments of wise old islanders who had come upon, or had heard about, a particular glyph on a rocky promontory, a secluded bay, or a shingle beach. Many authors helped to sustain my inquiry, but they never fully satisfied my appetite.[6] Then, one recent summer, I heard of a set of glyphs on the west coast of Vancouver Island that was so rare, so unmatched, that I simply had to see it.

The glyphs in question are near Clo-oose, a small, now abandoned village on the outer coast of Vancouver Island south of Barkley Sound, near where the Nitinat River flows into the sea. It is a beautiful, forbidding place, part of "the graveyard of the Pacific," where vessels, caught on a lee shore or in an unrelenting fog, would come crashing in, spilling out their human cargo to perish either in the surf or in the desolation of the wilderness. A life-saving trail was finally cleared from Barkley Sound to Port Renfrew at the turn of the century in order to give those who survived the surf a chance for life. But the cold, the rain, and the fast-flowing rivers soon reminded them that rescue, even if one made it ashore, was by no means a given. Former students who had hiked the trail reported noting the petroglyph site at Blow-Hole Beach in the Sierra Club guide, but they were unable to find its exact location.

What was so compelling about the Clo-oose glyphs was their subject: European sailing ships and, as at least two people have reported, a particularly heinous maritime massacre. The first reports of the alleged crimes reached government officials in Victoria in the early spring of 1869. Captain James Christenson, of the sealing schooner Surprise, was en route to Victoria from one of his coastal trading forays when he heard of a stranded vessel on the west coast of Vancouver Island. The ship had struck a reef and washed ashore just off the Native village of Hesquiat, north of Clayoquot Sound. Many had reportedly been drowned. When Christenson actually surveyed the wreck, what he claimed to have found would first horrify those in Victoria and then result in a call for blood.

In early February 1869, bound for Australia from Port Gamble (Washington) with a load of lumber, the trading barque John Bright ran into a heavy southeast gale not long after clearing Cape Flattery off the western entrance to the Strait of Juan de Fuca. Unable to beat its way off the lee shore of the west coast of Vancouver Island, the John Bright was slowly driven in and wrecked on one of the many reefs off Boulder Point (Matlahaw), south of Nootka Sound. Of the reported 22 people on board, it seems those who drowned were lucky. After Christenson's investigation, word spread that those who made it ashore were shot to death by the Natives of the nearby village of Hesquiat.

The press was involved from the start, and all through that summer of 1869 the John Bright affair was part of public consciousness. With a nineteenth-century penchant for the macabre, journalists repeatedly inflamed public opinion by reporting all the gruesome details covered in an official investigation, the ensuing trial, and the resulting awful punishments. Possibly no Victoria citizen was more affected by the events of that summer than was David William Higgins, owner and publisher of the British Colonist. He would go on to play a major role in British Columbia's joining Confederation and would, eventually, become speaker of the B.C. legislature. Higgins was so moved by the events surrounding the John Bright affair that in 1904, over 35 years after witnessing the trial, he was compelled to chronicle them in his book, The Passing of a Race. Higgins's account unleashed a series of events that was further complicated by a discovery in the 1920s. A Victoria reporter of the day provided illustrations for a fascinating story of newly discovered sailing-ship glyphs and other unusual images near Clo-oose. Next, a mystery person, signing himself simply D.H., responded to the newspaper article by unveiling an astonishing possibility: the petroglyphs of Clo-oose could well be an Aboriginal rendering of the story Higgins had written two *decades earlier. Ninety-five years after Higgins told Edwardian Victoria of the* John Bright *tragedy, I set out to find these glyphs and examine the validity of this theory.*

Most petroglyphs are of animal or human forms, although a single zoomorphic or anthropomorphic distinction isn't always accurate. Some glyphs contain both animal and human forms, as in the man-chasing-deer glyph of Lok Bay on Gabriola Island. Some are both, as in the strange mermaid glyph of Douglas Channel, near Kitimat, or the fish-and-mask face of Return Passage, near Bella Bella, halfway up the B.C. coast. All the forms and motifs do seem, however, to have stylistic peculiarities common to a particular time or region. To rediscover a piece of Aboriginal rock art that was directly related to a non-Aboriginal occurrence, such as the nineteenth-century coastal maritime fur trade, would be unique. I could remember seeing two striking samples of Aboriginal art that were analogous to the object of my quest.

On July 21, 1947, the Hudson's Bay Company vessel Nascopie *sank after striking a reef near Cape Dorset off the southwestern tip of Baffin Island. The Inuit artist and hunter Peter Pitseolak, who often used an old Kodak box camera to help him in making drawings, witnessed the event. I remembered seeing his telling photograph of the sinking of the* Nascopie *in an exhibition of Inuit art. The picture froze a "corner experience" in the lives of his people. The Inuit of Seekooseelak (Cape Dorset) are known to have dated the end of their way of life to that event. Pitseolak's simple comment, "What it carried helped the people before we had the government,"[7] spoke volumes of the hard and proud life of his people out on the land of the Eastern Arctic.*

Similarly, the Inuit artist Pudlo Pudlat spoke of the pale blue forms of the first airplanes that visited his west Baffin Island settlement as "an iceberg or a big hill of snow." In his acrylic "Airplanes in a Settlement," Pudlo saw the aircraft as huge birds and pale green serpents.[8] He, like Pitseolak, with an artist's idiosyncratic vision was doing something more important than portraying a simple event.

The sailing-ship glyphs of Clo-oose, like the works of Pitseolak and Pudlo, are significant as both artistic and historical works. Previous to them, the shamans and artisans who produced glyphs, often in a hallucinogenic trance, concerned themselves solely with subject matter and design motifs rooted deeply within their own tribal history. The

The vessel *Nascopie*, aground off Baffin Island in 1947, was one of many HBC vessels whose tinned and packaged goods signalled the end of a way of life that had prevailed in the Eastern Arctic for thousands of years.

sailing-ship glyphs of Clo-oose changed all that. If they still existed, they would be an eloquent and frightening expression of two cultures in collision. These particular glyphs would represent an Aboriginal view of a period when traders, colonial governments, missionaries, alcohol, and disease came to yet another remote coast and almost destroyed a people.

My working method would be simple. I would hike the West Coast Trail to Clo-oose and find the glyphs; then I would photograph and draw the entire site. Placing the sailing-ship glyphs within the context of other Aboriginal cultural forms and motifs, I would compare the rigging of the ships depicted with the sail-plans of vessels involved in the John Bright *affair. I would further research historical references pertaining to the Clo-oose glyphs and others like them. Finally, I would examine the references and compare them with the knowledge gained over years of research on such glyphs.*

The big problem was the location. It didn't seem right. The Clo-oose site of the sailing-ship glyphs is over 100 kilometres south of Hesquiat Harbour. What would this glyph be doing so far from its origins? Why would a shaman-carver choose to carve such a glyph here?

One possible answer lies in the topography of the outer coast of Vancouver Island, south of Esperanza Inlet. Immediately south of Hesquiat is the open, uninhabited coast, which itself is cut deeply to the northwest by Sydney Inlet. Here, huge first-growth Douglas fir rise steeply

Pudlo's aircraft flew between two times: the traditional and the modern. Depicted as a mythic figure, the airplane seems to have sinister connotations.

right from the water. Most of Clayoquot Sound is still like this today: uncut stands of forest growing down to the ocean. There are few cliffs and practically no flat rock shelves. Moreover, by 1864, after a series of Royal Navy gunboat attacks on at least nine villages, Clayoquot Sound was almost denuded of Native people. By the 1870s, Ahousat, safely tucked away in a niche on Flores Island at the edge of the sound, was becoming the central Aboriginal settlement.

The sandy shores of Long Beach, today part of majestic Pacific Rim National Park, further limit appropriate petroglyph sites for another 32 kilometres. There is only one known glyph site along this stretch of coast. At Quisitis Point, a rocky promontory midway between Wickaninnish Bay and Wreck Bay, there is a single glyph of a large fish eating a smaller one. Further away, at Pachena Point, the southern promontory of Barkley Sound, a small sandstone cave contains a glyph of a squatting man and a few small fish. Beyond that it is only when we get to Clo-oose, the now abandoned whaling village southeast of Nitinat Narrows, that the sandy coast gives way to small, rock-shelved coves appropriate to extensive carvings. Simply put, south of Hesquiat there are precious few rock formations that could sustain glyphs of any stature.

Another reason for the location of the Clo-oose glyphs became apparent when I made a brief 1996 visit to Ray Williams, chief of Yuquot (Friendly Cove). We didn't talk of the Clo-oose glyphs, but we did talk of the alliances made among Nuu-chah-nulth-speaking villages along the coast in the wake of the devastating smallpox outbreak of 1862. Such alliances are known to have existed before European contact. Indeed, Maquinna, the chief of Yuquot who greeted Captain James Cook, was brother-in-law to Chief Wickaninnish of Clayoquot Sound. I would also learn that the Ahousat informant Winnifred David, who recalled oral histories of first contact at Nootka to the linguist Barbara Efrat in 1978, was herself related to the Moachat of Nootka through her husband's grandmother. In other words, the thesis suggesting that Hesquiat stone carvers could have ended up near Clo-oose has merit.

The coup de grace came when I discovered a letter containing an early account of the glyphs, printed in the Victoria Daily Times on September 18, 1926. The letter, in itself a remote and mysterious morsel of history, confirms the friendliness among Nuu-chah-nulth villages on the outer coast after 1870. It speculates "that a native fully impressed with the enormity of the crime, perhaps even one of the men who participated in it, must have fled the scene, sought refuge in a nearby village, and as one who had been taught the lesson fully, may have drawn the story on the rocks."[9]

So I considered the topography, the alliances and inter-marriages, and the proximity of Hesquiat to Clo-oose as plausible reasons for the Clo-oose site of the John Bright *glyphs. It was all I had, and it did entail a certain rationale. In any case, for now it was enough. I became more determined than ever to study the petroglyphs of Clo-oose.*

CHAPTER 2
The Sound of "Nu-tka" and the Fight for Trade, 1774-1875

So here we are, the lot of us
builders and upsetters of apple carts
dispossessed and dispossessors.
Which found the life they hoped to find?
Which have shadows in their sunshine still?

          Hubert Evans[1]

The landscape is essentially vertical. Approaching the land mass of Vancouver Island from the open Pacific Ocean one sees literally a wall of mountains. Long, misty, blue-green fjords lead the eye up to them. With incredible cloud formations about their tops and ever-shifting patches of dark and lighter green, they look almost tropical. After the cold and the wind of the open sea, they are inviting. Often, low ocean headlands that are difficult to detect against the pale-green backdrop open up into huge, deep sounds that, more often than not, contain rocky, tree-clad islands. Everywhere, it seems, trees grow to the water's edge. Only in a small bay, tucked behind a peninsula, or at the very end of a long, steep-sided fjord, do the waterfalls and the mouths of rivers create land upon which to live. On a gentle summer day, resplendent with lapping water, reflected sun, and rainbow mist, an occasional deer or bear might forage here. In the winter, with the deluge that made the trees grow tall, life on this toehold pressed up against the mountains would certainly be a life lived "on the edge." This is, indeed, a beguiling place, but it is not a place to establish a civilization. And yet a certain people did.

They were the "Muwacath" or "Moachat"—"people of the deer"[2]— and they understood the necessity of incessantly migrating between the

Sydney Inlet, near Nootka Sound. Beguiling verticality on a rare summer's day.

Captain Cook's first harbour on the Northwest Coast gave him protection from the ravages of the open Pacific Ocean (bottom) and access to the treasures of Nootka Sound.

inner and outer coasts as food resources, and the climate, fluctuated sharply with the seasons. They were but one band of the "Nuu-chah-nulth," and behind them stood the "mountains in a row,"[3] the origin of their ancient name. It was to this place, the Moachat homeland, that the sailing ships portrayed at Clo-oose inevitably sailed. And so this is where our story must begin.

When his ship, the *Santiago,* dropped anchor off San Esteban (Estevan Point) in Nootka Sound on August 8, 1774, Juan Perez became the first European to hear the Moachat dialect.[4] The Native people circled his vessel cautiously in their canoes all night long; the next day "they drew closer, offering us sardines, and they exchanged otter and wolf

Captain James Cook (inset) recruited artist John Webber to accompany him on his third voyage to the Pacific and his only visit to what would become the British Columbia coast. Cook's relationship with the Moachat was initially easy and amiable. John Webber's feeling towards this most sophisticated and humane explorer is clearly evident here.

skins for Monterey shells."[5] The Perez visit was a brief one, for a rising gale would soon push the *Santiago* onto the nearby dangerous lee shore of Estevan Point. The Spanish captain was forced to cut his cable and head to sea.

In 1778 James Cook, on his third expedition into the Pacific, sailed towards these same northern latitudes with Captains Charles Clerke and John Gore aboard the *Resolution* and the *Discovery*. They too dropped anchor in an inlet the Spanish had already named San Lorenzo. In the tradition of the British explorers, Cook, of course, rechristened the vast inlet King George's Sound. And he encountered the Moachat at a location he charted as Nu-tka.

There is no hereditary village called Nootka among today's Moachat-speakers. The incorporation of the word "Nootka" into the English language was the result of Cook's misunderstanding of the Moachat word "nu-tka," which means "circle about." Native oral tradition records that upon Cook's arrival on March 29, 1778, he was told to "nu-tka" (i.e., "circle about") the open, rocky headland and shelter his battered ships in a safer anchorage facing the Moachat village of Yuquot. On Cook's charts, later published in England, "Nu-tka," the direction, became "Nootka," the place. And it was to this strange new place that the entrepreneurial instincts of maritime traders from Britain and the United States would soon be drawn.

As was the case with most of his meetings with Aboriginal peoples of the Pacific, Cook established a comfortable dialogue with the Moachat. Perez had stayed little more than a day; Cook stayed a month. Throughout April 1778, Cook traded, reprovisioned, and repaired his ships, first at the village of Yuquot and later in Ship's Cove on nearby Bligh Island. There, he careened the *Resolution* to refurbish the copper plating lining its hull.

European and Aboriginal perspectives on these early encounters are as different as are their respective cultures. Cook saw the Northwest Coast as a source of wealth, ripe for the plucking. Captains of commerce who read his *Voyages* would soon arrive in droves. Aboriginal peoples soon began to call the White traders "mamalni" because their houses "lived literally on the water."[6] Their initial impression ranged from fear to ridicule. In non-literate cultures, such as that of the Moachat, history is passed down through the generations by oral narratives that establish a person's particular status within the tribal unit. The linguist Barbara Efrat has done much to revive and preserve this oral tradition, and she recorded the narrative of Peter Webster of Yuquot, who told this story:

> I wouldn't say the first ship, but I do know that it was seen south-east side of Estevan Point. This Hesquiat seen something strange out in the open Pacific, looks like house poles out there ... They saw these guy wires for each mast. The blocks look like skulls. Us old people would say an Indian word that means "skull of a dead human," just the bones. And this is what they thought it was, dead people that was aboard that ship ... somebody composed a song right away.[7]

What Peter Webster's ancestors were looking at were the "dead-eyes"—rounded pieces of dark hardwood, each bored with three holes in a triangular pattern. The dead-eyes were spliced into the lower ends of the shrouds that held up the masts of the vessels at about the height of a person's head. The dead-eyes were then fastened to the ship's chain plates with adjustable lanyards. From a distance, the dead-eyes and their attached lines would look like the outline of a human skeleton. Shades of Coleridge's *Rime of the Ancient Mariner*!

The informant Winnifred David had married into a family with both Clayoquot and Nuu-chah-nulth origins. She related a significantly different story regarding first contact:

> The Indians didn't know what on earth it was ... So they went out to the ship and they thought it was a fish come alive with people. And one of the men was saying to this other guy, "See, see ... he must have been a dog salmon, that guy there, he's got a crooked nose" ... Those people, they must have been fish. They've come alive into people. Look at that one, he's a humpback ... They call it ca*pi, they're humpback fish. So they went ashore and told the big chief [Maquinna].[8]

For his part, James Cook's first impressions of the Moachat, though understandably less tied to notions of spiritual transformation, were equally concerned with outer appearances. "The men throw frequently over their other garments the skin of a bear, wolf, or sea otter, with the hair outward, and tie it as a cloak, near the upper part, wearing it sometimes before, and sometimes behind."[9]

Of their longhouses and technology, Cook was sure of his own cultural supremacy:

Their furniture consists of chests and boxes of various sizes, piled upon each other, at the sides or ends of each house ... Many of these boxes are painted black, and studded with the teeth of animals, or rudely decorated with figures of birds carved. To complete the scene of confusion, in different parts of their habitations are hung up implements of fishing, and other articles.[10]

With respect to the design and execution of their manufactures, and mechanic arts, they are more extensive and ingenious than could possibly be expected from the natural disposition of the people, and the little progress they have made in civilization.[11]

The Moachat dialect that Cook and his fellow seamen heard was one of several that made up the Nuu-chah-nulth language, which was spoken from Kyuquot Sound on the northwest coast of Vancouver Island to Port Renfrew in the south. The dialects were all mutually intelligible, and they constituted a language that Europeans once referred to as "Nootka."

The Nuu-chah-nulth language is closely related to Nitinaht, which is spoken on southern Vancouver Island, and to Makah, which is spoken on the Olympic Peninsula of Washington State.[12] The Belgian priest Father Brabant, who built the first mission at Hesquiat in 1874, noted eighteen different tribal units residing from the entrance of the Strait of Juan de Fuca to Cape Cook, all speaking the same language.[13] The relationship between various dialects of the Nuu-chah-nulth language down the outer coast of Vancouver Island is important to our story of the *John Bright* in that it provides yet another clue to the origins of the strange petroglyphs of Clo-oose.[14]

The European quest into the North Pacific was not without political purpose. The Spanish came to see what the Russians were doing; the British came to see what the Spanish were doing; and the Americans came to cash in on what everybody was doing!

What the Russians were doing was quietly establishing a trading monopoly in the North Pacific. Urged eastward in the early eighteenth century by the youthful and energetic Peter the Great, and his newly formed Academy of Sciences, Russian sailors soon charted the unknown arc of the North Pacific between the continents of Asia and North America. In their wake, Russia discovered not only the possibility of new colonial expansion and new northern commercial sea routes within the Asia-

Pacific basin, but also a vast fur-trading region that could readily offset the diminishing fur harvest in Siberia.[15]

Spain, however, claimed the Pacific and the west coasts of North and South America through the 1760 papal decree, the Treaty of Tordesillas, by right of the explorations by Cortes, Balboa, Juan de Fuca, and others. What Perez discovered in 1774 was that the Russians had been exploring and trading on the north coast since the 1740s. Further voyages north by Quadra and Maurelle in 1775, and Artega in 1779, confirmed Russian expansion south from Unalaska. The American War of Independence resulted in a brief hiatus of Spanish activity on the Northwest Coast, yet it convinced the viceroy of Mexico, Antonio Flores, that American settlement north of Mexico (California) was inevitable. So in 1788, Esteban Josef Martinez (who had been with Perez aboard the *Santiago* four years earlier) was ordered to take possession of Nootka Sound and establish a Spanish fortification at Nootka.

What the Spanish did not count on was the tremendous impact of the 1784 Admiralty-approved publication of Captain Cook's first, second, and third *Voyages*. One passage stood out: "There is no doubt but a very beneficial fur trade might be carried out with the inhabitants of this vast coast, but unless a northern passage is found it seems rather too remote for Great Britain to receive any emolument from it."[16]

Any hope of attaining the much sought-after prize offered for the discovery of the fabled Strait of Anian, or the Northwest Passage, for which Drake, de Fuca, Cook, and others had searched so long and so rigorously, was quickly fading. Indeed, Cook's old shipmate from his second voyage, Richard Pickersgill, had crossed the Atlantic and beat a course to Baffin Bay, hoping to meet Cook midway through what was still believed to be the "open" Arctic ocean. In so doing, Britain would have closed the ring on the Americas and discovered for the Empire the shortest route to Cathay and Jipango.[17] Such a route was never to be found, but other lucrative rewards appeared for the taking. Cook and Pickersgill never met, but Cook would find much Spanish activity at Nootka. Hence, the reward attached to the discovery of a shorter route to the Far East was eclipsed by the fur-trading opportunities that Cook envisioned. The *Voyages* were, for merchant adventurers, a wake-up call. They were read simply as a "blueprint for commerce."[18] When

Esteban Martinez arrived to claim Nu-tka for Spain, he found a sound full of foreign ships, all doing a rip-roaring trade. He was not amused.

The trading practices established on the Northwest Coast by those merchants who followed in the wake of Cook, Perez, and other early explorers destroyed any hope of a long-term working relationship with local Native peoples. Profiteering, political rivalry, and the outright plundering of both human and natural resources soon turned Aboriginal openness to outrage. The Native people of Nootka Sound became adept and shrewd at dealing with this new, unsavory commerce. Grievance became malice, and such rancour led to open hostility and violence. Had the unfortunate crew members of the *John Bright*, who came ashore at Hesquiat in 1869, fallen prey to what, by mid-century, had become cultural loathing on the part of Aboriginals? A knowledge of that early trading period is necessary in order to understand the wealth, the woe, and the will that became directly associated with the *John Bright* affair.

In that early period, the wealth gained in the new coastal fur trade was astronomical by any standard. James Hanna, the first British trader, had arrived in Nootka in his brig *Harmon* in 1785. Within five weeks, Hanna was able to sail to China "with 560 sea otter skins, which he sold in Canton for 20,600 Spanish dollars."[19] Nathaniel Portlock, George Dixon, and James Colnet, who once sailed with Cook, saw an opportunity and quit the Royal Navy altogether to form the King George's Sound Company. The single sea-otter pelt that they once bought for a few nails would now sell in Canton for 70 (Spanish) dollars.[20] By 1787 the *King George* and the *Queen Charlotte*, captained by Portlock and Dixon respectively, had unloaded 2,552 pelts in Canton and earned for the new company some $54,875.[21]

The profiteering and rivalry continued with a vengeance. In spite of Martinez, the British, by hook or by crook, were soon making their presence at Nootka known internationally. Within British ranks, the South Sea Company held the trade monopoly over the Northwest Coast. The British East India Company held the monopoly east of the Cape of Good Hope all the way to China.[22] Seeing that even more profit could be made in the Pacific, the East India Company formed a new venture headed by James Strange and David Scott. They sailed into Nootka Sound with a grand plan and two ships—the *Experiment* and the *Captain Cook*. The plan was to have the *Experiment*'s surgeon, John Mackay,

The Sound of "Nu-tka" 27

In order to gain a higher salary, John Webber signed on with Cook as an able seaman as well as a "Draughtsman and Landscape Painter" for the Admiralty. His illustrations were considered so powerful that he was asked to supervise the publication of over 60 engravings. Webber's accurate and critical eye is clearly evident in his eighteenth-century illustrations (above left). Both these and Edward Curtis's magnificent photographs of Moachat natives (above right), taken over a century later, capture the solemn dignity of the Nuu-chah-nulth people. A traditional costume of a woman of Yuquot shows the reed skirt, cedar shawl, and gathering basket used for a shoreline harvest. Equally impressive is the male fisher clad in a manner that may date back to thousands of years before European contact.

spend the winter of 1786 with Chief Maquinna at Yuquot. There Mackay would learn the language and customs of the Moachat, thus providing the new enterprise with a "bilingual" depot. It seemed like a good idea. As planned, Mackay went ashore, and Strange sailed away, never to return. Strange's new company failed to meet expectations, and the British East India Company turned its attention to tea. James Strange's Nootka brainwave was forgotten, along with John Mackay himself.[23]

To cross the Pacific (the Spanish be damned) and participate independently in this new commercial prosperity without the appropriate costly British licences was considered very bad form. The King George's Sound Company paid the fees, but many other British merchants did not. The question was: "Who is around to collect?" The attitude was: "Catch me if you can!"

To get around paying the required licence fees, and to cash in on the competition's monopoly, several notable British merchants disguised their vessels by flying foreign colours. When the British East India Company pulled back, other opportunists stepped in to fill what they believed to be a lucrative void. William Barkley quit the East India Company in 1786 and joined the scurrilous Bengal Trading Company to sail the *Imperial Eagle*, under Austrian colours, to Nootka Sound. Unfortunately, when he arrived he was spotted by James Colnet of the King George's Sound Company, who was there in the *Prince of Wales*. Colnet, who smelled a rat, sent Barkley a letter:

> On the Eighteenth [July 1787] I sent a letter to Captain Berkley [sic], by my chief mate, requesting he would shew him his Authority for trading in the Southsea Company's limits; my right for so doing jarred with him, it was refus'd but several letters & Messages pass'd, but it being in a language my chief mate could not understand we remain'd as much uninform'd as ever, but himself & Crew being mostly Englishman which is contrary to act of Parliament, it remains to be settled on our return to England.[24]

Colnet didn't press the issue at Nootka because the ships' crews had become friendly with each other. Moreover, the *Prince of Wales* and its companion vessel, the *Princess Royal*, received wine, tobacco, soup, and other necessities from Barkley's well-stocked *Imperial Eagle*.[25] Interestingly, Colnet met the abandoned John Mackay, whom Barkley had picked up earlier that month. Barkley somehow believed that Mackay had been left behind on July 27, 1786, because he was very ill with so-called Purple Fever. He also believed, as George Dixon recorded, that Mackay had become "satisfied with his way of life, and perfectly contented to stay, till next year, when he had no doubt of Mr. Strange sending for him."[26] Mackay himself didn't share Barkley's view: he was thankful to be finally rescued.[27]

Colnet, of the King George's Sound Company, allowed Barkley to leave Nootka. He traded, explored, and charted two sounds, one of which now bears his name. Finally, Barkley landed in Macao with some 700 pelts worth $30,000.[28] The *Imperial Eagle* was sold for $3,000 to pay for the "forgotten" licences. Barkley's own money, spent outfitting the vessel, was not repaid until some time later. Most significant, however, was the fact that all of his navigation equipment, and the irreplaceable new charts that he had made of Clayoquot and Barkley Sounds, went to John Meares, a shareholder in the Bengal Trading Company.

Meares's mentor with regard to business dealings was John Henry Cox, the founder of the Bengal Trading Company. Cox had convinced certain British East India Company officials in Calcutta to allow him to export cotton and (surprise!) opium to China. Soon a fine profit was had by all. Smelling even more wealth, Cox outfitted a ship, appropriately named the *Sea Otter*, and hired the successful John Hanna to sail back to Nootka for a load of furs. By late 1786, sea-otter pelts were selling in Canton for $100 each. That was more than three times the monthly salary of a first-class Chinese shipwright.[29] This was very big money indeed. On the strength of Hanna's first voyage, and the promise of a bright future, Cox convinced British East India Company backers to fund a new venture, the Bengal Fur Company. He then joined forces with the opportunistic, one-time Royal Navy lieutenant, John Meares.

Meares, it seems, was a better talker than he was a sailor. With a hidden, though controlling, interest in the Bengal Fur Company, and as captain of the *Nootka*, together with the old *Sea Otter* (now commanded by William Tipping) Meares sailed from Calcutta in late 1786. He avoided paying for the required licences charged against British ships by naming the foreign Bengal Fur Company as the owner and burying his own involvement. As it turns out, the best thing that can be said of Meares is that he was only a poacher. By all accounts, he was tough, he was a liar, and his practices at Nootka nearly brought two continents to war. The *Nootka* and the *Sea Otter* traded and dallied late into the season on the north coast, neglecting to keep the usual eye out for changing weather. As a result, they were forced to winter over in Prince William Sound. Other British vessels, such as Portlock's *King George* and Dixon's *Queen Charlotte*, were trading under licence in Nootka Sound that summer, but they understood the savagery of the Northwest Coast, and, perhaps as Canada's first snowbirds, they left for Hawaii for the winter.

Meares's trading expedition was a disaster. When Portlock and Dixon found Meares and Tipping in the following spring of 1787, 23 of Meares's men were dead of scurvy, and the rest were starving. Both ships were also locked in ice.[30] Rather than seize Meares's ship, as they might have done, they took pity on the abject condition of his crew and forced him to pay a bond and sign a declaration promising to cease and desist from further trading on the coast. They then let him and his crew go free. Meares, of course, continued a meagre trade, while the exhausted Tipping left for home. Tipping's misfortune continued. The *Sea Otter* was lost at sea with all hands: over 100 men perished. Cox lost his shirt, and the Chinese finally threw him out of Canton. The little justice inherent in Cox's expulsion came at a terrible cost. Worse, it didn't last.

Undaunted, by the fall of 1787 Meares was at it again. He had sold the *Nootka* in Macao and was refinanced by the same John Cox.[31] Meares bought two ships, the *Felice* and the *Iphigenia*, this time registering them as Portuguese, and, with even bigger plans, set off again for Nootka Sound. He finagled Chief Maquinna out of some land, befriended Chief Wickaninnish of Clayoquot Sound by supplying him with guns, and, with the 70 Chinese labourers he had brought with him, he constructed

A rogue and opportunist at best, John Meares almost started a war between the British and the Spanish.

a base that looked more like a fort. Then he built a schooner on site—the first to be built in North America. Times were good until the Spaniard Martinez showed up.

The trading rivalry at Nootka had reached international status. The British traders, known among Aboriginal peoples as "King George's Men" (after Portlock's ship), weren't the only ones freely availing themselves of the spoils during that summer of 1788. By then, Cook's *Voyages* had reached the ship owners of Boston, Massachusetts. Such comments as "sea otter pelts obtained by the expedition's two ships on the Northwest Coast had brought as much as $120 each in Canton," soon gained their attention.[32]

John Ledyard was an American from Connecticut who had been with Cook on his last voyage. He was now home in the United States, and he would have known of the eastern depression caused by the American War of Independence.[33] He and five Boston merchants soon put together a company and, in 1788, sent two ships—the *Columbia* and the *Lady Washington*—to Nootka Sound. The saga of the "Boston Men" had begun. The Aboriginal people of Nootka Sound prospered from this three-way competition by simply and shrewdly raising the stakes.

The Americans took full advantage of the growing rivalry between the British and the Spanish, not only by becoming artful traders, but also by acting as suppliers to the Russian posts north of the Queen Charlottes. On its way up to Nootka in 1788, after rounding Cape Horn, the *Lady Washington* put in at Tillamook Bay, north of the Columbia River. There, a black seaman from the *Lady Washington* and several local Natives were killed in a skirmish over weapons. The violence that was so much a part of the *John Bright* affair had already begun.[34]

The scoundrel John Meares, of course, saw the Boston Men as interlopers who were crashing a good thing. In September 1788, while visiting Captain Gray aboard the *Lady Washington* in Nootka Sound, he lied to the Americans about the profits that could be made. Haswell, the first mate aboard the *Lady Washington*, saw right through Meares. He noted: "The fact was they wished to frighten us off the Coast that they alone might monopolize the trade but the depth of their design could be easily fathomed."[35] Meares left for Hawaii five days later with a hold full of furs. He wasn't going to risk a repeat of what had happened to him the previous winter.

Entitled "The Spanish Insult to the British Flag at Nootka Sound," this rendering, first printed in 1790, depicts Martinez placing Captain Colnet of the *Argonaut* under arrest and seizing his ship. Later, on the verge of war over the incident, the Spanish abandoned all claims to the Northwest Coast.

The Americans told the Spanish, whom they met the following spring, about John Meares. First, however, in trying to assert Spanish sovereignty, Martinez fired a shot across the *Lady Washington*'s bow. Gray had to do some fast talking about his own presence in Spanish waters. Incredible as it sounds, Martinez actually believed Gray's story ("please sir, we are only collecting barrel staves"). Martinez continued on up into Nootka Sound to find the place crawling with people whom he believed were interlopers.[36]

The long and short of it was that Martinez seized Meares's second ship, the *Iphigenia*, thus sparking an international crisis. Spain had discovered that the real culprits were the British, not the Russians. Meanwhile, safely back in Canton, the wily Meares had met with members of the King George's Sound Company. After talks, they merged to form the Associated Merchants of London and India. These strange new bedfellows realized that, with the arrival of the Americans on the scene, they had better get their collective acts together or they would all lose everything. When Colnet, spearheading this new company, arrived at Nootka with his new ship, the *Argonaut*, it was seized and he was imprisoned.[37] The Spanish were quickly regaining the upper hand; the combined British company was rapidly going down the tubes; and the Americans were laughing all the way to the bank.

What did Meares do? He published his voluminous *Voyages* in 1790, in which he took credit for the information contained in Barkley's notebooks and charts. Then he had the audacity to scream blue bloody murder in a presentation to the British House of Commons, decrying his ill-treatment at the hands of the Spanish. In 1790, on the strength of Meares's "charts," the existence of his so-called "land" at Nootka, and his accounts of supposed Spanish indignities, the British Parliament prepared to go to war.

Spooked by British preparations, Spain destroyed the fortifications at Nootka and ordered Martinez home. Meares and all his crooked associates were paid handsomely for the "loss" and "seizure" of their possessions. Within four years, George Vancouver and the last of the Spanish explorers—Eliza, Quadra, Malaspina, and Galiano—shared information with regard to charting the inner coast, accepted the articles of the Nootka Convention, and went home.

The plunder continued. In 1800 the Boston Men alone took 15,000 sea-otter pelts. The newly formed Russian-American Company procured some 10,000 pelts. In the ten years between 1790 and 1800, just six to ten vessels could obtain a total annual average of between 10,000 and 12,000 pelts. In 1799, one ship alone could get 800 pelts in four days.[38] In the decade before 1800, the slaughter of some 100,000 sea otter made $3,000,000 in Canton. That works out to a staggering "one pelt every hour."[39]

Such rapacious and wanton slaughter not only brought the sea otter to the very edge of extinction, but it also prompted other abuses against both Aboriginals and White traders. History records that Aboriginal peoples were forced to trade at gun-point, that young Aboriginal women were subject to the most horrific indignities, that Aboriginal captives were ransomed off for pelts, that White traders were themselves captured and executed by Aboriginals, that the outright theft of Aboriginal goods was common, and that vengeful destruction of whole Aboriginal villages was an accepted form of retaliation.[40]

Whether or not the violence between coastal traders and Aboriginals was as wanton in the early nineteenth century as some believe is a moot point.⁴¹ Certainly, loss of face and lasting resentment occurred whenever a trading ship bypassed Nootka Sound for more profitable northern islands and inlets. Was the so-called restraint in the hostilities due to compassion on the part of colonial administrators? Or was it due to the intimidating presence of the Royal Navy? These are important questions with regard to how one views the *John Bright* tragedy, and they are addressed in a later chapter.

The fact remains, however, that this coast was a violent place during the years of the maritime fur trade. Certain acts of deadly violence entered the popular consciousness of the time and became part of the historical legacy that led to the outcome of the *John Bright* affair. As British and American sea traders moved out of Nootka Sound to inlets further up the coast, commerce with the Aboriginals became even more direct. Indignities felt by Aboriginal peoples led naturally to acts of restitution, several of which stand out. In the popular consciousness, the stereotypical guileless, gentle Aboriginal was fast becoming a menacing savage.⁴²

This view was further reinforced by the behaviour of the White traders themselves. Success in the highly competitive coastal fur trade demanded aggression and bluff. But this, unfortunately, was also accompanied by a complete lack of understanding of Aboriginal attitudes towards property. This resulted in the meting out of disproportionate and cruel punishment for what the Aboriginals saw as harmless misdemeanours. One Aboriginal actually made it into the great cabin of the *Resolution* and stole Cook's watch. Luckily it was recovered.⁴³ Had that act of Native "boasting" occurred before a less tolerant captain, particularly to a post-1800 trading captain, the culprit would surely have been shot.

The captains of the trading vessels that visited Nootka were not the captains of the Royal Navy. They did not have the education, the tradition, the ground rules, or the strict discipline that was associated with the Royal Navy. The trading captain's mandate was neither science nor exploration; it was profit, pure and simple. Yet even the Royal Navy's discipline and tradition did not always ensure the prevention of violence and mutiny. Cook died in Hawaii because he could not properly quell animosity between members of his crew and Native islanders. Captain Bligh, who was master of the *Resolution* on Cook's third and last voyage, was cast adrift from the *Bounty* some ten years later, along with eighteen officers and companions. Bligh's mutineer crew members preferred loitering amongst the young Native women of Tahiti to working an eighteenth-century sailing ship slowly back to rainy, repressive England.

The crews of trading ships were largely young, uneducated, rough men. Many were little more than rogues or profiteers, living outside British law in the far-flung outposts of empires. Many would "sign on" for a single voyage, desirous only of gaining a percentage cut from a full load of furs. That end would justify almost any means. Moreover, while at sea the men could avoid the moral constraints of a class-ridden Victorian society—be it in Boston, London, Macao, or Canton. For the crew of a trading barque, after months before the mast, there would be no Christian restraint when faced with the appeal of young Aboriginal women. The trading captain was concerned with profit, shareholders, and the safety of his vessel. If the behaviour of crew members did not directly affect the safety of these things, then the captain cast upon it a blind eye. Trading vessels had few officers and often no brig, as the former cost money and the latter took up space.

Traders such as John Meares, John Kendrick, and others would have no conception of the intricate lineal ties that designated Aboriginal landholdings. Maquinna could no more "sell" Meares land than Meares could "sell" Maquinna Whitehall. Similarly, the deed for eighteen square miles of land near Ahousat in Clayoquot Sound, which Kendrick "bought" from Maquinna in 1791 for six muskets, a sail, some gunpowder, and an American flag, is ridiculous in the extreme, even though Maquinna's and Wickaninnish's signatures appear on the document.[44] Kendrick's own vile trading practices were cut short by his death in Hawaii, where he was shot by a friendly British vessel that was engaged in saluting him. Such irony was small mercy, however, for others like him readily filled his place.[45]

It is incorrect to say that Aboriginals did not "own" land. They did recognize ownership of village sites, fishing places, berry and root patches, and tracts used for trapping and hunting.[46] The subtleties of hierarchy and kinship that defined ownership and use of such lands was unknown to Meares and others who wished to "discover" and "claim" Aboriginal territory. A similar dearth of understanding greeted Aboriginal cultural codes regarding the possession of simple goods.

Within Aboriginal communities, the possession of most goods was communal: things rotated through tribal units. All too often, White punishment was wildly out of line with Aboriginal "crimes." Such ignorance soon led to injustices, which, in turn, led to retribution. And neither White society nor a White judge, such as "the hanging judge" Matthew Begbie, could tolerate what the Aboriginals deemed to be justifiable homicide.

The story of the Aboriginal attack on the American trading vessel *Boston* in Nootka Sound in 1803 is a case in point. It was keenly remembered by those who would mete out justice in the *John Bright* affair some fifty years later. Seen through Aboriginal eyes, such as those of the Moachat informant Peter Webster, the burning of the *Boston* takes on a decidedly different colour.

> According to my father, my father got all the news from his cousins that were at Yuquot ... I believe it was the Spaniards that settled right in the reserve of Yuquot. They opened a blacksmith shop. And these Spaniards, mamalni, they sure must have mistreated the Native Indian young girls. They used to pull them into the blacksmith's without any romance, I think that is what the mamalni call it, you know, trying to flirt, or something. Some of the Indian girls refused what these guys wanted. The blacksmith had that red-hot iron always ready for those that refused. There'd be more than two boys, mamalni boys, open up the girl's legs and poke that red-hot iron right into the poor Native Indian girl's vagina. The poor parents couldn't revenge to the mamalni because they had no weapons of any kind ... This is the reason why [the men on] that ship [the *Boston*] was murdered. They didn't care who it was, only that a ship would come in ... I haven't read anything about this what I'm telling. They wouldn't admit it. Nobody will admit it.[47]

The unfortunate *Boston* sailed smack into a call for Aboriginal vengeance. Peter Webster continued:

> According to my old man's stories about Jewitt and Thompson, the Indians in that time couldn't pronounce the name right. This Jewitt was called cuwin and Thompson was called tamsin. When [the men on] the ship [*Boston*] was murdered. The Indians displayed their half load of fresh spring salmon which was caught that morning. They pretended to try to give fish to these ship people. They must have all had weapons, that's what they call it,

The American trading vessel *Boston* in Marvinas Bay, Nootka Sound. Marvinas is a corruption of the Moachat word "mawina"—"a village along the way"— and the bay was situated between the two significant Native villages of the sound, Yuquot and Tahsis. The *Boston* was captured here by Chief Maquinna, ostensibly in a dispute over trade.

> the adze today. They all got on deck ... I guess they had the weapons on the right side, because they had them hidden. Now they killed all the men that was on deck. They didn't know what they were to do with the ship. They started looking around in the ship and there were two men found way below mending their sails. That must have been Jewitt and Thompson.[48]

Jewitt's own narrative, written as a secret journal during his two-year period of captivity, confirms that, as Webster relates, the slaughter was the result of a build-up of injustices. Yet he also adds that the theft of 40 sea-otter pelts by the captain of a passing trading schooner, as well as the *Boston* captain's personal insult to Maquinna himself (supposedly over a defective musket), were also probable reasons for what occurred. Why were John Jewitt and John Thompson saved from the massacre? They were in the right place at the right time. Being below, they missed the initial fury of the attackers. Moreover, they had special talents: Jewitt was a blacksmith, Thompson was a sailmaker. Soon after, the *Boston* was looted clean and burned to the keel. Jewitt then began his journal (a very fine read).

When the American trading brig *Lydia* arrived in Nootka Sound in July 1805, Chief Maquinna was held on board as hostage until Jewitt and Thompson were allowed to "escape." The *Lydia* arrived at Fort Clatsop up the Columbia River in November 1805, where Lewis and Clark had arrived two weeks before. The following spring it sailed for Macao, then Canton, arriving in Boston, Massachusetts, in June 1807. There, Jewitt published the journal that he had kept at Nootka Sound, married, moved to Connecticut, and parlayed his encounter with the Moachat into several successful theatrical performances. Further to this, his journal was published in London in 1816. He died in Hartford, Connecticut, in 1821 at the age of 37. John Thompson was not so fortunate. He either died in Havana, en route to Boston, or in Philadelphia soon after.[49]

By 1812 the Northwest Coast maritime fur trade was in full swing. From 1803 to 1813 the Russians and the Americans engaged in joint trading ventures. The North West Company, based in Montreal and rival to the Hudson's Bay Company (HBC), had reached the coast of no-man's-land—the Oregon Territory. The Boston men supplied these posts, especially the post at Astoria, and carried their furs to China. Naturally, they also ventured north, where they met the Russians. It was to be, for a time, a most fortuitous meeting. The Russians were inexorably moving and trading down the coast. They brought plenty of Aleut labour with their baidarkas (sea kayaks), but they lacked ships. The Boston men had ships but insufficient labour to carry out the one-to-one barter.[50] Hence the Russian-American collaboration was highly profitable. In one year of the first decade of the nineteenth century this joint venture yielded over 24,000 sea-otter pelts.[51] More than that, with the reconstruction of the Russian base of New Archangel (now Sitka) in 1804 (it had been destroyed by the Tlingit in 1802), the Boston men acted as its sole provider. When its Siberian supply line collapsed, the American traders also carried their furs to Canton—for an appropriate profit, of course. Who needed Nootka Sound?

Given that there were upwards of 250 American ships visiting the Pacific coast from New Spain (Chile) to Alaska annually in the early

The longhouses of the Moachat at Yuquot (Friendly Cove) remained until the first years of the twentieth century.

1800s,[52] and given their rapacious practices, Aboriginal hostility towards the traders was certain. Consider, for example, another renowned precedent to the *John Bright* affair. The Boston ship, the *Tonquin*, had two strikes against: its captain, Jonathan Thorn, and its landfall in Clayoquot Sound.

Like so many other maritime trading captains of the period, Jonathan Thorn had procured a leave from the navy. He left New York in late 1810 for Fort Astoria at the mouth of the Columbia River. His hardhearted manner soon revealed itself. He left a group of passengers stranded on the Falkland Islands in December simply because they loitered ashore, returning for them only because an angry passenger held a gun to his head. Arriving at the Columbia River, Captain Thorn sent two boatloads of crew members to their deaths merely because he was so anxious to find a way over its notorious bar. Then, after leaving Fort Astoria in 1811, he chose to trade at Clayoquot Sound.

Unknown to Thorn, the whaling captain G.W. Ayres of Boston had, some years before, shanghaied several Clayoquot for a sealing expedition off the coast of California. He promised them all safe return. The Clayoquot were abandoned among island seal colonies and killed or enslaved by other Aboriginal tribes while trying to get home. Again, Ayres was ignorant of everything but profit. At that time, the Nuu-chahnulth collectively shared the responsibility for the taking of a life. When their relatives failed to return, Aboriginal law allowed them to avenge their deaths. Enter the *Tonquin*.

To the Clayoquot that summer of 1811, as to the Aboriginal people involved in the case of the *Boston*, one American ship was the same as any other. Thorn might have spared his crew, but he was a ruthless, tight-fisted trader. More, he publicly bad-mouthed a local chief, causing an unforgivable loss of face. The slaughter was horrific, but that was only the half of it. Fleeing crew members had lit a slow fuse leading to the ship's powder magazine. When it blew, some 200 Clayoquot, along with the wounded and dying ship's company, were blown to smithereens.[53] Those who lit the fuse and left the ship via the stern's great cabin windows were hunted down and killed. It had come to this.

By the 1830s, the maritime fur trade on the Northwest Coast was all over. Rifle fire, echoing down the myriad coastal inlets, had become the mutual medium of exchange. The HBC had absorbed the North West Company, and the land-based fur industry had begun. The heyday of American intrusion into Russian coastal territory was finished. Unrestricted direct trade with the Tlingit made the Russians sit up and take note. The so-called British "blockade" of the Northwest Coast during the War of 1812 resulted in American privateers simply dumping goods at New Archangel now Sitka, Alaska at rock-bottom prices. By 1814, Baranov, the governor of Russian Alaska, was ordered to keep out the Boston men completely. By 1818, north of 51 degrees, the Russian government issued a decree banning all foreign vessels from approaching within 115 miles of the Northwest Coast.[54] Though this decree was overturned in 1824, the sea otters were gone, and the new means of trade, the fur seal, was in grave danger. The perceived threat of Aboriginal violence was becoming more and more common. Armed lookouts were often ordered aloft to the cross-trees of the masts of trading ships. The preferred trade good had become the rifle, and the Natives were using it against those with whom they traded. By 1825, "only four to six American and British ships annually traded on the Northwest Coast."[55] By the 1830s, the careful management of the HBC, with its policy of using both land posts and ships, such as the *Beaver* (launched in 1835), created markets and competition that the privateers simply could not match.

What remained, however, were those indefatigable human qualities of greed and memory. The private maritime traders would shift their attention to whaling, and within a scant 30 years would bring these great ocean leviathans to the edge of extinction. As they were failing, the ravenous traders would turn their attention to the slaughter of the Pacific seals and the rain forest. Soon these, too, would be despoiled.

Between 1774 and 1870 the maritime fur trade on the Northwest Coast amounted to little more than hucksterism. Yet Aboriginal culture survived virtually unscathed and even prospered during this period. This, in itself, is powerful testimony to the complexity, adaptability, and subtlety of a social organization that had flourished for thousands of years. Aboriginal culture, however, could not survive the onslaught of White settlement. As the articles of trade shifted from sea otter, metals, and guns to fur seal, blankets, and whisky, the trading life became more difficult. Aboriginal and White traders alike became increasingly embittered. However, the White traders, like the White settlers, were here to stay. What they saw as unwarranted Aboriginal violence led to the clarion call for intervention, for gunboats, and for outright White supremacy. This, along with smallpox, would bring the Aboriginal peoples to their knees. By the 1860s, the memory of the White citizens of Victoria vis-à-vis the encounters between White traders and Aboriginal peoples had changed. The murder of a single European skipper had been transformed into a slaughter; the awful shipwreck of a lumber trader had been transformed into a massacre.

The history of the coastal fur trade, as seen through the eyes of those firm and settled citizens of Victoria, was a history of necessary subjugation. They saw progress and profit as Christian virtues. Those who would stand in the way of such ideals were savages. Within this atmosphere, the Aboriginals who were believed to be responsible for the *John Bright* tragedy didn't have a chance.

CHAPTER 3

Pilgrimage

Come to me
Not as a river willingly downwards falls
To be lost in a wide ocean

But come to me
As flood-tide comes to shore-line
Filling empty bays
With a white stillness
Mating earth and Sea.

                        F.R. Scott[1]

I could hear the familiar sound of John Gellard's old Volkswagen chugging up the hill near the house, and I hurried to finish my coffee. John, my old friend, teaching colleague, and amateur photographer, had insisted that his van (which had once climbed logging roads in the Kootenays) was easily up to the long gravel highway to the trailhead on the outer coast of Vancouver Island. True, it was noisy and the heater pumped warm exhaust fumes straight into the cab, but the ground clearance was ample, and it did have plenty of room. Hell, it was August, hot, and we were finally away. I knew that if I could survive the drive, I could survive the trail. I would later rue my nonchalance.

    The trail in question was the West Coast Trail, one of the most spectacular hiking adventures on the North American continent. Pertinent pages of old newspapers, books, diaries, and maps were copied and packed away, along with cameras and enough food and gear for a week. We would leave the van at Bamfield and begin the three-day hike down the West Coast Trail to the old abandoned whaling station of Clo-oose.

Vancouver Island, the largest of all islands on the west coast of the Americas, lies about ten miles off the mainland of British Columbia and protects the gentle inner coast from the full force of the Pacific Ocean. Its long, thin land mass was pushed up from the seabed to heights of over 7,000 feet by the relentless, subductive grinding of the Pacific Plate, which is slowly slipping beneath the continent upon which Canada stands. A small ribbon of flat coastal plain—thin on the west, more substantial on the south and east—surrounds the long mountains of Vancouver Island, creating several wonderfully distinct climatic regions. The road to Bamfield and the West Coast Trail would cross the spine of this ancient Long Barrow.

Lush and almost subtropical, the garden communities of the inner gulf, such as Qualicum and Lantzville, sport a Mediterranean climate and vegetation. As we travelled westward towards the mountains, the rolling Alberni Valley revealed simple, orderly clusters of yellow fields and small farms, where cows grazed beneath Garry oaks and blue smoke from an occasional tractor hung in the afternoon stillness. With woodland swamps and village markets, it might have been Appalachia or the Annapolis Valley, save for the glistening icecap of the high mountain ridge known as Forbidden Plateau. Suddenly, the long hills called us up into a cooler, darker green dominated by 800-year-old Douglas fir. The eastern rainshadow of the mountains was no more, and from here to the sea the austere crags wore shrouds. Far above, where the switchbacks could no longer go, the rain forest still ruled.

Port Alberni lies at the end of a long fjord, some 40 miles from the open ocean. Alberni Inlet nearly cuts Vancouver Island in half. The former lifeblood of Port Alberni, the forest industry is now restricted by environmental priorities; however, tourism, sport fishing, and hiking remain strong. From here you can hike into the Drinkwater Canyon and see the 1,443-foot cataract of Della Falls, the highest in North America. From here, too, you can load a kayak onto a charming coastal freighter, the Lady Rose, and be transported to a marine life paradise called the Broken Islands in mid-Barkley Sound.

At Port Alberni we left the main highway and began the last dusty 50 miles to the tiny coastal fishing village of Bamfield. The great primeval forests disappeared decades ago. Yet high above the clear-cut slopes, we could still see the tall virgin hemlock and cedar, overwhelmed as they

44 Glyphs and Gallows

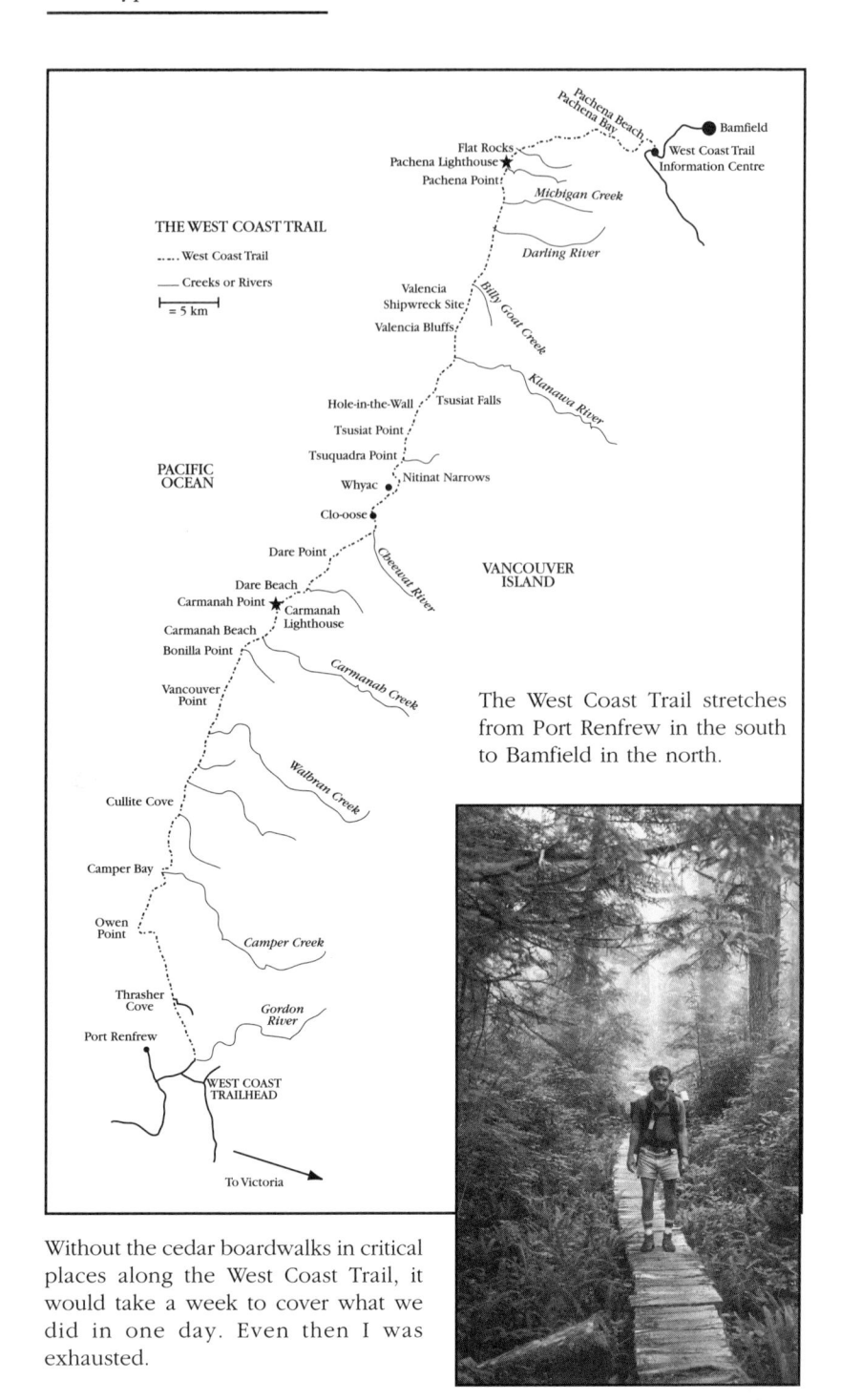

THE WEST COAST TRAIL

····· West Coast Trail
——— Creeks or Rivers
⊢———⊣ = 5 km

PACIFIC OCEAN

VANCOUVER ISLAND

Pachena Beach
Pachena Bay
Bamfield
West Coast Trail Information Centre
Flat Rocks
Pachena Lighthouse
Pachena Point
Michigan Creek
Darling River
Billy Goat Creek
Valencia Shipwreck Site
Valencia Bluffs
Klanawa River
Hole-in-the-Wall
Tsusiat Falls
Tsusiat Point
Tsuquadra Point
Whyac
Nitinat Narrows
Clo-oose
Cheewat River
Dare Point
Dare Beach
Carmanah Point
Carmanah Lighthouse
Carmanah Beach
Bonilla Point
Vancouver Point
Carmanah Creek
Walbran Creek
Cullite Cove
Camper Bay
Owen Point
Camper Creek
Thrasher Cove
Gordon River
Port Renfrew
WEST COAST TRAILHEAD
To Victoria

The West Coast Trail stretches from Port Renfrew in the south to Bamfield in the north.

Without the cedar boardwalks in critical places along the West Coast Trail, it would take a week to cover what we did in one day. Even then I was exhausted.

were by the smaller, lighter fir that had been hand-planted during the 1950s. Down to the road's edge, huge old grey stumps, the natural tombstones of a bygone frenzy, were still visible between the road-dusted cover of alder and huckleberry. It was dark by the time we reached Bamfield, brine-soaked and cool by the calm, black sea. Exploration of the marine station and the boardwalk that hugged the shoreline of this northern terminus of the West Coast Trail would have to wait for another visit. By seven the next morning, we were each carrying 50-pound packs and were headed for the ocean.

From Bamfield to the lighthouse at Pachena Point was an easy, though heavy, four-hour trek. The graceful boughs and fine needles of the western hemlock told us that we were still inland and had a long way to go before we reached the coast. The sparse understory was full of patches of huge sword fern, and the swamp hollows were crowded with skunk cabbage so big you could sit in them. I knew the Natives used to boil the roots of skunk cabbage for food in times of famine, and I thought of the driving sleet of a southeast gale in winter. How many times, I wondered, did the trader and amateur ethnographer William Banfield[2] walk this same route after his arrival on the outer coast in 1862?

At Pachena Point, the trail left the quiet of the forest. We headed out to the roar of the surf and hiked along a great flat section of rock that marked the ocean's edge. Reaching Michigan Creek at noon we paused in the sun for tea, crackers, cheese, an orange, and a piece of chocolate. With the exception of one object that caught my eye, we were surrounded by nature. As I became more absorbed in an old rusting boiler some 100 yards off, just above the rising tide, I seemed to have no choice but to investigate it.

In the tidal surf at the mouth of Michigan creek lies what is left of the old wooden steamer that gives it its name—a Scottish-made boiler and propeller shaft. I heard the Michigan's story from a park official at Pachena Point. It was bound north for Puget Sound, out of San Francisco, on the foggy, bitterly cold night of January 20, 1893. Just before midnight, it struck a rock shelf off Pachena Point and began to break up. For two days those trapped aboard the groaning vessel stared out at the breakers, until one heroic seaman named Simons swam through the surf with a line that he had fashioned into a breeches buoy. He saved all hands, pulleying them ashore just inches above the murderous surf. As the survivors began a two-week ordeal while they awaited rescue, it was reported that local Natives carried away the Michigan's cargo of cases of whisky.³

We needed to get on. The remains of the Michigan urged us southwards, towards the glyphs and towards the thickening, low band of raincloud. The old boiler struck me as symbolic of a long line of opportunistic traders who, in a previous time, had brought sailing ships and, along with them, another sort of ruin to this empty, faraway coast.

The West Coast Trail began in 1889 as a simple telegraph line from Victoria to Bamfield, from whence it continued as an undersea cable to India by way of Fiji. Hence, at the end of the nineteenth century, Britain was connected to all its overseas colonies. The weakest link in the so-called chain was right here along this desolate coast. The cable was simply strung from tree to tree between Port Renfrew and Bamfield. In winter, thanks to the gales and snow, the cable was down more often than it was up. Bamfield gained an international reputation, and Clo-oose gained a population. Somebody had to keep the telegraph trail open and the line up. A cannery at Clo-oose provided even more work for the growing number of White families. The Nitinaht, who had a reputation for violence, kept a low profile in their nearby village of Whyac.

These thoughts remained with me as we hiked along the beach past Tsocowis Creek and Billy Goat Creek, inching our way southward towards

Pachena Point Lighthouse in the 1920s.

Four days out from San Francisco, Captain Graves admitted to "losing his bearings" in the fog off Cape Flattery. Set north by an onshore current, he heard the ominous breakers at Pachena Point too late. First Mate Marshall crossed the strait in a lifeboat to dispatch the American tugs *Discovery, Sea Lion,* and *Tacoma* from Port Townsend. When he returned, the *Michigan* was already in pieces

the hoped-for glyphs. The sweeping white sandy beaches and tide pools, which were teeming with life, made this part of the coast seem gentle and idyllic in the warm, late afternoon sun. Yet in a surge channel near Billy Goat Creek lay the remains of an old square-rigger—the barque Janet Cowan, which had grounded on New Year's Eve, 1895. Seven deaths and eleven days later, rescue began. The same storm that took the Janet Cowan also took out the telegraph line that might have saved more of its crew.

We left the beach at Billy Goat Creek, broke through a botanical barrier of salal, and climbed up over a windy promontory. It was then that I saw only too clearly the power of the Pacific as it surged against the distant impassable headlands. Below me, down an unscalable 100-foot cliff, lay what was left of the SS Valencia. It missed the entrance to the Strait of Juan de Fuca in the darkness of January 22, 1906, and hit the rocks off Shelter Bight. In all, 126 lives were lost. The sky soon hazed over, and the wind changed direction. I put on a fleece and looked out to sea. The novelist Brian Moore was right: it is a landscape that dwarfs all human endeavour.

48   Glyphs and Gallows

The West Coast Life-Saving Trail was constructed after the wrecks of the *Valencia* and *Janet Cowan* in 1906. This bridge at Pachena Point was one of the early improvements on the trail, which was twelve feet wide from Bamfield to Shelter Bight, and four feet wide to Carmanah.

It grew colder then, and the line of dark blue clouds was nearer. We forged freezing Klanawa River barefoot, water up to our knees. The tide was rising fast but was still low enough so that the cable-car crossing above us was not yet necessary—food, rest, and warmth, however, were. We stopped. That night in my tent I listened to the wind and the muted roar of the distant surf. I thought of how this place must have been before lighthouses, before charts, before radio, before telegraphy—in darkness and in winter.

There is no shelter for ships, large or small, along the whole outer coast of Vancouver Island. The rocky approaches to Barkley, Clayoquot, and Nootka Sounds in the south, and to Kyuquot and Quatsino Sounds in the north, are difficult to see in rough weather. Besides these long-fingered fjords, there is nothing. The few exposed and shallow bays, such as Esperanza and Hesquiat, are certain death for a sailing ship unable to beat weather in a southeasterly storm that pushes everything ashore.

Sailing northward from San Francisco, the safest route, then as now, would have been well off shore, away from the shallows and turbulent outflow of coastal rivers such as the mighty Columbia. Once past the

In the days of the telegraph cable, crude log bridges spanned many of the creeks that spilled out into the Pacific across the West Coast Trail. The major rivers, such as the Klanawa, then as now, could be forded only by a seat hung from a cable (or a boat).

notorious river bars, it would have been necessary to keep a sharp eye on the ship's patent log. Closing the shore would have been a worrying business, crew members straining from the cross-trees to find the rock pinnacle of Cape Flattery at the end of the Olympic Peninsula, the southern opening of the long Strait of Juan de Fuca. How easy it would have been, in fog or darkness, to have missed this critical starboard turn—to have turned too soon or, having been deceived by the southerly sweep of the current, not to have turned at all. Such an easy error would have been tantamount to driving a ship into a rock face. How easy it would have been to have miscalculated distance travelled, especially with an uncertain ocean current. How easy it would have been to have missed a changing compass variation as a vessel sailed over an unknown magnetic sea-mount. They say there are over 40 known ships per mile littering the seabed along the length of the West Coast Trail between Port Renfrew and Bamfield, all of which sank since trade began on this coast around 1800. Lying there in the dark, listening to the howling wind, I wondered why there weren't more.

It was fog—cold, concealing, drenching fog that greeted us next morning. Tea would have to wait for fresh water at Tsusiat Falls. We pushed on mainly to keep warm. Strange to think that even on land fresh-water springs and creeks are practically non-existent. In 1906 the lack of fresh water and the uncertain operation of the telegraph were reasons enough, especially after the horrific wrecks of the Janet Cowan and the Valencia, to turn the old trail into a life-saving route. Thankfully, that year a new lighthouse at Pachena Point would point its life-saving beam seaward and warn mariners that they were north of the lights at Cape Beale or Carmanah. Such a fix would have undoubtedly saved thousands of lives.

That day we stayed in the forest, just beyond the salal. We preferred muck up to our knees to pea-soup drizzle down our necks. At Bamfield, as at Clo-oose in 1906, there would be a lifeboat station, warm clothes, and perhaps hot coffee for shipwrecked sailors lucky enough to be plucked from the deep. My body shivered. I needed hot tea.

A day later found us at Nitinat Narrows. Here the river from Nitinat Lake meets the Pacific Ocean. At low tide, all hell breaks loose. Tidal currents roar seaward through the gap at eight knots! Whirlpools are everywhere, as great ocean swells, generated by week-long offshore storms, surge upriver against the combined effects of an outflow current and ebbing tide. Huge standing waves gave me reason to be thankful that I was, at least, on shore. There was no way to cross the Nitinat River save with the aid of a local Native who ran an aluminum skiff ferry for hikers. We waited, and waited, and waited. And then we waited some more. When he finally came, the next day, our numbers had swelled to a merry band of intrepid hikers from all over the world. We shared nuts, chocolate, sardines, history, and stories. A five-minute crossing put us one hour from Clo-oose.

I had been thinking about the glyphs all morning after finally being ferried across Nitinat Narrows. Again it was cold and foggy, and again I was glad to be in the forest away from the open shore. At least here there was no wind. The closer we came to the assumed location of the glyphs, the more sceptical I became that they could ever provide answers to the questions I had posed to them. Soon I was beginning to doubt that I would ever understand the glyphs at all.

Miterwort grew everywhere in the rich, sodden soil, upturned from roots of the giant fallen cedars. Skunk cabbage glistened green against

Pilgrimage 51

Walking the beaches on the West Coast Trail without careful attention to the tide tables could result in being trapped at the foot of an unscalable cliff on a rising tide.

Besides the Life-Saving Trail that was established after the wreck of the *Valencia,* Clo-oose received a lifeboat station run by local volunteers. However, the surf at Clo-oose was often too high for the boat to be launched. In January 1909 a gale carried the lifeboat from its moorings and it was lost. The station at Clo-oose was soon abandoned.

the fallen black trunks that lay scattered in a bog. I thought I saw the remains of a muskrat-house, half hidden by grey and spindly trunks standing well into the swamp. Everywhere there was the rich smell of decay, as death and life intermingled about me. All the forces of the universe were working here, and I slowly gained a more fatalistic attitude towards the problem of the glyphs. At the very least, I had become a detective in a 130-year-old mystery, my clues lying in a wonderfully abstract art form, and at the same time, I was engulfed by a natural world about which I knew far too little. I mentioned to Gellard that I felt like John Hanning Speke hiking through the unknown country of East Africa in 1862, literally stumbling upon the luxuriance of Lake Tanganyika. He told me to shut up and keep walking.

The intermittent wooden bridges and split-cedar boardwalks across the frequent streams and bogs south from the Nitinat River were a blessing. The replacement boards were of the same axe-hewn type that, at the turn of the century, had run from the village of Clo-oose, on to Clo-oose Lake and the nearby Native village of Whyac. I pulled from my pack a section of a topographic map and a photocopy of a short article that had appeared in the Victoria Daily Times *in 1926.*[4] I had found it by chance in one of my many archival searches, and it sent me home grinning like the Cheshire cat. The article described another late summer hike from Victoria to Clo-oose, with the objective being to see the strange sailing-ship glyphs. The party was led by a Mr. Halket, who first chanced upon the rock art in 1914. Since the life-saving trail had only been completed some five years before, Halket was probably among the first White people to ever see the glyphs. In his party was the well-known Victoria journalist Robert Connell, who was undoubtedly the first European to have ever written about them. He never had the luxury of a split-log walkway, but he would have understood the need for one. Poor old Connell would surely have been up to his waist in mud.

I trudged on, occasionally passing through trees felled by winter storms and later cut in two by passing wardens. The more recently toppled ones I had to climb over. Small spruce logs had been dragged to the trail and had become the underlying timbers to which the flat, three-foot cross-members were nailed. I chortled to myself; Connell would have liked this.

My knees brushed against the dripping sword ferns that grew in profusion on each side of the boardwalks. The broad oval leaves of trillium

Pilgrimage 53

Clo-oose was viable right up to the 1960s. After whaling ceased early in the twentieth century and later plans for development fell through, only a few cottagers remained. Today there are a couple of summer cabins dating from the 1970s; beyond this, the place has been reclaimed by the forest.

and lily-of-the-valley were everywhere. Bunchberry bushes hung heavy with scarlet berries, and I remembered the small, tell-tale white flowers that looked so much like dogwood. Here and there huge banana slugs were inching their way across my human-made path. The place was a visual feast of greens of every imaginable hue. My hand ran across long, thick, smooth leaves, while my feet felt the knots and fissures of the split logs. Above me in the trees was the scolding "seet-seet, seet-seet, seet-seet, trrrr" of what I believed was a yellow warbler. Above the forest cover was the ever-present sound of the wind.

If one could avoid tripping on them, the boardwalks did make the hiking easier. They also allowed my mind to wander, captivated by the wild excess of the surrounding forest. My task, though I was losing heart, was to predict from a torn and limp green-paper topographic map that lay across my palm just where, exactly, we should leave the trail. The thing was, I had worked out that the distance from the Nitinat River to the supposed site of the glyphs should be under an hour's walk. But I hadn't slept well for the last two days because I'd been worrying over the glyphs. My pack was growing heavier and my bones were sore. I was beginning to wonder if the small "x" I had marked on the map had anything to do with reality at all. Glancing at my watch, I decided we had hiked enough. It was now or never. To be sure, I sat and read aloud bits of Connell's article: "The trail was covered with fallen trunks and upturned roots." [5]

"That helps a lot," said John.

We could both hear the sea. I described where Connell and his party had found themselves in a small cove, where a honeycombed sandstone bluff sloped gently in a series of shelves towards the sea. I locked the image into my mind and pored again over the sodden green map.

"It can't be more than another hundred yards," I offered cautiously.

We walked on a bit further, paused, grinned, then pushed through the few feet of brush to the beach. Unbelievably, we found ourselves at the southern edge of a small, almost enclosed cove, as described by Connell.

"Good Lord," said John, "we've found it! It's all here! Look! The honeycombed ledge near the salal! And see! The small oval beach between two rocky promontories!"

Excitedly, I climbed the northern ridge of rock for an overview. I knew the glyphs were here, but would they be completely eroded? I scrutinized the sandstone shelf for an outline in the flat, foggy afternoon light. Suddenly, I spotted a shape I had seen a thousand times before, albeit only in old sketches. It was remarkably preserved. Others, more strange than I could ever have imagined, leaped out as if from nowhere, and the whole shelf suddenly became one huge mural full of glyphs. Unbelievably, we had found them; more to the point, they were still intact. Literally inches from my feet lay the long-sought-after sailing-ship petroglyphs of Clo-oose.

CHAPTER 4
Victoria, 1869: Afraid to Know Itself

Alas, poor country!
Almost afraid to know itself!
It cannot be called our mother but our grave,
where nothing
But who knows nothing is once seen to smile
                    Macbeth*, Act IV, sc. iii* [1]

On June 10, 1869, on board the HMS *Sparrowhawk* (the same Royal Navy gunboat that plays a central part in our story), Frederick Seymour, the first governor of the newly amalgamated Colony of British Columbia (the mainland colony and the Vancouver Island colony were now one), had drunk his last. Dead at 49, he had lived an unfulfilled life. Seymour was ineffective in settling disputes between his Whitehall superiors and the exuberant legislators in Victoria, yet he had gained some success in settling internecine conflicts on the frontier.

Jurisdiction on that frontier, however, was still felt to be the purview of the HBC, since it had already established exclusive trading rights with all Aboriginals on the mainland west of the Rockies.[2] When the Canadian-American border treaty forced the HBC to vacate the Oregon and Washington Territories after 1846, it gained proprietorial rights to Vancouver Island. The Honourable Company promised, of course, to encourage settlement and to acknowledge British civil authority through a governor appointed by the Colonial Office. Richard Blanshard, the first governor of Vancouver Island, arrived in March 1850 but left the following year, openly admitting that the HBC on the Island was a fiefdom—a closed system.[3] James Douglas, partisan chief factor of the HBC's new headquarters at Fort Victoria, soon learned of his appointment as the second governor of the Colony of Vancouver Island. Philosophically opposed to universal suffrage, Douglas reluctantly established a representational assembly in 1856.

When Seymour was appointed governor after Douglas's retirement in 1864, much had changed. The aftermath of a gold rush, swarms of settlers, a political union, and talk of Confederation made his tenure difficult. Held in scorn by many citizens of Victoria in 1866 for choosing New Westminster as the sole seat of government once the Island and mainland colonies were united, Seymour was often absent from Victoria. By 1868, outraged citizens of Victoria had restored the capital to this island city, and Seymour was forced to return to a city he had previously shunned. Years of living the high life in government houses as a colonial administrator in Tasmania, Antigua, Nevis, and Honduras had left their mark on Seymour. A guest to one of his infamous soirees in Victoria once noted that he was "intoxicated *before* sitting down to dinner."[4] Undoubtedly, "Panama Fever," picked up on a previous civil service posting in British Honduras, exacerbated his condition, but alcoholism was what finally did him in.[5]

James Douglas (left) and Frederick Seymour (right) represented two very different approaches to the problems of colonial Victoria.

Slow to act when action was necessary, Seymour stalled for two years before accepting Victoria over New Westminster as the new capital of the combined colony. He didn't like Victoria; he called it "ill at ease with itself,"[6] and he referred to its citizens as "half-alien and restless."[7] Married less than a year to an English clergyman's daughter, Florence Stapleton, Seymour returned, with misplaced affability, to the colony from a visit to London in 1866. The convivial and confused Seymour held lavish parties aboard his private yacht *Leviathan* and at his damp and drafty mainland residence. Even as he pursued his plan to draw British Columbia into Confederation, the Canadian prime minister, Sir John A. Macdonald, himself known for imbibing the juice, wrote a letter to the British government in early 1869 suggesting that Seymour be recalled.[8]

Although Aboriginal people seemed to appreciate Seymour's soft and civilized manner, many in the White community did not. He was infirm in dealing with the back-stabbing gentility of his own kind, and he took a particular dislike to the unscrupulous seal traders on the outer coast. And he did not have much patience with those sailors who sold whisky for furs. As his enemies grew, Seymour neglected to deal with Victoria's growing debt, was opposed to the new colony of British Columbia joining Confederation, and was too much a "bonhomme" to be wary of all the changes that enveloped him. He was taken ill en route to Bella Coola from Skidegate on the Queen Charlotte Islands, where he had just resolved yet another skirmish between local Aboriginals and American whisky traders. Officially, Seymour died of dysentery, but everyone in Victoria knew as well as did the HMS *Sparrowhawk*'s surgeon, Dr. Comrie, that, plain and simple, Seymour died of drink.[9] Comrie reported in his log: "Gov. Seymour who had for some time been debilitated, called upon me for medical advice June 6th and I found him suffering from great gastric irritation, nervous tremours, sleeplessness and other symptoms of alcoholism."[10] Had Seymour not died that gentle summer of 1869, he surely would have been muscled out of office by his political opponents.

Governor Seymour is *the* classic inert protagonist in our story. Lacking Macbeth's panache and self-reflection, he gladly "danced" his way into oblivion. Essentially an innocent, Frederick Seymour personified Victoria itself. Unable to reconcile its many conflicting interests, in 1869 Victoria was a terrible contradiction. The colony could no longer hide its face from the moaning winds of change. Saddled with a debt of almost $300,000 when Vancouver Island merged with the larger British colony of British Columbia in 1866,[11] and with an $80,000 overdraft from the Bank of British North America (at 12 percent interest),[12] it faced starvation, isolation, and American annihilation. In the midst of such calamity, the least Victoria could do—and this is the background of our story—was deal firmly with troublesome Aboriginals. That it did, and with great indignation.

The effects of the twin gold rushes, first on the Fraser River in 1858 and then in the Cariboo in 1860, changed Victoria completely. No longer could it remain a gentle British colonial outpost whose citizens were fast becoming "more English than the English."[13] With the stampede to the goldfields, there came thousands of Americans and hundreds of Chinese by way of San Francisco. From the east, hundreds more arrived in huge wagon trains. These were the "Overlanders" from Ontario and Quebec. In the spring of 1859, Victoria had been little more than a peaceful settlement. By the end of the summer of 1859, hundreds of tents could be seen sprawling from the Inner Harbour to the grander homes around the edge of the upper-class area of Rockland. Land speculation was rife. Land that, before the gold rush, "couldn't find a buyer at $5 an acre, soared to one hundred times this price, and soon became $3000 an acre."[14] Victoria grew from a population of 200 in 1842 to over 5,000 by 1850, not to mention the 20,000 transients who saw it simply as a watering hole on their way up the yellow brick road.[15]

Judge F.W. Howay, later County Court Judge of New Westminster, noted in his journal:

> Beginning in April, the rush continued through May, June, and July. It was at its height when nearly ten thousand adventurers are said to have left San Francisco for the Fraser River; during the first ten days of July, six thousand more sailed. It is estimated that the total number who came by land and water, was between twenty-five and thirty thousand ...Victoria became a city overnight, crowded with every type of humanity.[16]

By 1869, many of the disillusioned adventurers had either gone home or retreated to the coast. Immigration grew dormant, and for a decade the population remained firm. In due course, the growing town had become distinctly ghettoized. Jewish merchants, auctioneers, and tailors had opened shops on Johnson Street. The Chinese had settled two streets over in "little Canton." Kanaka Row and Humboldt Street were home to the Hawaiians; while the English, of course, lived up in the many hills that surrounded the city.[17] The roads had not improved much in fifteen years. Pavements did not exist, even of wood, except along Government Street, where conditions were a little better. "Horses, cows and pigs roamed at pleasure; and very boggy streets bore placards which informed the public that no bottom was available. Through the mud padded Songhees Indians, indolently hawking clams, salmon ... and berries."[18] The Right Reverend George Hills brought the Church of England to tame Victoria's English elite; Father Brabant brought the Roman Catholic missions to tame the upcoast "savages"; and the nuns arrived and established St. Ann's Academy to tame the children. Of course, the pious were not the only ones intent upon taming the beast within. Matthew Baillie Begbie and the Admiralty brought British law and order to address any sinner the churches somehow missed. And they all brought smallpox.

By 1869, three-quarters of British Columbia's Aboriginal population was gone. One hundred thousand people had become 25,000 in less than ten years. When smallpox hit Victoria in 1862, all local Aboriginals, including wives of Whites, were ordered to Ogden Point and quarantined.[19] In consequence, many headed straight to their home villages. White miners received no such dictate: they were free to travel and carried the dreaded disease, which spread like pearls of death up through the Fraser River and Thompson River camps to the goldfields. The effects of smallpox were to be felt directly in Victoria and throughout the colony until the 1880s. Though the Aboriginal population suffered most, the dreaded pox claimed significant numbers of all groups—rich, poor, Aboriginal, and White alike. When visiting upcoast Aboriginals caught the disease in Victoria in 1862 and refused an order to leave the city, the local constabulary set fire to over 100 of their harbourside shanties.[20] Those who were forced, in consequence, to return north carried the disease with them, thus wildly exacerbating the problem. Aboriginal susceptibility to smallpox, in turn, placed the lives of White settlers in further jeopardy, thus serving to add even more legitimacy to an already negative White attitude towards Aboriginals.

Those miners and settlers who survived the first wave of smallpox may have counted themselves lucky, but they weren't particularly happy. All were a very long way from home, and many were lonely. Old Anglican rector Lundin Brown of Lillooet knew of the difficulty they had in "fighting the good fight" against temptation. Nights were crisp in the mountains, and a man wanted a woman to keep him warm. It wasn't long before Brown had organized what came to be known as the "brideships." On September 17, 1862, the steamer *Tynemouth* hove into view in Victoria with 60 eligible young Englishwomen, aged fourteen and up, all no doubt anxious to start a new life. Many of the women had pre-arranged employment in Victoria, while others had specific plans to marry. Others had their own plans. Few of the women could anticipate the welcome that awaited them. Of course, Brown did manage to provide the 60 hopefuls with a shipboard "governess" during the outbound voyage, in order to protect his valued entourage from what must have been the drooling mouths of the *Tynemouth*'s crew. Nights can be cold at sea as well.

Victoria was abuzz with anticipation. A young reporter was able to get aboard the vessel, anchored off Esquimalt, and relate the news to a city that, for a moment, held its collective breath. With a flair for the dramatic, the journalist filed his report with the *British Colonist*, September 18:

> We went aboard the steamer yesterday morning and had a good look at the lady passengers. They are mostly cleanly, well built, pretty looking young women—ages varying from fourteen to an uncertain figure; a few are young widows who have seen better days. Most appear to have been well raised and generally they seem a superior lot to the women usually met with on emigrant vessels. Taken together, we are highly pleased with the appearance of the "invoice" ... They will be brought to Victoria and quartered in the Marine Barracks, James Bay, early in the morning by the gunboat Forward. A large number of citizens visited Esquimalt yesterday and endeavored to board the vessel, but were generally ordered off and returned from their fruitless errand with heavy hearts.[21]

At least one historian has recorded a suspicion that some of the women may have been prostitutes in London, or, once seeing the size of a miner's poke, soon became involved in the trade in Victoria.[22] A second brideship, the *Robert Lowe*, arrived in Victoria early in 1863. This time, however, only 36 women took the proverbial plunge. Nonetheless, the arrival of the *Robert Lowe* led to 1,000 people gawking at the disembarkation, forcing the poor women to "run the gauntlet through them amid the utterance of coarse jokes."[23] Somewhat like the "Filles du Roi" (the King's Daughters), recruited by France for marriage to Quebec farmers between 1663 and 1673, the brideships of Victoria were to provide a stabilizing, humanizing element by introducing women into a social unit made up primarily of rough bachelors. It didn't work.

Settlement, law, order, and "culture," in and around Victoria, were the only answers to the enormity of the frontier and its existential vacuum. Craigflower Farm, Constance Cove Farm, Viewfield Farm, Fairfield Farm, Upland's Farm, and Cadboro Bay Farm, which totalled thousands upon thousands of acres of prime Victoria landscape, were all run by astute English HBC managers who, from the start, had rejected the British government's injunction of settlement. Independent settlers were forced further afield. Conflict and violence, occasionally resulting in the murder of these settlers by displaced Aboriginals, was inevitable. Inter-tribal violence was common among Natives on the coast, as it was among Natives elsewhere. However, the White community took these internecine raids and generalized them into savage acts committed by all Natives upon all people. The unfortunate Songhees were the recipients of this growing cultural animosity. Those who wandered into Victoria from their nearby reserve were regarded as a "depraved eyesore."

There was a horrific retribution raid by the Cowichan on the Bella Bella at Ganges on Saltspring Island, in 1860. White settlers became caught in the crossfire. The Lamalchi of Thetis Island carried out numerous and violent raids during 1863 on passing Cowichan canoes and the cargo boats of White settlers. Blacks, themselves fleeing the slavery of the American South, were attacked by the Quamichans on South Pender Island in 1863. In consequence, Victoria drew into itself, thankful of the colonial presence in Esquimalt of the Royal Navy and preferring to concentrate on D.W. Higgins's column in the *Weekly Chronicle*, which dealt with parliamentary antics in the colonial legislature. But the violence continued. A settler was shot by firelight, and his wife was axed by the Lamalchi at Miner's Bay on Mayne Island in 1863. The Royal Navy destroyed the Lamalchi camp at Village Bay on Mayne Island later that same summer.[24] And on and on it went, until 1864, when a rampage, a pillaging, and a massacre would bring outright war in the Chilcotin. Victoria looked on in horror.

The highly educated English-cum-American wholesale grocer Alfred Waddington had arrived in Victoria in 1858 to open a branch of his San Francisco business at Government and Johnson Streets. As would-be miners poured into Victoria that gold-rush summer, it didn't take Waddington long to spot an opportunity. Astute developer that he was, he had bought a sizable piece of open land lying roughly between Johnson and Yates Streets. Soon he was busy: "Dividing the land along Waddington Alley into small lots, he erected buildings of redwood he had imported from California and leased them out to a variety of tenants, including a fish market, a bakery, a blacksmith, the Sacramento Restaurant, and the Bowling and Refreshment Saloon."[25]

Alfred Waddington, like Amor de Cosmos and David Higgins, was a strong advocate of union with Canada. In pursuing this aim he became embroiled in a deadly confrontation with the Chilcotin.

Ever the utopian dreamer, Waddington believed strongly in the idea of a trans-Canada railway for British Columbia, and he worked tirelessly for it in Victoria, Ottawa, and London until his sudden death due to smallpox in 1872. In 1864, his latest scheme was to build a road through to the Cariboo from the head of Bute Inlet. The intent was simply to divert money away from the mainland city of New Westminster to his own growing business interests in Victoria. As it was, gold from the interior plateau of New Caledonia headed south, going slowly overland through the difficult and dangerous Coast Mountains to the burgeoning mainland city near the mouth of the Fraser River. Waddington's plan was as simple as it was brilliant. He would cut a shorter 70-mile road straight west from the Chilcotin through the Coast Mountains to the head of Bute Inlet and ferry goods, people, and money south to Victoria directly via the Strait of Georgia. To progressive Victorians, who were fully aware of what the mainland city was doing to their profits and

Attack on a Native village in Clayoquot Sound
by HMS *Sutlej* and HMS *Devastation*.

who were ever mindful of a business opportunity, the idea seemed sound.

Waddington soon had a syndicate of Victoria businessmen eager to back his venture, a government go-ahead in the form of a charter and a plan. What he didn't have, like so many coastal traders before him, was any appreciation of Aboriginal rights to land. The proposed route from the Chilcotin to Bute Inlet would pass right through traditional Chilcotin hunting lands. For Waddington, as for so many others, the land was simply there for the taking. That Aboriginals should resist such progress was simply indefensible. In the spring of 1864, however, all went awry. On April 30, with the road already 40 miles east from the head of the inlet up the valley of the Homathko, all hell broke loose. Fourteen members of Waddington's party were massacred in their tents at dawn by a Chilcotin band out to protect its sovereignty. Waddington's friends in Victoria, who still daily confronted the "shiftless" Songhees in front of their businesses on Government Street, were aghast.

Response from Victoria was swift. Seymour dispatched the frigate HMS *Sutlej* north to Bute Inlet. Aboard was a volunteer force of vengeful Royal Engineers, friends of the slain. It was quickly renamed the New Westminster Volunteer Rifle Corps.[26] Of the six Chilcotin brought to trial, "Hanging Judge Begbie" committed five to the gallows.

Meanwhile, back in Victoria, farmlands were being carved into city lots as the winners from the goldfields retreated to the coast. Most arrived to spend and "put on airs." Bad taste exacerbated by money was everywhere. The streets of Victoria soon became a collage of nonconformity. The stone, pillared Bank of British North America was not far removed from the clapboard Willows Hotel. The Oriental Hotel on Yates Street allegedly housed ladies who played through the night, while the Victoria Eleven Cricket Team played in Beacon Hill Park through the day. If the circus of stuffy, appointed legislators in the ornate set of buildings known as "the Birdcages" wasn't enough, then you could attend a real circus imported from San Francisco. Victoria's first banking house, Macdonald's Bank at Yates and Wharf Streets, had already suffered its first big robbery,[27] and *Uncle Tom's Cabin* graced the Victoria Theatre. The young women from St. Ann's Academy who attended dances put on by the Royal Navy probably shouldn't have. Meanwhile Stotts Boarding House remained *the* preferred place of residence for respectable young men. For their evening pleasure, Lowe Brothers, Commission Merchants at Yates and Langley, was still importing French wines and cigars. As an expression of the permanent presence and power of British interests, between 1858 and 1871 Judge Matthew Baillie Begbie hung 27 men: 22 Indians, 4 Whites, and 1 Chinese.[28] When in Victoria, Begbie lived the life of a dashing bachelor about town. He was elected first president of the Victoria Philharmonic Society, was knighted, and later became a noted horticulturist.

In 1869, Victoria already had a library, a hospital with an Aboriginal ward, an hourly carriage service from Victoria to Esquimalt across one of its two new bridges, and a Masonic lodge. There existed a carefully regulated non-sectarian public school system, several religious academies, and a sizable Chinatown that was redolent of the "aromas of unnamable viands, burning joss sticks, and damp bamboo."[29] The city also boasted several clothiers, a gas works, streetlights, a fire station, and Madame Pettibeau's Fort Street Seminary for Young Ladies.

The streetlight that illuminated Carroll's Liquor Store also shone on the city's many saloons and brothels. Government Street was a melange of former gold-rush shanties, old hotels, and new businesses. Goodacre and Dooley's Butcher Shop (Queen's Market, on the east side at Johnson Street) and the Star Saloon adjoined the Theatre Royal and the stately edifice of Caresche, Green and Company's Bank. In the last days of Victoria's colonial period, though the government was nearly bankrupt, small businesses had gained a promising foothold. By 1869, Victoria

The staff of Goodacre and Dooley's Butcher Shop proudly stand before their new sign, which honours their distant monarch, Queen Victoria.

could boast four breweries, two distilleries, a soap factory, two lumber yards, two sash factories, two tanneries, an iron foundry, and a shipyard.[30]

As the spring of 1869 gently wore on into summer, what was really being illuminated in the minds of thoughtful Victorians, beyond the excesses of the city and the fears of the frontier, was the rapidly changing political landscape. For the two preceding years the *British Colonist* had been rife with the debates over Confederation. Earlier, in 1866, it had been just as strident over the Act of Union between Vancouver Island and the mainland. The catalyst for the renewed debate over a "sea-to-sea" dominion was two significant events that occurred only months apart in 1867. First, on March 30, American Secretary of State William Henry Seward concluded negotiations to purchase Alaska for $7,200,000. Second, on July 1, 1867, Quebec, Ontario, Nova Scotia, and New Brunswick federated to become the Dominion of Canada.

Confederation was an issue close to ordinary people, and those living in Victoria were no exception. The popular voice was expressed by the newspapers of the day. The literate gentlemen of the Victorian Age were nourished by political opinion. Newspapers not only encouraged that opinion, they advocated it. They aroused passions and elevated prejudice. In Victoria, a small printing press that had survived a journey around Cape Horn became the first organ of public opinion.

The man to start that press was himself a lover of liberty.

Amor de Cosmos was a journalist who left Nova Scotia in 1851, lured to California by the rumours of gold. It seems that de Cosmos left Halifax somewhat of a Mormon, and by the time he reached Utah he had internalized a considerable amount of Mormon philosophy—all except the idea of marriage or, worse yet, polygamous marriage.[31] Drawn to Victoria in 1858, after gaining financial success as a photographer in California, he was dismayed by an island colony whose so-called legislative assembly was little more than a dictatorship of HBC magnates. There and then he set about his life's work: to bring a democratic, completely elected, responsible government to an amalgamated colony and to bring that colony into Confederation. More, he bought the press and founded a newspaper, the *British Colonist*, with which to do it!

The Honourable Amor de Cosmos

It didn't take long for de Cosmos to ruffle the feathers of the colonial administration. In his first edition of December 11, 1858, he attacked the long-standing HBC hierarchy presided over by Governor Douglas: "Unfortunately for these colonies Gov. Douglas was not equal to the occasion. He wanted to serve his country with honor, and at the same time preserve the grasping interests of the Hudson's Bay Company inviolate."[32] By December 18, de Cosmos had made the *British Colonist* his pulpit. The oligarchy that ruled Vancouver Island, he charged, was full of "toadyism, consanguinity, and incompetence, compounded with white-washed Englishmen and renegade Yankees."[33]

The government, led by HBC chief factor James Douglas, reacted by trying to close down de Cosmos's newspaper, but this eccentric with an attitude had gained immense popularity by the simple means of giving voice to a common opinion. De Cosmos, like others, wanted a free press, a free trade, and a new form of political freedom—a national constitutional monarchy. Through his press, and at a series of public meetings, he denounced the government's action and further legitimized the idea of British Columbia joining Canada. Such actions would eventually lead de Cosmos into public life. Evoking the mid-Victorian liberalism of Joseph Howe, the Nova Scotia freedom-fighter whom he must have heard in his youth, de Cosmos would require the help of former enemies before British Columbia would join the rest of Canada. As a public official, de Cosmos would serve first as an elected representative in the Vancouver Island House of Assembly (1863-66). Later, he was elected to the British Columbia Legislative Council (1867-68), the Legislative Assembly (1871-74), and the Canadian House of Commons (1871-72). For just over a year he was the second premier of British Columbia (1872-74).[34]

The landed gentry of Victoria, the established church, and the high poo-bahs of Victoria's very private denominational school system had good reason to fear de Cosmos during the latter half of the 1860s. Selling the *British Colonist* when he entered public life,[35] de Cosmos's rhetoric had helped to inspire the formation of other Victoria newspapers, such as D.W. Higgins's pro-Canadian *Weekly Chronicle* and Leonard McClure's short-lived annexationist *Telegraph*. The 72 resolutions that were approved at the Quebec Conference of 1865 soon resulted in a vociferous debate in the newspapers across British North America. By 1866, Higgins's *Chronicle* and the *Colonist* had merged, and together they were intent upon soundly defeating Governor Seymour's anti-Confederationist views.

The clamorous voice of that merger came from another dynamic, 28-year-old Nova Scotian—a man who had arrived in Victoria only four years earlier. David Williams Higgins had seen the gold rush first-hand from a camp near Yale on the Fraser River. By 1861 he was back in Victoria, first as an employee of the mercurial Amor de Cosmos and later as the owner of the *Weekly Chronicle*. He stated the parameters of the coming debate quite clearly: "Let the people of the Colonies only understand that by annexation they must abandon that happy mean they now enjoy between the arbitrariness of English institutions on the one hand, and the tyranny of the many in democratic America on the other."[36] Higgins would soon, however, become a prime player in moving British Columbia towards Confederation. He would also become the leading newspaper publisher of his day and a respected politician. More important for us, his time in New Caledonia gave him a sense of the

The only business section in town in the 1860s was here at the intersection of Government and Fort Streets. Even at this early date, Victoria is already showing the restrained and confident architecture of its British origins. Notice, however, the wooden sidewalks. The photo on the right page is looking east on Fort Street from Government Street, while the photo above looks north along Government Street from Fort Street.

times and its racial conflicts. He was captivated by the human dramas he had witnessed both in Yale and in Victoria, and he would chronicle many of them in later life. Indeed, D.W. Higgins was *the* prime eyewitness reporter regarding the events of the *John Bright* affair, and he had a direct hand, as we shall see, in pushing the story into the public domain.

For the moment, however, he was absorbed in the issue of Confederation. By Confederation year, the new colony of British Columbia was feeling neglected, isolated, and vulnerable. The debate in Victoria divided newspapers into Annexationist and Confederationist camps. By 1867, under the control of David Higgins, the *British Colonist* expressed the growing sentiment:

> We know we speak the mind of nine out of ten men in the Colony ... men who after struggling for years to awaken the Home Government to a sense of the wrongs under the weight of which we are staggering, have at last sat down in despair at the gloomy prospects before them ... The people disgusted, disheartened and all but ruined ... are loud in their expression of a preference for the stars and stripes. The sentiment is heard on every street corner ... at the theatre ... in the saloon ... and the feeling is growing and spreading daily.[37]

American Annexationists living in Victoria suddenly got a shot in the arm, as did the British, who felt the only way to preserve their British heritage was for British Columbia to join Canada.

Governor Seymour wanted to stall a council debate on Confederation until the dispute over the remaining HBC holding in "Rupert's Land" in the North-West Territories could be resolved. What he was really trying to do, however, was to subvert an inflamed public opinion and to gain time to produce signatures for an anti-Confederation petition he would send to Ottawa. Higgins would have none of it.

Meanwhile, the fox (or, rather, the eagle) was at the gate. American troops were in Alaska, and one American politician—Senator Banks—echoing the voice of many, introduced a bill in the American Senate allowing President Grant "to annex the British North American colonies whenever he desired, in exchange for paying their debts."[38] Setbacks could ruin the day, especially when, on the Prairies, Louis Riel was in the process of installing himself as president of Assiniboia, asserting the rights of his beloved Métis. In 1869, British North America was being carved with many knives.

If Seymour and the controlling oligarchy of the colony could not be roused into action, David Higgins, ever the journalist and storyteller, knew the power of public opinion. He presented a plan to Amor de

This sombre perspective of what was to come for Native peoples was captured by period photographer Frederick Dally in this 1869 landscape. It was taken from the site of the Songhees village across Victoria harbour.

Cosmos that would circumvent Seymour's unrepresentative council altogether. The plan called for a direct lobby that would enable Canada, not recalcitrant British Columbia, to precipitate negotiations with the citizens of the western colony.[39] D.W. Higgins, among others, went to Ottawa. Prime Minister John A. Macdonald bought the idea, and a defeated Governor Seymour turned his attention to less raucous conflicts on the outer coast. He would never return to Victoria. Three short years later, on July 20, 1871, British Columbia entered Confederation.

⚓ ⚓ ⚓ ⚓ ⚓

These, then, were some of the forces, themes, personalities, and memories that the good citizens of Victoria would be subject to that fateful summer of 1869. The business elite had no time for Karl Marx's *Das Kapital* or Charles Darwin's *The Origin of Species*, both available at Spencer's Stationary.[40] Although that was the year John Stuart Mill had written *On the Subjection of Women*, few in Victoria read it. More to the taste of Victorians were Louisa May Alcott's *Little Women*, Dostoevsky's *The Idiot,* and the leftover spicy bits from the impeachment trial of U.S. president Andrew Johnson. Matthew Arnold's *Culture and Anarchy*, also published that year, was, for many, far too close to home.

Leaving home was becoming both less challenging and more frightening. On the one hand, G.A. Hansen had isolated the bacterium

The Songhees near Victoria quickly adopted European clothing styles.

that caused leprosy, paving the way for a vaccine and less risky foreign travel; on the other hand, Robert Whitehead had just invented the underwater torpedo. Though the grass still grew "between the boards of wooden sidewalks,"[41] you could get to Chicago in a hurry via the recently opened first rail link across North America—the Union Pacific Railway from San Francisco. Compared to San Francisco's 170,000 inhabitants, its gambling casinos, and its stately Spanish homes, Victoria, with its 5,000 inhabitants, appeared to be little more than a bucolic backwater. The world may have been getting smaller in 1869, with the opening of the Suez Canal and the launching of the *Cutty Sark*, but Victoria's past was ominous, and its present still uncertain.

As we have seen, the tranquil closed composure of pioneer life under the aegis of the HBC had been shattered completely. In less than a generation, American free spending and British frugality had created a schizophrenic city, where resentment turned with full fury against coastal Aboriginals. The one constant in this brooding time was the unflinching belief in the civility of the Empire and its God-given right to effect law and order on the frontier. The agent of that order on this far-flung ocean shore was the British Admiralty. And it is the Admiralty that will take us to Hesquiat, to the next piece of our puzzle, and, ultimately, to the wreck of the *John Bright*.

CHAPTER 5
Dead Reckoning[1]

Nobody stuffs the world in at your eyes.
The optic heart must venture: a jail break
And re-creation.

Margaret Avison [2]

I walked out alone to the end of the rock promontory north of this nondescript little indentation in the many miles of rugged coastline and looked back over the place in which we found ourselves. I was frankly amazed that we had even found the petroglyphs, an immovable art treasure on a desolate coast that some refer to as the edge of nowhere. Yet the roar of the ocean up and down a surge channel behind me, and the sight of this beguiling little cove with its priceless offerings, soothed my initial anxiety. It was good to sit and rest my weary bones. My mind went back to the 70-year-old letter in an old newspaper, the fascinating clue that first linked the petroglyphs of this place with the tragedy of the *John Bright*. It was that small news clipping in response to an even briefer article about the glyphs of Clo-oose that had started me on this whole crazy journey.

The sailing-ship glyphs, in particular, were absolutely compelling. I smiled at John Gellard, who was on his hands and knees studying them carefully. Suddenly, my mind flashed to Pachena Point and to the wreck of the *Michigan,* whose boiler I had seen the first day of our trek, rusting away on the foreshore. It had reminded me of Pitseolak's striking photograph of the *Nascopie,* aground and sinking off Cape Dorset on faraway Baffin Island some 50 years after the *Michigan's* own sad end. For me, the old boiler simply represented an event; the Inuit's photo, like the glyphs that now lay before me, represented an event transformed into art.

Renewed, I headed back towards the beach; the desolate coast seemed a little softer, its isolation not as overwhelming. People deeply in touch with nature had lived here and taken the time to create works of art. I felt an outrage towards those artists of my own heritage who had dismissed Aboriginal art as primitive. John motioned me towards a new discovery, and I went over to see that he had found a set of strange bird figures. With glyphs of fish, seals, birds, ships, and strange human forms graven into the sandstone shelves all about me, I was perplexed. What was it, exactly, that these stone carvers were trying to say? Watching the waves crash into this barren shore, it struck me just how wrong those early Europeans were to portray the B.C. coast as a place of abundance. The Aboriginal peoples who had once prevailed here and had created a body of art certainly were not savages. Moreover, the art that lay beneath my feet was not simply an art born of plenty. There was much more to it than that.

Yet as we had hiked, roots, skunk cabbage, sprouts, bulbs, and berries seemed to be everywhere along the thin coastal plain. Moreover, we saw the tracks of deer and bear as we wove in and out of the forest. Shellfish, mollusks, and crabs were abundant in the many tide pools, and grey whales spouted offshore. The massive conifers lent themselves to the making of huge whaling canoes, longhouses, and totem poles. Was it the majesty of the Aboriginal village sites, the middens of clamshells, and the dignity of the chiefs that seduced early writers and artists into believing that life here was easy? Certainly, many artists, like the Irish-born Paul Kane, for example, saw relatively less strife on the Coast than they did on the Plains. Interestingly, their renderings, their art and novels, had an artificial, contrived air about them.

As I watched the sky thicken to grey and felt the temperature plummet, I knew that this place was not always the Eden that some had made it out to be. Salmon did run in the hundreds of thousands, but only in the fall. Waterfowl and whales came and went with the seasons. The climate suffered severe cycles of change. The ragged shoreline and rock-strewn coast hid, from unwary Natives and early mariners alike, dangerous tidal currents and other perils. It is indeed a beguiling place, but it is also an unforgiving place. If the weather turned nasty, and we were socked in here for over a week, then we could be in serious trouble. For two centuries shipwreck survivors had reached this shore only to die of

74   Glyphs and Gallows

This small, circular, well-protected cove (above left) lies just south of Stanley Beach, approximately one and a half miles from Nitinat Narrows. The glyphs face the ocean and are on one sandstone shelf in the middle of the picture. Cliffs, dangerous inshore shelves, immediately south of the Clo-oose Blowhole site (above right), extend all the way from Pachena Bay to Carmanah Point. During storms and at high tides, the surf roars up this particular surge channel at Glyph Cove (below), forcing its way up through various holes and galleries in the rock. The noise created, especially during high tide on stormy nights, is both unnerving and haunting.

starvation or exposure. The primitive trail we had walked was not known as the West Coast Life-Saving Trail for nothing. In earlier times, an extended family of Natives living here could easily have suffered death through accident, illness, severe weather, or hunger.

Indeed, for coastal First Nations in the nineteenth century, starvation was not uncommon. At the turn of the nineteenth century, an anthropologist wrote of the Haida: "They often, through feasting or improvidence, eat up all the dried berries before spring, and were it not for a few bulbs which they dug out of the soil in the early springtime, while awaiting the halibut season, numbers of Indians would really starve to death."[3] *Even Father Brabant, who built the first Roman Catholic mission at Hesquiat on the west coast of Vancouver Island (and, as we shall see, had much to say about the wreck of the* John Bright*), witnessed near starvation. In 1878 he noted: "[There were] two successive springs at Hesquiat when pickings were lean and children cried out with hunger, until the weather eased enough for the fishermen to go out."*[4]

So it was a generous coast to be sure, but it was by no means an Eden. With the coming of the European colonials, many Aboriginals sought to live, work, and gain status in such garrisons as Victoria, Nanaimo, and New Westminster. Did the tragedy of these merging cultures lie in the Aboriginals being seduced by European materialism? Partly. But the real tragedy was that Europeans completely misread the social structure of coastal Aboriginals.

The lavish Aboriginal potlatches were misinterpreted and condemned by Europeans. They were not, as thought, bacchanals; rather, they were a way of solidifying social status as well as an effective means of dealing with the shortages brought on by cyclical extremes. The potlatch provided two ways for Aboriginal peoples to gain high status: through the displaying of ancestral prerogatives and through the giving away of wealth.[5] *Through the potlatch, surplus food was converted into wealth and wealth was converted into status. Better marriages and other culturally significant ties were often the result of such increased status.*[6] *Everybody benefited, while those on the edge of starvation saved face.*

Within Aboriginal cultures, the shaman had knowledge of traditional rites and ceremonies associated with the gaining of status as well as knowledge of traditional medicine. Most often, it was the shaman who was involved with the creation of oral history (myths), the practice of religion, and (indirectly) the production of art. Standing here upon this wild and lonely shore, overlooking this shelf of images, I wondered if the art of the petroglyphs was about exorcising those demons that threatened a good but tenuous life in this harsh and unforgiving land. Aboriginal culture was complex: as violent and as humane as any. And it was a system finely tuned to operate within the northern coastal rain forest— with all of its geographic permutations and climatic uncertainties.

Most of the first Europeans did not care to know about Aboriginal culture. What they did know about it they feared: there were "savages" living on the frontier. This perception clashed with "enlightened" European notions of an ordered universe. I wondered just how this misreading was accomplished—a misreading that transformed an adaptive and creative race of people into either demons or simple-minded children, depending on the needs of the Empire.

The nineteenth-century penchant for "progress" seemed too easy an answer to why such educated men (including judges, admirals, journalists, and governors) treated the Aboriginals with such contempt. I thought about the treatment of the Natives implicated in the John Bright affair and looked over to the glyphs. I began to think about the role of art—especially the role of the European romantic artist who painted the new frontier. I was thinking particularly of the works of the artist Paul Kane. He had studied art in the United States and was inspired by the romantic steeds and heavy prairie skies of the well-known American painter John Mix Stanley.[7] He had even travelled all over Europe copying the excessive madonnas of Raphael and Murillo. In 1846, back in Canada and painting decidedly within the romantic tradition, he began his famous trip across the continent with HBC chief factor Sir George Simpson. Simpson loved his work and commissioned twelve of them. In Kane's paintings, the York boats descending the Saskatchewan River look like Roman galleys. His Indians are often depicted as Napoleon-like, on splendid rearing stallions.[8] One painting, Norway House, depicts a fur-trading post at the north end of Lake Winnipeg. The HBC flag proudly flies from the flagstaff beneath billowing summer clouds. All is royal blue. Beside the fort are York boats, and to the left, paddling off into oblivion, are two Indians in a canoe. They are shown as dwarfed by the imposing White garrison that has pushed them deep into the wilderness.[9] Kane had made the Natives refugees in their own homeland.

Paul Kane visited Vancouver Island in 1847 after crossing the Strait of Juan de Fuca from the Olympic Peninsula. Here he depicts a battle between the Makah (part of the Nuu-chah-nulth language group) and the Clallam, a Salishan people from further south on the peninsula.

In "War Party" Kane depicts a romanticized vision of Aboriginals heading off to engage in internecine warfare.

I knew that by 1847, Kane had visited Vancouver Island where, among other things, he had painted salmon weirs at Sooke, Mount Baker from Gordon Head, the Native village at Esquimalt, and even Fort Victoria itself. He made one sketch based upon an account of a battle at I-ch-nue (just west of Sooke), in which the Clallam had burned the longhouses of the Makah (a Nuu-chah-nulth tribe that had moved across the Strait of Juan De Fuca from Cape Flattery to Vancouver Island).[10] The dark smoke from the burning house is depicted in marked contrast to the beckoning, white totem poles of the once proud village. In two paintings,[11] Kane depicts two distinct and profound nineteenth-century ideologies: (1) the Aboriginal is a "Noble Savage" who will simply disappear from the landscape upon giving way peaceably to nineteenth-century ideas of progress and (2) the Aboriginal is a "murderous savage" whose presence despoils a potentially Edenic landscape—a landscape that it was up to enlightened Europeans to recover. Paul Kane's work was very popular; he was lionized in London, he published a book, and the British and Canadian governments commissioned many of his works.

I thought, too, of Peter Rindisbacher, who was another European (Swiss) artist. He painted the Canadian west before Kane. Arriving in the Red River area in 1821, he painted a small watercolour of the governor of Assiniboia addressing a group of seated, attentive Chippewyan chiefs.[12] Portrayed Napoleon-like, with his arm in his shirt, the British governor dominates one side of the picture, while the British flag dominates the other. The painting has all the qualities of a Sunday School lesson, with the docile, obedient, child-like Natives absorbing the truth from their new masters. Rindisbacher, like Kane, was also very successful, selling much of his work to HBC officials, both in the Canadas and overseas. The style of both Rindisbacher and Kane, and of a host of others, supported the then prevailing world view—a world view that enabled British immigrants to assume cultural superiority over Aboriginals and that, to no small extent, legitimized genocide.

Over a pot of tea (it was now late afternoon and cold), John and I began a conversation about nineteenth-century British social history and the impact that "Canadian" painting of the colonial period might have had on the local intelligentsia of the time. I condemned the romanticism that had tainted the paintings of Paul Kane and those before him. Either the Aboriginal was left out of the wilderness image altogether or was

Chilcotin children becoming confirmed into the Roman Catholic Church. Anaham, 1940s.

Shaman performing Native healing at Kitwanga in 1910.

portrayed as a primitive. Here I was, at the end of a millennium, able to reach out and touch the petroglyphs—work that White artists, even a century ago, should have acknowledged. Why were we only now willing to condemn racism and celebrate the art of the Nuu-chah-nulth and Haida? I wanted to build a pedestal for the creators of these glyphs and to demolish the one upon which we have placed narrow-minded nineteenth-century European artists. To be sure, the fact that the latter did not attempt to understand the art of Aboriginal peoples cannot be blamed for the state of social consciousness in 1869 Victoria, but it certainly did not help. Any way you look at it, these artists missed an opportunity to help European invaders understand the cultures they were so quickly eliminating.

⚓ ⚓ ⚓ ⚓ ⚓

The day had been long and the rewards great. Tomorrow we would delve deeper, intent on understanding these rock images as best we could. Near at hand the sea had calmed slightly, and my final thoughts turned to the sailing-ship glyphs. Was one of those glyphs a rendering of the HMS Sparrowhawk? *The Royal Navy had been here, at least in spirit, and the petroglyphs of Clo-oose had made its stay eternal.*

CHAPTER 6
The Admiralty on the Northwest Coast: 1812-1869

Rule Britannia!
Britannia rules the waves,
Britons never, never, never shall be slaves.
          Thomas Augustine Arne (1740)

Rule Britannia!
Britannia rules the waves,
Britons never, never, never, shall be marri-ed
to a merma-id
At the bottom of the deep blue sea.
          Sea shanty version, sung at
          Solihull School, Warwickshire (1952)

After Lord Nelson's triumph over 33 French and Spanish warships on October 21, 1805, at Trafalgar, Britain became the undisputed ruler of the world's oceans. It was a claim that survived until the middle of the First World War. The unofficial national anthem, "Rule Britannia," however, continues to be sung after 250 years—most recently while Britain's warships returned from the Falklands in 1982 after a confrontation with Argentina. This song affirms that Britain and its "Empire" will forever be protected by the Royal Navy. Simply, in the century after the end of the Napoleonic Wars (1815), Britain's foreign policy was defined by its supremacy at sea. Britannia, the Roman name for England and Wales, had become anthropomorphized into the great mother goddess—a woman wearing a helmet and carrying a shield and trident. To the anthem "Rule Britannia," Britain had gone to sea, the goddess's trident surely being equated with

Esquimalt Harbour, c. 1860, where ships of the Royal Navy symbolized British supremacy on the west coast.

Neptune's. As a symbol of nationalism, Britannia came to represent an empire upon which the sun didn't set for over 100 years.

The sea shanty version of the same song is, however, more telling. The lines of the shanty "never married to a mermaid, at the bottom of the deep blue sea" are more than schoolboy bombast. They proudly assert that Britain, in gaining mastery of the seas, has defeated both death and nature itself—an idea that, as we have seen, helped shape its nineteenth-century attitude towards all Aboriginals living in its overseas Empire. That attitude provides us with a more critical understanding of the Royal Navy's mandate on our coast at the time of the wreck of the *John Bright*.

The Royal Navy's Pacific Station at Esquimalt had, by 1869, many roles that had been inherited directly from James Cook's voyages in the Pacific nearly 100 years before. Because of Cook and the Royal Navy, Britain extended its overseas Empire immeasurably. Colonies and military outposts in New Zealand and Australia, as well as in the Pacific islands, soon came within the governance of Britain and the vigilance of the Admiralty. Because of Cook and the Royal Navy, Britain was able to extend its trade from China to the Pacific Northwest. When settlers, soldiers, miners and rogues, talkers and traders, and railways and roads created the British Columbia that we know, they did so under the ever-present protection of the Royal Navy. "Empire," "expansionism," and "economics" became, as we shall see, Britain's new watchwords. They did so, however, at a terrible cost.

By the time of the tragedy of the *John Bright* in February 1869, the Royal Navy's Pacific mandate was very broad. British ships in the Pacific had overseen the operation of the HBC from the mouth of the Columbia River northward. Then, when President James Polk's doctrine of "Manifest Destiny" loomed ominously over British territory, and when American Democrats cried "54-40 or fight," the Royal Navy's strength and reputation assured a compromise. The Oregon Treaty was followed by a fracas over a pig in the San Juan Islands, which again threatened to cause war. Once more, the presence of the Royal Navy prevented bloodshed. However, in this instance, British naval superiority was not enough. In the San Juan dispute, the British were out-manoeuvred by international diplomacy. When the Crimean War spilled over from the Black Sea, and Russian interests on the Northwest Coast were once again revived, the ships of the Royal Navy stood by to mitigate fear. The Royal Navy saw to it that settlers made it, in less robust ships, to our wild, western shores. They stopped whisky traders, and they protected the growing numbers of settlers from Aboriginal outrage.

The Royal Navy did all these things with a flair for ceremony, custom, and discipline as well as with an unflinching belief in its new-found place in nature. The "tight-assed" Admiralty of the nineteenth century was not far from parody, as Gilbert and Sullivan well knew. But the officers and men in gunboats such as HMS *Sparrowhawk* were not just the dutiful agents of a larger Imperial polity. When they had to deal with unruly and outraged Aboriginals in such isolated coastal villages as Clo-oose and the Nass River,[1] they were, more ominously, the agents and inheritors of a new quasi-religious nationalism. Along with such dispatchers of British justice as Judge Begbie, not to mention the merciless assault of smallpox, the Royal Navy assured that Aboriginal life on this coast was doomed.

First, the Empire. As of April 1, 1869, Royal Navy estimates of ships and men on station at Esquimalt show some thirteen ships with a complement of 2,968 men.[2] Initially, they were there because the independent trading companies that had established themselves up the long ribbon of the Northwest Coast from California to Alaska were so successful that they began to arouse national interest. Though independent White traders from Russia, Spain, the United States, and Britain were often in open and bloody conflict with Aboriginals (and

HMS *Sparrowhawk* was on station in Esquimalt from 1865 to 1872. Though the *Sparrowhawk* was a steam-driven vessel, its rig was that of a hybrid barque. Its thin smokestacks would have been obscured under sail. Note the clipper bow and fan-tail stern.

Below, a group of naval officers, sailors, and a woman on board HMS *Sparrowhawk*. The officer standing beneath the ship's clock is thought to be Captain Henry Wentworth Mist.

each other) since the middle of the eighteenth century, it wasn't until such conflict aroused large-scale territorial claims that nation states became involved.

The War of 1812 between the United States and British North America had, surprisingly, repercussions on the remote Northwest Coast. It is here that the Royal Navy became involved, so it is here that our investigation must begin.

The interior plateau of British Columbia (named New Caledonia by Simon Fraser, as the country reminded him of his mother's descriptions of the Scottish highlands)[3] had its string of North West Company fur-trading posts almost as soon as Alexander Mackenzie and David Thompson mapped the region west of the Rockies at the turn of the nineteenth century. For these successful new posts, the Nor'Westers needed a depot on the Pacific Ocean. Meanwhile, in the vastness of the Oregon Territory, John Jacob Astor, a wealthy German-American, had, by 1810, his own plans for his Pacific Fur Company. Like the Nor'Westers, he too sought to establish an ocean base at the mouth of the Columbia River. Thompson's descent of the mighty Columbia was a journey of map making, surveying, and diplomacy. He identified a factory site at the confluence of the Fraser and Nechako Rivers (Fort George); however, as important as this was, time was even more important. When David Thompson reached the great river's mouth, the "stars and stripes" already flew boldly over Fort Astoria.

Yet life was not so good in Astoria. The Columbia River Bar proved to be a nightmare for American reprovisioning ships from Boston. One such ship, the *Tonquin,* deliberately sent two longboats and their crews to their deaths while seeking a way across the notorious bar. Finally, Captain Thorn abandoned his attempt to make Fort Astoria and, as we have seen, sailed north to trade in Clayoquot Sound. Soon Fort Astoria was being run by the British—friendly, tough little Nor'Westers, most of whom were from the Shetlands—and "Canadiens" from Quebec. Then, on January 15, 1813, a Pacific Fur Company manager newly arrived from Fort Spokane told them that for the past six months the United States had been at war with Great Britain.[4] Oops!

By failing to appreciate the wrath of the Pacific Ocean when it met the Columbia Bar during the winter months, and thinking, instead, that the absence of ships was due to a coastal blockade, the abandoned, frightened, and hungry American traders sold Fort Astoria to the resident "Canadians." They thereby forfeited, by reciprocally agreed-upon terms, the first and only title of land that the United States held on the whole Pacific coast.

The Royal Navy soon arrived, but there was never any blockade. However, one blunder generated much animosity between the two countries for the next 50 years. HMS *Racoon*, under the command of Captain Black, sailed into the Columbia River in late 1813. Not realizing that Fort Astoria had been sold to a group of Canadians, he proceeded to indulge in an old Royal Navy tradition. On December 13, 1813, after dinner, accompanied by Royal Marines and members of the ship's company, Black went ashore and, as the Nor'Wester eyewitness Gabriel Franchiere noted, "took a British flag that he had brought for the purpose and raised it to the top of the staff; taking a bottle of Madeira, he smashed it against the pole, proclaiming in a loud voice that he took possession of the establishment *and the country* in the name of his Britannic Majesty."[5] Black then, in the name of the king, renamed Fort Astoria, which became Fort George (not to be confused with the one further north). Suddenly a terrific business deal for the Canadians had become, by formal ceremony, an act of war.

The terms of peace at the end of the War of 1812 restored Astoria to the United States, but the damage had been done. Things might have been quite different had the Royal Navy not stuck its ceremonial foot in it. As it was, a simple trading transaction was superseded by an international political action. Because of Black's act, the United States became strategically interested in the Pacific Northwest. In consequence, in order to protect its own interests, Britain would also soon require a Royal Navy outpost in the North Pacific.

The 1821 merger of the HBC and the North West Company brought relative peace to Pacific Northwest commerce for some 20 years. Britain and the United States had agreed to share the Oregon Territory. By 1834, the amalgamated HBC stretched across half a continent, from Fort William on Lake Superior and York Factory on Hudson Bay to Fort Vancouver on the Columbia, Fort Nisqually on Puget Sound, Fort Simpson at the mouth of the Nass River, Fort McLoughlin at Bella Bella, and Fort Taku on the Stikine River. Adroit company management had ensured peace with the Americans, drawn Aboriginal trade away from the

Russians, and given serious consideration to establishing posts in the Yukon. With the steamship *Beaver* on hand—able to deter interloping Boston traders, to navigate coastal inlets, and to approach island harbours regardless of wind or current—who needed the Royal Navy? Not the HBC. At least not until its ship, the *Dryad*, found a Russian navy gunboat blocking the Stikine River, protecting a new Russian trading post that had clearly been built outside its territorial limit.[6] It was 1834, and the Russians were coming.

The Admiralty in London began to think very seriously about its influence in the Pacific. The audacious HBC had expanded to Hawaii, where a fleet of ships delivered exotic wares to the Royal Navy, among others. The Admiralty's annual reconnoitre of the Pacific certainly proved that it was not alone.[7] What the members of the Admiralty found disturbed them sufficiently for them to build a naval base at Valparaiso, Chile, in 1837. The French, moving into Polynesia, laid claim to the Marquesas in 1842. The Spanish were as far north as San Francisco. The Russians, in consequence, farmed 100 miles north of there at Bodega Bay and were firmly established in Alaska. The Americans, already in Hawaii, were by 1842 inexorably pushing west on the newly established Oregon Trail.

If Britannia was to rule, it was time for action. Or, in the parlance of the British government, time for the scientific expedition and the hydrographic survey. In other words, it was time for a high-level presence. The Admiralty dispatched HMS *Blossom* (26 guns) to the Bering Sea, hoping to greet Franklin after his exit from the Northwest Passage. It sent the surveying ship HMS *Sulphur* (eight guns) to Oregon, HMS *Rover* to Mexico, and HMS *Beagle*, along with a young naturalist named Charles Darwin, to the Ecuadorian coast of South America.[8] The result of these government-sponsored expeditions during the first half of the nineteenth century was the creation of whole new paradigms of knowledge in astronomy, geography, navigation, and biology— paradigms that are still relevant today. The Royal Navy's own intelligence along the Pacific coast, however, revealed even more pressing demands for Britain and its economic interests. For the time being, the Russians on the Stikine River would have to wait.

The Lewis and Clark Trail opened up an absolutely colossal area of land west of the Rocky Mountains. By the 1840s, drawn by news from retired HBC employees of a land with a moderate climate, rich in water and soil, settlers and Methodist missionaries from the eastern United States flooded into the area. The trouble was, it was virtually a "terra nullius"—an empty land. To the Europian mind, it had no boundaries, no borders, and no people. What it did have was furs, a few HBC posts, and a long and open coastline that was only occasionally visited by passing ships of the British or American navies. The Pacific Northwest was a land created through exodus.

An 1818 treaty defined a British-United States border from Lake Superior to the Rockies along the 49th parallel. What lay beyond was undefined. The Spanish surrendered their rights to this grey area in 1819. The Russians departed in 1825, when they achieved exclusive rights to a 30-mile strip of land north of 54-40 degrees latitude (north of Queen Charlotte Sound above Vancouver Island) to the 60th parallel of latitude and all lands west (i.e., Alaska and its "panhandle"). West of the Arkansas River then, after 1848, was the Oregon Territory, a huge area that lay, empty of White habitation, on the North American Pacific coast. As mid-century approached, much to the chagrin of the occupying HBC, American settlers arrived in the thousands. Suddenly this Oregon land had two takers.

It didn't take long for Governor Pelly of the HBC to write to the British foreign secretary asking for a clearly delineated border between British North America and the United States west of the Rockies. Pelly claimed that the HBC's thirteen posts in the region, along with the absence of American settlers, should secure the border to the Columbia River and the sea. British North America then would consist of all of Canada, Washington, northern Idaho, and a goodly piece of Montana.[9] The United States would gain all the fertile lands south of the Columbia River, which, at the time, were also without settlement.[10] By 1844, Democratic presidential candidate James Polk, speaking on behalf of the settlers in Oregon, was having none of it. The United States not only wanted Oregon, it wanted the Colony of British Columbia as far north as Prince Rupert. The new border was to become the battle cry that swept him into office: "54-40 or fight"! And there certainly would have been a fight had not the Royal Navy been there to call Polk's bluff.

The Foreign Office instructed the Admiralty to send a warship, the sloop HMS *Modeste* (18 guns), to the Northwest Coast in July 1844.[11] If war broke out, then the problem of sending British troops overland to the Pacific, or by sea to the mouth of the Columbia River, would be horrific. Sir Robert Peel, the British prime minister, considered the latter action but was convinced by Britain's foreign minister, Lord Aberdeen, that the Royal Navy's reputation, its presence and show of force, and its gunboat diplomacy would stave off all-out war.[12] Tensions mounted.

There were calls for a military post at Lower Fort Garry in Red River. There were plans drawn up for "three batteries of guns at Cape Disappointment, Oregon, and a huge naval base at Fort Nisqually in Puget Sound."[13] What actually occurred was a slow, careful, and unrelenting display of British naval power. The British frigate HMS *America* (50 guns) was sent to Port Discovery, near the end of the Strait of Juan de Fuca. If necessary, it was to commandeer the HBC's *Beaver*.[14] The commander-in-chief of the Pacific, Rear-Admiral Sir George Seymour (no relation to Governor Frederick Seymour), in the massive flagship HMS *Collingwood* (80 guns), left Tahiti for Hawaii, where, along with HMS *Talbot* (26 guns), it ensured that a decidedly British influence would be felt.

The Americans in Hawaii would soon alert Washington to the arrival of more Royal Navy heavy firepower. The small paddlewheel sloop HMS *Cormorant* (six guns), along with a merchant vessel (the coal tender *Rosalind*), was sent north from Valparaiso. The frigate HMS *Grampus* (50 guns) was ordered out from England, and HMS *Juno* and HMS *Spy* were to meet Seymour's flagship off Mexico. HMS *Fisgard* (46 guns) was prepared to enter the Columbia River, while HMS *Daphne* (18 guns) and the heavy frigate HMS *America* (50 guns) were, by now, in Fort Victoria's harbour. Much to Seymour's disgust, HMS *America*, under commercial pressure, suddenly left Victoria "without orders"—its hold full of merchant's money. Victoria was short of an armed frigate, but its wonderful money was on its way to London. The Admiralty was not amused.[15]

Interestingly, while in Hawaii, Rear-Admiral Seymour met the enemy in the person of his American counterpart, Pacific Commodore John F. Sloat of the United States navy. Seymour learned that the American warship USS *Columbus* and the frigate USS *Constitution* were being sent to the Northwest.[16] The situation was becoming grave. At the time, the intelligence given to the rear-admiral of the Pacific indicated that the United States navy had eleven ships in the Pacific, the French navy sixteen, and the Royal Navy fifteen.[17] Britain's refusal to commission more ships, even in the light of a possible joint French-American conflict, led eventually to the resignation of the first lord of the Admiralty, the Earl of Ellenborough, in July 1846.

Ironically, the tide turned away from war when the American chargé d'affaires, Louis McLane, met with the British foreign minister on January 6, 1848. After the meeting he wrote to his government in Washington, warning it that Britain *was* prepared for a massive build-up of naval power.[18] It was a poker game in which one bluff was called by another. Simply, the United States made a deal because it believed there was a gun being held to its head.

The Royal Navy's gunboat diplomacy[19] not only saved Britain and the United States from another costly war, but it also secured the future of the British colony of Vancouver Island. The HBC abandoned Fort George (Astoria) in favour of Fort Vancouver, which was some miles further up the Columbia River and, more important, on its northern bank. HBC chief factor Dr. John McLoughlin was certain the Americans would adopt all lands south of the Columbia, while the British would retain possession of modern-day Washington. With time, even that seemed uncertain, so in 1842 McLoughlin sent his accountant, James Douglas, north in search of an ideal backup site for the HBC's Pacific headquarters. As fate would have it, the idyllic setting of Fort Victoria and the magnificent harbour of Esquimalt would provide a final Pacific home for both Britannia's bastion of commerce and its Royal Navy.[20]

British ships-of-the-line continually visited Fort Victoria and Fort Vancouver during the next nine years. "Empire" as well as "economics" had been secured by the appointment of the HBC's chief factor, James Douglas, as second governor of the new colony of Vancouver Island. Douglas had brought about the "comforting presence"[21] of the Royal Navy. Hence, in the late 1850s, the management of the newest resource (coal) and, later, the American scramble into the goldfields was largely peaceful. However, due to the outbreak of the Crimean War, the presence of the Royal Navy would soon become permanent. The Russians had come once too often.

In June 1854, Britain and France declared war on Russia. Without resistance, Russia had fortified Ayan (on the Sea of Okhotsk in the

Northeastern Pacific) and Petropavlovsk (on the Kamchatka Peninsula). The whaling grounds of the North Pacific basin, a secure foothold on new fur-bearing regions, and easy commerce with China and Japan had gone virtually unheeded. During the hostilities, Governor Douglas had secured neutrality from Russian posts in the North Pacific, but, being both HBC chief factor and governor, he was a man who wore two hats. When he demanded British support for an armed force should the Russians decide to attack Victoria from Sitka, the Admiralty laughed at him, deeming Fort Victoria so unimportant that the Russians would never consider wasting firepower on it. They blamed Douglas for trying to foist the increasing cost of defending settlers against Aboriginals on Whitehall instead of where it belonged, on the "honourable" HBC.[22] They were right.

Ships in Esquimalt Harbour were a comforting presence to English colonists.

It was only when one-third of a combined force of 700 French and British sailors succumbed trying to take Petropavlovsk by land that Douglas was heeded. When the battle was over in 1854, three British ships—HMS *President*, HMS *Pique*, and HMS *Virago*—left Petropavlovsk and retreated across the Pacific to Esquimalt to get aid. The need for a permanent North Pacific shore facility in North America was clearly evident.

Rear-Admiral Bruce made his formal request for such a facility in a letter to Governor Douglas dated February 1855: "Your excellency will probably be able to provide a building upon the arrival of the squadron that may serve as a temporary hospital for the sick and wounded, the want of which was so seriously felt last year."[23] In response, Douglas built three huts, at a cost of 932 pounds, at Duntze Head. By 1857, when Captain James Prevost of HMS *Satellite* formally took over the "Crimea huts," they were well used. The first hut did become the requested hospital, the second was used for stores, and the third housed both the office of the hydrographic survey and the residence of the attending surgeon, Samuel Campbell. By 1860 the Admiralty had sent three hospital attendants and a large supply of medical stores to this "temporary location." When a Royal Navy magazine was established on Cole Island (near the head of Esquimalt Harbour) later the same year, it was well on its way to becoming a permanent Pacific station.[24]

And it was "luxury, absolute luxury," compared to the Chilean South Pacific station, where sailors were first stationed aboard older decommissioned frigates such as HMS *Nereus*, moored in scorching Valparaiso, and later, aboard HMS *Naiad* in the more sheltered, although flea-infested, harbour of Coquimbo in nearby Callao. The language, the currency, and the culture were daunting. Life at anchor aboard the old hulks in this sweaty Southern hemisphere was cramped, hot, and boring. When news reached Valparaiso of a "land naval establishment being formed in the fir-tree covered Island of Vancouver on the Northwest Coast, there was much rejoicing amongst officers and ratings alike."[25]

In the 1860s, enlisted officers and gentlemen of the Royal Navy drooled for the opportunity to be posted to the Admiralty's new Pacific station at Victoria. Hell, there were women, official government balls, and people actually spoke English! One of those lucky gentlemen, a sub-lieutenant aboard the hydrographic survey vessel HMS *Pylades,* a new steam corvette on station in Esquimalt between 1859 and 1861, was a son of the English novelist Charles Dickens.[26]

In 1863 a permanent Royal Navy hospital replaced the Royal Engineers quarters at the head of Skinners Cove. Soon there would be a graving dock, a foundry, proper officers quarters, a parade ground, and a fine, cool, all-weather anchorage. The business of Esquimalt—providing security, first for trade, second for the colony and, hence, the Empire—had begun in earnest. When it was heard that American settlers planned to colonize the Queen Charlotte Islands, Admiral Moresby could readily place a Royal Navy vessel there. As it was, the paddlewheel

On the deck of HMS *Satellite*, ca. 1857. The two Royal Navy gunboats, HMS *Satellite* and HMS *Sparrowhawk*, had much to do with the winning of British Columbia and the execution of "justice" at Hesquiat.

sloop HMS *Virago* (six guns) and the old sailing frigate HMS *Thetis* (38 guns) proved sufficient to fly the white-ensign and protect British sovereignty from what the Admiralty called "marauders without title."[27] When hordes of American miners swarmed up the Fraser River during the gold rush of 1858, they swelled the population of Victoria from 500 to 6,000. They brought with them their own frontier disregard for order and a penchant for brawling, while a new steam corvette, HMS *Satellite* (21 guns), and a surveying sloop, HMS *Plumper* (12 guns), stood off the Fraser River as a psychological deterrent. The miners were sold licences of passage, clearly demonstrating British sovereignty. More, the Royal Navy provided an early version of the Coast Guard. It patrolled the sea lanes from the western approaches of the Strait of Juan de Fuca to Victoria and New Westminster, providing safe passage for the many passenger ships bound for the mainland colony.[28] When gold was discovered in the Cariboo and north on the Stikine in 1860, the paddlewheel sloop HMS *Devastation* (six guns) provided miners with safe passage through Russian territory (the mouth of the Stikine River lay in the Russian panhandle) into the hinterland. It later brought many of these same miners, disheartened and frozen, home.[29]

In January 1849, the British government leased Vancouver Island to the HBC for seven shillings a year, with the stipulation that the company foster wholesale English settlement of the Island in order to safeguard it from encroaching Americans. To keep an eye on things, Britain appointed a colonial governor, Richard Blanshard, an ambitious young London lawyer with connections to the British Colonial Office. He had no colonial experience but was so keen to get the job that he offered to work for nothing until colonial rule was fully established.

Richard Blanshard's keenness to be a colonial governor lasted little more than a year.

On arrival in the colony, Blanshard failed to understand the HBC's status in Victoria. His attempts to sell land to British settlers failed primarily due to his personal and public animosity towards Chief Factor James Douglas.[30] Achieving only rebuff from HBC employees, Blanshard epitomized the split between the "stand-offish" attitude of the English aristocracy and that of the less educated, coarser HBC "riffraff." Pulling in little revenue, Blanshard was quickly going broke. Within a year, emotionally drained, he resigned.

James Douglas became the colonial governor on August 30, 1851. Douglas's authority was almost total. As a chief factor he had become used to a deference that approached deification. "Old Squaretoes" appointed an executive council that, in due course, would be criticized for simply abiding by his wishes. Douglas didn't care. He believed that "people do not naturally take much interest in affairs of Government as long as affairs go on well and prosperously, and are content to leave questions of state to their ruling classes."[31]

This 1860s painting by J.A. Startin shows the *Plumper* anchored in Port Harvey, Johnstone Strait. The survey ship served on the coast from 1857 to 1861, before being replaced by HMS *Hecate*.

HMS *Hecate*, an 860-ton paddlewheel sloop, is pictured here at Esquimalt in an 1862 E.P. Bedwell painting. In early 1862, the ship had the distinction of spending time frozen fast in James Bay during one of Victoria's coldest winters. That December the ship returned to England, and the British government hired the steamer *Beaver* from the Hudson's Bay Company to continue survey duties.

This E.P. Bedwell painting of the Royal Marines camp at Roche Harbour on San Juan Island in 1861 includes a Royal Navy ship and the ever-present Aboriginal canoe.

Bullheaded as he was, Douglas virtually single-handedly created, out of the wilderness, a strong British social infrastructure. After securing the Royal Navy's commitment to protect the coast from its base in Esquimalt in 1855, he soon set about creating a military land force from volunteers and the various materials at hand. He would take law and order where Royal Navy ships could not, or would not, go. By 1858, Whitehall supported his plea for a contingent of Royal Engineers to be stationed on the mainland. The Fraser River gold rush had become the impetus for Britain to make the mainland a new Crown colony, separate from Vancouver Island. Douglas created other military units on the Island, like the Victoria Pioneer Rifle Corps—a unit composed mainly of Black men who had fled discrimination in California. They became known locally as the "African Rifles."[32] Of course, given Victoria's less than enlightened views on race, they weren't allowed to march in parades when royalty visited.

By 1859, Douglas's puffery and temper led to a conflict with the Royal Navy over a problem brewing in the San Juan Islands. Though the Washington Treaty of 1846 settled the Canadian border question at the 49th parallel, the actual demarcation line through the "middle" of the San Juan Islands was a little less clear. It seemed the negotiators never bothered to check Vancouver's charts because, as the Royal Navy knew, there were three channels through the islands: Rosario Strait, Haro Strait, and a reef-laden, almost impassable route in-between.

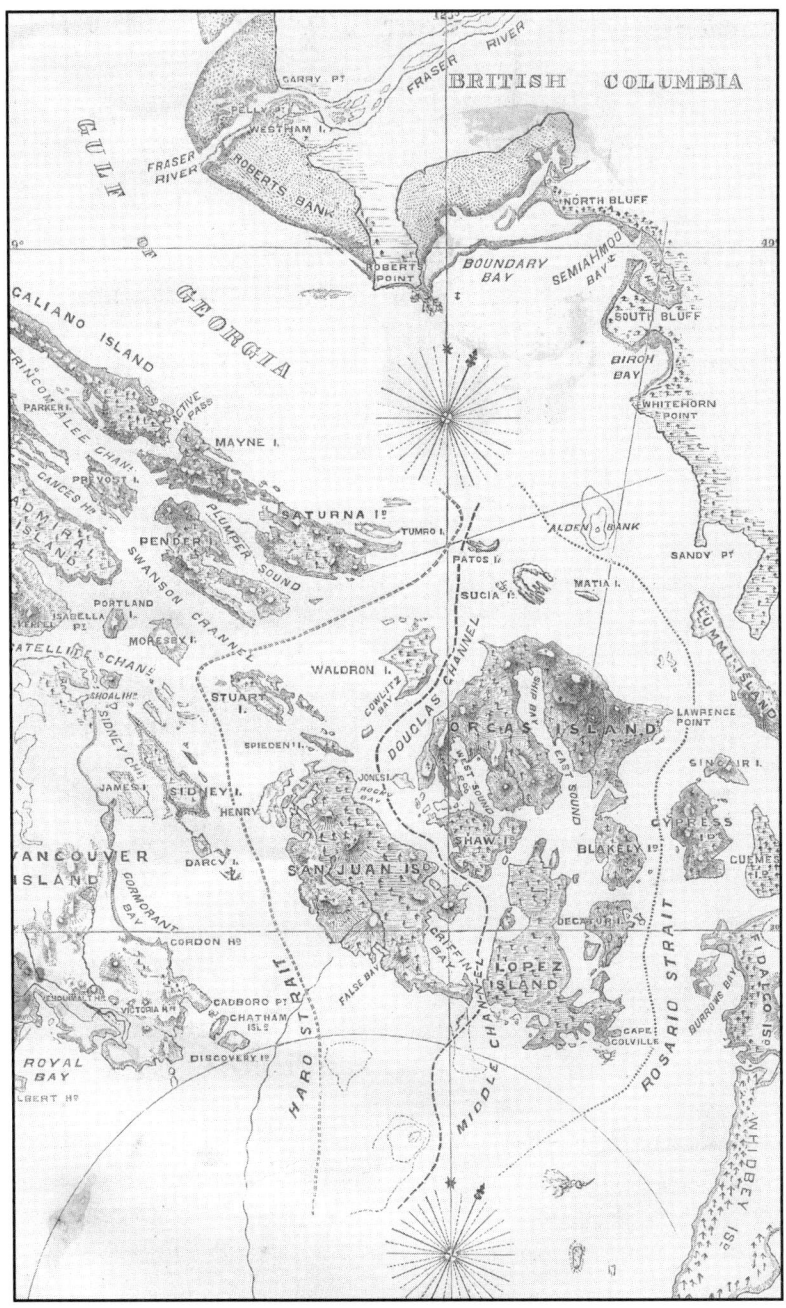

While the "Pig War" went into history as one of the world's most pacific confrontations, it did require a definitive stand by the Royal Navy against American expansionist policies of the day.

Historically, the British felt that San Juan Island belonged to them. It was included in Vancouver's charts, and the British had been using the wider, easier eastern route of Rosario Strait to send its larger ships north to the Strait of Georgia and the lucrative new coal industry in Nanaimo since 1850. By 1853 the HBC had already established a fishing station and a sheep farm there. By 1854 the new American Washington Territory claimed the islands. When an American returning from the Fraser River goldfields in 1859 squatted on the HBC farm and shot a pig, all the ingredients for an international incident coalesced. The HBC's complaint became "British persecution on American soil." The United States countered by sending a land force from Fort Bellingham to San Juan Island to take formal possession and protect American sovereignty.[33] Britain had to act, something that the irascible James Douglas was itching to do.

James Douglas called in his war council. He saw the American troop landing on HBC land as a personal affront and called for British warships and troops to oust them. The Admiralty was under strict orders to avoid an incident, knowing full well that the United States had sided with Russia in the Crimean War. Existing tensions between London and Washington could therefore easily erupt into yet another costly war. Wisely, Douglas was for the moment over-ruled by Michael de Courcy, the senior naval officer, who realized that the joint occupation of San Juan Island could only result in bloodshed.[34]

When the Americans saw British ships-of-the-line in the general area, the American military commander on San Juan Island called in the United States navy. This time the Americans would not be deterred by a show of force on the part of the Royal Navy, as they had been in 1844 during the "54-40" issue. At this juncture, Douglas ordered the Royal Navy (which, as governor, he *did* have at his disposal) to stop American soldiers from making further landings. An officer of the Royal Navy who refused a direct order from the Queen's representative was committing an act of treason. Disaster loomed.

Geoffrey Phipps Hornby, captain of HMS *Tribune*, was ordered to stop the USS *Massachusetts* from disembarking more American troops. The two ships met in Griffin Bay on San Juan Island. At the last moment, as the British were about to fire on the United States navy, Hornby, because of his own diplomatic negotiations with the American military commander, refused Douglas's command.[35]

Geoffrey Phipps Hornby was successful, but he had disobeyed the governor's direct order. Heady stuff! Luckily for him, and for ourselves, Rear-Admiral Baynes, aboard the 84-gun HMS *Ganges,* praised Hornby's restraint, as did other military personnel. Unlike Douglas, Baynes was not a hothead, and he informed Westminster of the situation. Settlement of the San Juan boundary soon followed. The Royal Navy's Pacific base at Esquimalt was further reinforced, and Governor Douglas's war-mongering, at least against the Americans, was stopped dead in its tracks.

The British colonies on the Northwest Coast had been saved by the gunboat diplomacy of the Royal Navy. Commerce had flourished under its protection, and it had played a major role in the winning of British Columbia. However, when it comes to the Royal Navy's treatment of Aboriginals, we get a story of a different colour.

On August 6, 1866, Queen Victoria signed a proclamation uniting the two colonies of British Columbia and Vancouver Island. The boom of the gold-rush period was over, and the economic downturn was well begun. Population declined, and the debt of the two colonies rose to such an extent that union was the only practical answer. The frontier had attracted a very strange set of bedfellows. Social misfits, remittance men, ambitious people intent on "rising above their station," and even mail-order brides were drawn here by the opportunities provided by free enterprise. Those who were disturbed by the terrible social costs of laissez-faire capitalism, as witnessed in the slums of London, were quieted, once here, by an almost lovelorn response to the purity of a primitive wilderness. Yet, ironically, the Aboriginals who inhabited this new world bred fear rather than hope for salvation. The missionaries saw them as superstitious children who lied, stole, and committed adultery. It was believed that only Christian education could eradicate their vices. When Aboriginals retaliated against unfair trading practices or the illegal occupation of their lands, the prevailing outcry of most Europeans was: "Punish the heartless savages and teach them a lesson for the future."[36]

And so the men of influence, be they chief factors, governors, officers of the Royal Navy, elected officials, or newspaper publishers, faced a stark reality. The frontier prophecy of renewal initiated by romanticism and propelled by notions of progress had become mythic. As one historian stated, "Many frontier prophecies became self-fulfilling only by acts of violence and oppression that imposed on disempowered peoples and places the marginal rules they had been assigned in the march of progress."[37] Lesser men inheriting the myth, men with grievances and desirous of any opportunity to succeed, would surely have created a bloodbath in British Columbia similar to the one that occurred in the American "wild west." As it turned out, we did not have a bloodbath, but we certainly had government-sanctioned violence.

In March 1850, three Scots who had fled the harsh and brutal conditions surrounding coal mining at Fort Rupert (Port Hardy) on the northeastern tip of Vancouver Island were murdered by Newitty (Kwakwaka'wakw) from Bull Harbour. Fearing the action was indicative of growing Aboriginal hostilities, Chief Factor Douglas, ever concerned for his company's commercial success, wrote to Factor George Blenkinsop at Fort Rupert, stating that he expected him to take decisive action, "otherwise our position on Vancouver's Island will be insufferable and the civil government worse than a dead letter."[38] Blanshard must have suffered Douglas's goading rhetoric from the day he arrived in Victoria. Chief Factor Douglas was determined from the outset, by virtue of his disdain for settlement, that Britain should pay for the protection its farmers and settlers were demanding. Blanshard visited Fort Rupert in HMS *Daedalus* and decided that the Kwakwaka'wakw surrounding the fort constituted "one of the most warlike Tribes on the Coast."[39] True to his ancestry, he was determined to act. And, needless to say, Sir Fairfax Moresby, KCB, Commander-in-Chief of the Pacific, gave Blanshard his wholehearted support.

Almost a year after the murders, Blanshard appealed to the Newitty to release the murderers for 30 Hudson's Bay blankets. Their refusal brought with it both new contempt and their own threats. Blanshard ordered the Royal Navy to destroy the Newitty camp. Soon after, boats from HMS *Daphne* "stormed and burned" the village completely.[40] Six years later, in 1857, safely home in England, Blanshard's true colours came out while he was testifying before a British parliamentary committee that was examining the HBC.

> Committee: "Though it may seem to be an inhuman statement to make, the sooner they get rid of the Indians the better?"
>
> Blanshard: "I believe it is what, in the United States, people call improving them."[41]

Committee: "Improving them off the face of the land?"

Blanshard replied: "Exactly so."[42]

James Douglas may have been right in his early assessment of Blanshard. Despite his own biases, Douglas was never inclined towards fomenting Aboriginal injustice or censure (he was himself married to a mixed-blood woman); he sought only order and commerce. He coped with settlement because he knew it would bring disorder. And disorder was a two-way street.

In 1853, two years after the "miserable affair" at Bull Harbour, two Cowichan were hanged at Gallows Point, Protection Island (just off Nanaimo), for allegedly killing a Scottish shepherd. Fair enough, except that the hanging was conducted in full view of the Nanaimo tribe as a warning against further acts of violence against British law and White settlers.

In 1856, Governor Douglas deployed nearly 500 officers and men from HMS *Monarch* and HMS *Trincomali* to Cowichan Gap (Cowichan Bay) to capture and execute Chief Tathlasut for the wounding of a White settler, Thomas Williams. That Tathlasut's bride had been raped, ostensibly by a White settler, seemed immaterial to the punishment and its intended message.[43]

In 1864, in response to the burning of the trading sloop *Kingfisher* and the alleged murder of its crew, Rear-Admiral Denman investigated and sent HMS *Devastation* to destroy three Native villages at the head of Clayoquot Sound.[44] That summer of 1864 saw Clayoquot Sound literally ablaze, when at least eight other Aboriginal villages and a total of 64 of their precious canoes were shot to pieces by Navy gunboats (see photo of HMS *Sutlej* in Clayoquot on page 63) when bands of local Clayoquot allegedly stole goods from trading schooners.[45] The Clayoquot would not see the same "justice" meted out to unscrupulous traders. Indeed, could they read English, they would have seen that the *British Colonist* of October 17, 1864, reported that the shelling of Clayoquot had been "conducted according to the strict rules of civilized warfare."[46]

In 1865 Fort Rupert, with a population of 1,500 Natives, was itself assailed by Royal Navy guns under the auspices of Captain Tournour and the new steam corvette HMS *Clio*. In this instance, the navy was sent to ferret out those responsible for an inter-tribal murder. The

Esquimalt Harbour in the 1860s.

Kwakwaka'wakw of Ku-kultz closed ranks and rejected surrendering the culprits. In consequence, the village was destroyed.[47] In 1866 the chiefs of Fort Rupert demanded compensation for the loss of their village, but Arthur Kennedy, the hard-nosed governor of the colony, simply refused.

Through British eyes, White colonial settlement and White commerce had to be defended at all costs. The agent of that defence was, naturally, the Royal Navy. And, though there were humane naval commanders such as Prevost and Richards who decried the retributive measures and acted with compassion and caution, the Admiralty in general supported the punitive action of the day.[48] When it came to Aboriginal peoples, there was no Captain Hornby (the person who refused Governor Douglas's order to fire on the U.S. navy during the San Juan Island dispute), no spokesperson for a more compassionate way. Governor James Douglas disliked the violence and wanted Aboriginals treated in law as British subjects. He drafted local treaties at Fort Victoria, Fort Rupert, and Nanaimo, and he tried to institute an Indian Land Policy under which reserves would be protected from legal pre-emption and encroachment.[49] However, Douglas's successor, Governor Kennedy, felt differently. Kennedy's successor, Frederick Seymour, had only just begun his conciliatory approach when he died in office. In consequence, few treaties, or similar equitable arrangements, were concluded as settlement began in earnest.

In general, the Royal Navy officers, governors, magistrates, and other White administrators on this coast between 1850 and 1869 seemed not to have been overly influenced by the liberalism that was permeating Britain under the Gladstone administration. There was little attempt made by colonial lawmakers to penetrate Aboriginal culture, and there was no willingness to integrate Aboriginal ideas into British justice. These were hard, pragmatic men with a job to do and with little cultural sympathy for the Aboriginal. Many of these men had administered Natives in Africa, Polynesia, or the Caribbean, and the calluses of the frontier were well formed. Most were aristocratic, educated, conservative-minded men who believed wholeheartedly in the idea of the Empire. "Primitive" peoples, wherever they were found, were considered to be "savages," and, like the missionaries, colonial administrators "sought to end their habits of lying, stealing, and adultery."[50] These administrators and their agent, the Admiralty, had implicit faith in the "morality" of British law. They were self-proclaimed "virtuous" men who, like Douglas, found clarity and certainty in firmness. They were taught to appreciate the "velvet hand," but all too often they donned the "steel glove."

Governor Arthur Edward Kennedy

One historic police action that represents all that was wrong with this ethos of "dominion" is the one that was directed against those who were believed to have been involved in the aftermath of the wreck of the trading barque known as the *John Bright*.

CHAPTER 7

The Riddle of the Glyphs:
A Tryst With Nature

This is the world, which is fuller
and more difficult to learn than I have said.
You are right to smudge it that way
with the red and then
the orange: the world burns.

Once you have learned these words
you will learn that there are more
words than you ever can learn.

                        Margaret Atwood [1]

There is a confidence in stone. In the border country between England and Wales, where I grew up, I can remember seeing great stone markers used by the Romans to designate the old roads to and from Chester. I have since found these round, engraved stone posts in the wilds of Brittany, and, like the stone runes of Denmark and Norway, they give the land a sense of security, a history, and a timelessness that I find comforting. "People have lived here," the stones proclaim, "since memory and stories began." When I discovered the same Aboriginal reverence for stone on this coast, in this land that I was told had no history, I knew I was on to something important. Suddenly here lay the same sort of markers, more exquisite than those of my youth, that pointed to landscape, to reverence, and to memory. The petroglyphs took away my fear of the frontier and replaced it with awe.

    Think of it—ingenious lines, compelling circles, and sparse archetypal images—ancient indentations, crafted on coastal rock shelves, that could *actually represent something so momentous as the passing of a race. When I saw them first, I was dumbfounded. The silent, curious simplicity of the "messages" of the petroglyphs, I thought, were much like the carved hyphens found between the dates of birth and the dates of death on ancient Christian tombstones. For those buried without an epitaph, without the remembered written word or phrase, that single cryptic mark between dates is all there is to evoke the pathway of a life. I remembered, on an earlier glyph foray, seeing such a gravestone, almost totally obscured by crab grass, at the rear of an old dilapidated mission church on a north coast reserve. There was a weathered name I couldn't decipher, and two dates—only seven years apart—separated by that enigmatic hyphen. I tried to envision the experience of the brief life of the lost child. Was it smallpox or an accident? The loss of the infant was made even more poignant by its having been placed in unsanctified ground. Aboriginal glyphs evoke that same sort of feeling. They are remembrancers of lives past. I am drawn to conjecture upon the quality of the lives of those who understood these obscure marks. However, unlike the simple hyphen, petroglyphs, more often than not, are very beautiful. They transmit, through their strange codes, a significant part of the spiritual essence of a whole culture. It was that thought that turned my initial curiosity into an obsession.*

Petroglyphs: What do they mean? How can we crack their silent codes? How do we get at meaning? Do they have meaning beyond that contained in the beauty of their mysterious shapes?

Glyphs are carvings made largely on permanent, immovable stone shelves or boulders. The rock "canvas" itself may be varied. Often it is soft, coarse-grained sandstone; sometimes it is hard limestone, basalt, or even granite bedrock. All surfaces are chipped away by abrading, pecking, or scratching. Petroglyphs may be likened to inverted bas-relief outlines, where the design is grooved into a suitable material with a special "hammer-stone." This incised line, though imperfect in its edge, would be pecked into the rock surface for days, often for weeks.[2] This is not a painter's art. The strength and focus required to peck a perfect circle or whole curvilinear design (such as the magnificent rain god of Kulleet Bay near Ladysmith on Vancouver Island) without faltering is considerable. Often, the pecked line or form would be rubbed smooth so that it would stand out more clearly from the natural roughness of the

106   Glyphs and Gallows

The upside-down figure in the top right of this photo of the well-known Nanaimo site is thought to be a Haietlik, a mythical snake figure that is perhaps related to the more northern Wasgo of the Haida. In Clayoquot mythology, the Haietlik's alligator-like body and large mouth were shaped like a spear, so that when Thunderbird wished to kill a whale, it would throw a Haietlik at it.

rock. If the rock were dark like volcanic basalt (which is common throughout the Columbia Plateau), then a scratching technique was used to cut through the patinated ancient surface in order to expose a lighter interior that would contrast markedly with the older, chemically altered, darker surface.

Whoever they were, these artisan-shamans, they had good eyes. Clefts, cracks, or other naturally occurring faults in the rock (such as depressions, flakes, natural roundness, or ridges) were readily used to execute an intended design. A surface depression in a beach boulder in Lok Bay has been superbly crafted into a perfectly round ceremonial bowl. Nearby, on a smoother boulder, are the incised figures of a running man and a deer. At the Clo-oose site, a natural rock cleft has become a vulvaform, around which the outline of a large-breasted female figure has been skilfully crafted. The undulating surface of a cliff face at Sproat Lake provided a natural surface upon which to depict a swimming

The Riddle of the Glyphs 107

The rain god of Kulleet Bay. Like glyphs on Cortes Island and at Matlahaw Point near Hesquiat on the outer coast, this magnificent glyph is graven on a human-sized boulder at the southern end of Kulleet Bay. Beth Hill, like E.L. Keithahn, believed that this glyph may have had to do with the invoking of the seasonal rains that ensured that the salmon made it up freshwater streams to spawn. (Copied by the author)

Haietlik—a serpent-snake figure common in Northwest Coast mythology. Everywhere there is a sense of artistic control and a clear mastery of rock-art technique, and there are common techniques, styles, and motifs. Indeed, the works are expressive of forces and themes common to the whole Northwest Coast culture area. If we are to understand petroglyphs, then we must become knowledgeable about, and sympathetic towards, a vastly different civilization. The petroglyph art form rivals any other ancient art form.

Strangely, the glyphs do not appear near Aboriginal settlements. Villages may be nearby, but sites are distinct from them.[3] Isolation seems to be a key. Early glyph researchers theorized that these sites may have been out-of-bounds for uninitiated, ordinary villagers, as there is little information about them in the common tribal memory. Yet more recent investigations by anthropologists and their Aboriginal informants reveal that much is known about petroglyphs in relation to local ceremonies and customs.[4] Many of the sites are found where there are abundant salmon (e.g., the Gibbs Creek site on the Fraser River, the Jack Point glyphs near the mouth of the Nanaimo River, and the remarkable stylized bear in the gorge of the Englishman River near Parksville). The whale glyph at Ozette, Washington, and the Blackfish at Degnan Bay point to

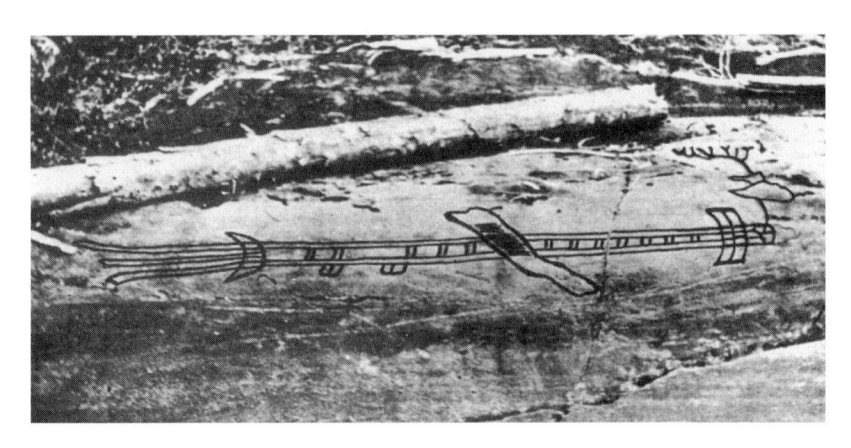

Abstract serpent petroglyph at Great Central Lake.

ceremonies connected with the annual salmon and whale hunts, respectively.

Some sites are found near the location of special events. For example, the head glyph near Fort Rupert is said to be connected with the ritualistic eating of a slave during a winter Hamatsa ceremony.[5] *Like those on the ocean edge, inland sites such as the Church site or Cliff site (Wharf Road) on Gabriola Island are also isolated from known Aboriginal settlements. Here, as by the sea, the sites are hushed, save for birdsong and the rustling of leaves. The absolute abundance of glyphs at specific places suggests that they were special sites—Aboriginal shrines—enhanced by their isolation and enriched by their profusion. Such sites are made more evocative by the very presence of previous petroglyphs—each perhaps rendered during a different time, each building on the mysterious essence of the other. The result is that some locations have the same spiritual memory and function as do the caves of Lascaux, the circles of Stonehenge, and the cloisters of Canterbury Cathedral.*

Dating a petroglyph is almost impossible because it is, in essence, a void in a rock; that is, it is what is left after something has been displaced. It is difficult to tell exactly when that which is missing was removed. Yet there are clues. Glyphs carved on rock that has undergone patination reveal their age in a striking fashion. Due either to micro-organisms or the oxidation of iron and manganese salts, the surface of basaltic rock darkens over time.[6] *A hammered or scratched petroglyph would remove the ancient natural colouration, leaving the lighter image outlined in marked contrast to the surrounding rock. Hence, glyphs that appear lighter on a given surface may be assumed (given constant climatic conditions) to be more recent than those repatinated closer to the original colour of the rock surface. Such "differential patination" has been used on glyphs at Buffalo Eddy, Idaho, to suggest an approximate chronology for the heavily repatinated naturalistic (anthropomorph-zoomorph) glyphs as opposed to the more recent graphic (triangles, circles, and dots) glyphs found at the same locale.*[7]

Dating petroglyphs from surrounding datable archaeological deposits (such as volcanic ash) or from their similarity to existing datable objects (such as pendants, buckles, and other stone or bone objects) has also had some limited success.[8] *It has been reported that the most accurately dated petroglyph in British Columbia was one found on Protection Island off Nanaimo in 1977. Carbon-dating of charcoal midden material covering a glyph of a killer whale placed it at approximately 345 years old.*[9]

Some have suggested that hydrographic history may be used to date glyphs.[10] *With the slow increase of the high-tide level over the millennia (the rise of the sea level in the last 6,000 years has been placed at approximately six metres),*[11] *glyphs such as those at Fort Rupert and Return Passage, Bella Bella, are now submerged at high water. If we accept the assumption that the glyphs were likely carved at a time when they would have been completely above the high-tide mark, then referring to tidal heights over the long term is another possible way of dating petroglyphs.*[12] *The difficulty of this method lies in trying to measure the occurrence of seemingly haphazard placements of glyph sites above unknown historical high-water marks. Furthermore, there is a plethora of sites within the intertidal zone, which, many believe, are either connected to fishing rituals or play a part in a belief system premised on the notion of transformation (wherein humans may take on animal forms and vice versa).*

Others have suggested erosion rates, the growth rates of lichen upon bedrock over time, soil deposition, and stylistic differences as relative measures for dating petroglyphs. Yet each is fraught with difficulty. Climatic conditions change over time. Boulders once exposed are washed over, turned, and buried, escaping the natural ravages of wind and tide, while others at the same locale remain in their original positions, deceptively appearing more weathered and older. Periods of summer drought, or the shade cover of forests, affect soil buildup and the growth rates of rock moss and lichen. Stylistic differences at a particular petroglyph site may have more to do with the idiosyncratic differences of contemporary artisans than with changes in cultural influence.

Petroglyphs carved within the contact period are a little easier to date than are those that were carved earlier, because often a Native elder will remember them or they will be part of a direct European historical record. Yet here, too, clues often mislead the incautious. Beth Hill once told me of a copper glyph on Chisholm Island in Maple Bay. In the nineteenth century, copper sheeting was used widely to cover the underwater exterior of ships in order to prevent teredo worms from eating their way through the hulls. Such copper sheets became highly prized symbols of wealth and prestige among the Kwakwaka'wakw and were often turned into objects of art, then copied in wood and stone. To find a copper glyph among the southern Gulf Islands seemed odd to Beth, so she did some rigorous sleuthing. It turned out that a glyph aficionado living in Victoria made the glyph in the 1950s as a hoax and as a piece of experimental anthropology.[13] As I said, one must be wary.

Yet there is clear evidence of genuine glyphs having been made within the nineteenth century. Hill reported that the father of a Mr. Tranfield (who helped them in their search for glyphs in the early 1970s) had seen a deaf-mute Native make some Englishman River petroglyphs in 1886.[14] The Fort Rupert face glyph was dated between 1849 and 1882, was documented by Boas, and was witnessed by some HBC factors. The sailing-ship glyphs of Clo-oose contain representations of mid-nineteenth-century brigs and barkentines as well as a clear representation of either the HBC vessel the Beaver or the steam-powered HMS Virago. Such images date that particular glyph, only one among many, as having been drawn sometime between 1830 and 1890. And that is about as accurate as it gets.

Petroglyphs have been discovered on the Northwest Coast of North America from Southwest Alaska to Oregon. They exist along with pictographs in Quebec, southwestern Ontario, Minnesota, Alberta, and the American Southwest. Most likely they have been a part of Native culture since their makers travelled with nomadic hunting tribes across the then Serengeti-like land bridge of Beringia, some 12,000 years ago. In British Columbia, it is most probable that glyph art flowered during the period around 500 AD, when "a shift occurred in society from art in a religious context to art which could serve the growing need of families for status symbols."[15] Others also believed that it was near the end of this Middle Developmental Stage (3,500 to 1,500 years ago)—when detachable barbed fishing hooks, stone bowls and sculpture, and items of personal ornamentation appeared—that petroglyphs regained much of their popularity.[16] It was during this same period that villages became larger and more permanent and that the labret, head deformations, and burial goods became marks of status. At the same time, flaked stone implements were being superseded by tools of ground stone. A culture with highly decorative stone war-clubs, mortars, and batons could also refine the hammer-stone, thus providing petroglyph art with a new sophistication. Could it have been the shamans who sensed this cultural shift and so took over rock-art production in order to enhance their influence?

Whatever happened, the production of Aboriginal art blossomed during the later Middle Developmental stage. Accordingly, petroglyphs returned after their initial earlier appearance and remained strong right into the period of first contact. There is a rich tradition of petroglyph art in British Columbia that reaches back for at least 1,500 years. Unlike most of the totem poles, stone bowls, and steatite (soapstone) carvings that have disappeared or have found their way into museums, many petroglyphs are still visible on exposed coastal bedrock. They remain to be pondered over in the places where they were made—in nature, in antiquity.

Why were they made? The reasons for petroglyph art are tied to its meaning. As Gottlieb, the abstract-expressionist, has said: "There is no such thing as a good painting about nothing."[17] Most anthropologists now agree that petroglyphs were made for a variety of reasons: to record tribal myths, to entice the salmon to run, to record the rituals of secret societies, to enhance the training of shamans, to invoke spirit power, to record significant events in tribal history, and to display tribal crests. These reasons are known largely through the work of some of the finest ethnographers in the history of anthropology (e.g., Franz Boas, John Swanton, Philip Drucker, E.L. Keithahn, and others), all of whom had direct access to the memories of those Native informants who were alive when petroglyphs were still being made. It is due to the work of these investigators that later B.C. anthropologists (both professional and amateur), such as Ed Meade, Doris Lundy, Ray and Beth Hill, Mary and

Ted Bentley, Roy Carlson, and Joy Inglis, were able to begin the monumental task of stylistic classification and interpretation.

The religion of Northwest Coast Aboriginal peoples was, not surprisingly, rife with belief in the supernatural, in guardian spirits, in beings that transformed themselves into animals and vice versa, and in loathsome and dangerous beasts that hid in the forest and in the sea. The Nuu-chah-nulth and others who lived on the outer coast belonged to a part of the world in which the forces of nature were often violent. Death lurked closely every time a hunter or fisher set about to kill a formidable foe such as a bear, a full-grown male deer, a whale, or a large halibut. The rain forest and the sea were dangerous places, even without such creatures. It is no wonder, then, that this ever-present tension between life and death, between wildness and intelligence, would show up in myths, ceremonies, dancing, and feasting. It was the function of the shaman to mediate these two great oppositions. For the Nuu-chah-nulth and others, the sacred existed everywhere—within the longhouse and within the belly of the whale or bear that must be faced and killed. It is known that Tlingit halibut hooks, totally practical objects, were highly decorated with shamanic art.[18] A belief system that urged its followers to face the chaos, to enter the unknown element, to embrace the wildness through spirit quests and in initiation rites, was premised on the idea that the unknown could be felt, seen, and understood by following the appropriate rituals. In such oral cultures, images obviously played a critical role, and wealth and status were very much associated with giving thanks.

  The Sliammon informant Rose Mitchell once told a wonderful story of the glyph at Manson's Landing on Cortes Island. The story is testimony to the invocation of spirit power and the training of shamans. A young man was too lazy to catch fish for his new wife, preferring instead to lie in bed. Humiliated, the young man's father banished him from his clan. Months after his disappearance, it was felt that the young man had committed suicide. Later, they found evidence of boughs used for sleeping beside nearby lakes. A year passed. One day a freshly killed deer was found drooped over a fallen tree, beside which sat the young man. He had gained spirit power and could now provide his village with any meat or fish it desired. He demonstrated his newly gained power by having porpoise, seal, salmon, and deer all readily come to him and be killed. He was reunited with his wife and a great feast was held, at which his *father named him "Tl'umnachm"—"canoe always loaded with food." Out of respect for his new power, the young man carved a glyph of a whale on a nearby rock. That glyph is still there today.*[19]

If guardian spirits gave comfort to a precarious life, then it is reasonable to assume that people would want to make manifest such forces within their religious and artistic iconography. If Christianity soothed the plundering masses with images of the Virgin Mary, Jesus, and the Christ-child, then images of beings with special powers should also be expected to proliferate within non-Christian traditions. And, indeed, the petroglyph is one example of this proliferation. It has been estimated that well over 300 glyphs in the lower Columbia River Basin are of human figures that have arcs (or rayed lines) emanating from their heads.[20] *The Shaman's Pool on Kulleet Bay, near Ladysmith, the Dancing Shaman on Gabriola Island, and the strange square, rayed face at Clo-oose are but a few of the more striking rayed images that I have seen along the glyph-strewn south coast. Anthropologists generally accept that such glyphs are representative of the idea of supernatural power and are associated with the work of shamans.*[21]

In 1909, John Swanton was told a myth about Raven, the trickster, and his exploits among the Tlingit. Being hungry, Raven wanted to catch a salmon that was cavorting about in a bay. Finding a piece of jade in an abandoned camp, Raven added the figure of an eagle to its already designed surface. Raven then moved the incised jade to the shore where the jumping salmon would see it. There, the Jade-eagle would speak to the salmon, enticing them in. Wily Raven, of course, soon had a feast.

In 1940, E.L. Keithahn noted that petroglyph boulders were often found at the mouth of salmon-spawning streams, their designs facing seaward. The rising and falling tide would submerge the glyphs daily, their designs and messages mingling with the sea.[22] *The connection between hunting rites, rites of initiation, the religious dimension of Native culture, and the carving of glyphs has been well established.*

The stylistic properties of petroglyphs, their forms and motifs, have also been described and classified. Graphic elements such as concentric circles, chevrons, and pits co-exist with zoomorphic depictions of fish and birds, often with ribs and bones exposed. However, the absolute dominance of human figures, with disproportionately large faces, overwhelms. The faces are round, ovoid, or square and display huge

Compare this rare family group dominated by the sexually explicit mother-figure (found at Cliff site on Gabriola Island in the inner Gulf Islands) with the full-breasted woman and copulating figures found at Clo-oose (see chapter 10).

eyes. Often, one eye is closed. Many faces contain huge tongue-like protuberances and open mouths. Frequently, the heads are depicted with strange projections, or rays, that have been likened to haloes. More often than not, the anthropomorphic figures squat in Polynesian-like, or frog, positions. Phallic and vulvic images are everywhere. The figures are little more than outlines, or stick figures. Legs are drawn, but feet seem not to matter. A hand may have three fingers. On a given rock shelf, these figures might compete with mythic beasts—strange serpent figures called Wasgos or Haietliks. Beside these there are strangely beaked mythic birds and/or whales. The regional variations in these elements are becoming clear.

Though the subject matter is being described and understood, that in itself doesn't help us very much. We are still left to puzzle over the messages that the designs and forms themselves contain. That is, of course, assuming that the idea of "message" can be applied to this kind of art. It is one thing to say that a salmon glyph ensures a successful run of fish, or that a phallus figure connects humanity to "Mother Earth," but do these forms have a further visual script that is not supplied solely through a knowledge of their cultural associations? Are there deeper meanings, and deeper structures, that we are missing? Is there a way past the limitations of simply describing an Aboriginal cultural event or ceremony and applying it carte blanche to nearby glyphs whose styles and forms have also been described to death? What do we do when simple representation breaks down? What can we make of a glyph that doesn't seem to represent a myth, a spirit figure, or a crest? More directly, what specific ideas are associated with which specific forms? Do the different forms at a particular site relate to each other in the same way as do, for example, the forms in a mural, tapestry, or tableau?

It is this question of the pictorial literacy of the petroglyph that truly intrigues me. Is there a language going on here that may be "read"? These questions challenge our propensity to make patterns, and they mock our logical connections between images and ideas. We become bifurcated. We must leave the glyphs and look into the nature of perception, into our notions about human creativity, and into how we create symbolic systems. As one anthropologist has said of another kind of Native art, "it has to activate the imagination, create the metaphor, bring into existence the new primary class for which there is no name." [23] Time for symbolism and a leap of faith.

It is well known that in the art of the shaman, the bird was symbolic of "out of body flight." [24] Among the Coast Salish, ghosts were often owls.[25] The mask, especially that of the Swaihwe among the Cowichan and the Nanaimo peoples, was symbolic of purification and good luck.[26] Among the Aboriginals of the Baranof Islands, Kun-ook, the guardian of fresh water, was often represented as a wolf.[27] The glyph of a Wasgo, located near the mouth of the Nanaimo River, is part whale and part wolf.[28] The closed eye of many glyphs recalls the Norse myth of Odin, who gave one eye for insight.

Glyphs with overt sexual references are not uncommon along the outer south coast, in bays and on headlands along the way to the site of Clo-oose. Indeed, the Clo-oose site has no less than three distinctly sexual figures: a female figure created around a large natural cleft in the rock; a carving of two figures engaged in head-to-tail copulation; and, a short distance away, a figure with a huge phallus, itself holding a head. En route to Clo-oose from the north, in a cave near Pachena Point, is a circular glyph with a divided oval, along with two other smaller divided ovals and a lone fish. The divided oval is known to many cultures as the female vulva. Are these forms symbolic of male/female sexuality or are they something more? Clearly, Northwest Coast Natives dreamed their demons and put many of them on rocks.

These symbolic representations are at the centre of the riddle of petroglyph art because they present us with universal human paradoxes. If Aboriginal art is full of the oppositions of birth and death, love and hate, individuality and social responsibility, then it must be seen as having the same concerns as do our art forms. This being the case, we are forced to see Native culture not as an ethnographic curiosity to be studied and commented upon with due academic distance, but as a vital, passionate, and deep reflection of ourselves.

No anthropologist has done more to further this view and to break new ground in the interpretation of Native art than Wilson Duff. His essays, "Kwakiutl Killer Whale Coppers," "Stone Clubs of the Skeena River," and "Thoughts on the Nootka Canoe,"[29] provide us with remarkable speculations. However, it is in his compelling little essay on meaning in northern Northwest Coast art, "The World Is as Sharp as a Knife," that his insights are truly revealed.[30] In his short life, Duff's major interest was the art of the Haida. Unfortunately, Haida art does not include the petroglyph, so it is up to us to apply Duff's ideas to the rock art of Clo-oose.

Duff applied psychoanalytic theory and structuralist literary criticism to the explanation of stylistic forms. Like Freud and Lacan, Duff believed that the human heart was fraught with dark, libidinous passions, defence mechanisms, and guilt.[31] In order to be expressed, sexuality, he believed, "had to be beautified and sublimated into art."[32] With this basic assumption, his quest to understand symbolic systems began with a hard look at how human sexuality was represented in Northwest Coast art.[33] He found, as expected, sublimated male and female genitalia expressed in Tsimshian stone clubs, Salish stone seal bowls, Haida totem poles, and so on. In northern Aboriginal sculpting, Duff uncovered a covert, idealized sexuality—an "underground" manifestation of sexual taboos in visual puns, visual metaphors, and wonderfully humorous and metaphorical sexual play. Duff wasn't preoccupied with sexuality; he

Could the metaphors inherent in the paintings of these cedar chests also be inherent in rock art?

was just interested in how a common human prohibition was expressed in art. In bringing a Freudian (and Jungian) analysis to aesthetic principles, he was opening the door to passion, to emotion.

I had seen many glyphs over the years, and none held such an attraction for me as did the sailing-ship glyphs of Clo-oose. Their connection to our own coastal history was what intrigued me most of all. It was as if they were speaking out about something that must not be forgotten. I had been discouraged during one of my many searches in the archives in Victoria, and I popped into the adjacent provincial museum to sit before the amazing totem poles in the rotunda. Wandering around the museum bookshop afterwards, I spotted, almost hidden on a bottom shelf, the writings of Wilson Duff. He had been waiting. Serendipity. My enthusiasm returned.

Duff, like Lévi-Strauss, provided me with a new dynamic for seeing the relationship between Aboriginal art and myth. He enabled me to relate Native art to our own universal concerns. If Eros and Thanatos (desire and death), and all their everyday transformations/permutations, *exacted a genuine toll on Aboriginal life, then there must be many other oppositions waiting to be discovered. Duff believed that all this was evident in the stone sculpting, wooden carvings, and decorative boxes of Northwest Coast art. For Duff, such oppositions as Raven/Bear, Eagle/Raven, Presence/Absence, Eater/Eaten, Inside/Outside, Whole/Part, and so on provided a path into, and out of, the artistic experience.*[34] *Coastal carvings, including the glyphs, that express such combinations, such intelligence, while all the while building upon culturally known visual clichés and transforming them from dream, to myth, to archetype are, without dispute, the very stuff of art.*

There is much more in Wilson Duff, but we must stop. We have enough, and the sailing-ship glyphs of Clo-oose call us anew. The glyphs at Clo-oose appear to be nowhere near as complex as an argillite carving or a Bill Reid sculpture, but simple they are not. Other Western historical allusions at the site, such as the HBC vessel Beaver, *intrigue me now not so much for the thrill of historical confirmation, but for the echo of very human themes. The paddlewheel steamer may well be the* Beaver, *but it is also a symbol and a summing up. As I prepared for a second journey to the glyph site, I could feel my old boyhood passion for history, for codes, and for clues returning.*

Rock art requires level-headed interpretation; cautious speculation fits the durable quality of form. We will look for mythic beasts and birds, and I know that the site contains many of them. We will look carefully at the delineation of the human figures and their location among zoomorphic forms. Is there a reason for their proximity to each other? We will examine the relationship between the styles and motifs. We will look carefully at age. We will not shy away from the plethora of sexual images, which are all over the site, nor will we ignore those of death. The whole site will be our data. It will be difficult not to be overly subjective, not to fall prey to a self-fulfilling prophecy. It will be interesting to see if the application of psychoanalytic principles and/or structural analysis yields us something new. Could we delve more deeply into the meaning of the petroglyphs at Clo-oose by treating them not only as images, but also as texts waiting to be read?

CHAPTER 8
The Wreck of the *John Bright*

How I would like to believe in tenderness.
Sylvia Plath[1]

Aside from D.W. Higgins's published recollections of the *John Bright* affair in 1905, little new has been added by later writers. Yet it seems to have regularly caught the attention of BC coastal chroniclers for over 100 years. It was the talk of the coast for five years after it occurred in 1869. Thomas McKenzie of the clipper ship *Thermopylae*, rival of the infamous *Cutty Sark*, said of it that "no greater tragedy is recorded in the annals of shipping in the North Pacific than that which befell the crew of the *John Bright*."[2] Since then, a decade has not passed without at least one article appearing on the subject in the popular press. Why this is so is intriguing. The story certainly has elements of the macabre, as does the gruesome tale of the ghost ship the *Flying Dutchman*.[3] It is also shrouded in mystery, like the strange disappearance of the crew of the infamous *Mary Celeste*.[4] Yet it is more than a good fireside yarn of peril on the high seas. It is, first, a story about a relatively small stretch of coast upon which British colonialism was able to establish a beachhead. It is a compelling tragedy of clashing cultures, illustrative of colonial law and order and its effects upon Aboriginals and Whites alike. It is a sea story, to be sure, pitting humanity against the elements and showing that courage and cowardice often reside together. But it is also a microcosm of the hard life of the early trader, the sealer, the settler, and the Native, all of whom had little time to be afraid. It is a story full of vindictiveness, evasion, and vested interest. And it is a modern story, reminiscent of a Kurosawa film, containing several different, often contradictory, points of view. Last, it is a story without a conclusion. We are left speechless and powerless, gazing at our own stupidity. We find in it connections to our own fatal flaws. As such, it is a story worthy of art—worthy of an Aboriginal petroglyph. Indeed, the *John Bright* affair is a tragedy of truly classic proportions.

In Victoria, it was treated with crass journalism, which stoked the fires of prejudice. The limited facts available on the loss of the *John Bright* were soon recruited to aid many causes. They were used as a pretext to bash an undemocratic government; they were used against those in the new colony of British Columbia who wished to join the United States; and they were used to legitimize seeing Aboriginals as something less than human. With all of these ancillary crusades eroded by time, what remains is a story of sheer romance. The *John Bright* affair belongs to the last days of the clipper ships, to young love, and to thwarted opportunity. It is a tale of self-reliance, self-deception, and dreadful naiveté.

There are few really detailed versions of the *John Bright* tragedy. The only contemporary written accounts are those of the Victoria daily papers of the period and the unpublished notebooks of Judge Joseph Needham, who tried and convicted those directly involved. The person on whom we must rely for a central narrative, however, is D.W. Higgins. An active newspaperman in Victoria in 1869, 30 years later Higgins embellished his account of the ship's demise. A Haligonian by birth, Higgins left the east coast colony of Nova Scotia for the California gold rush and arrived in Victoria in 1858, after a stint as editor and proprietor of a newspaper in San Francisco. He spent five years in Yale at the height of the Fraser River gold rush, pursuing gold, news, and, most important, the stories of the pioneers. Upon moving to Vic-

The *John Bright* story remained in the consciousness of D.W. Higgins for over 40 years.

toria in 1863, Higgins became a fervent Canadian nationalist and a public figure. He purchased the *British Colonist* from the colourful Amor de Cosmos and turned it into the main opposition to the American annexationists. The quintessential gentleman adventurer, Higgins prospected, mined, traded, owned a theatre, became a theatrical impresario, and "filled every position in a newspaper office from devil to editor."[5] By his own admission, he made copious notes of events and of the speech, habits, and frailties of those about him who were making history. Never one to hide from a fight,[6] Higgins became an MLA and served as the second speaker of the B.C. legislature. In his retirement during the early 1900s, he published two remarkable books, *The Mystic Spring* and *The Passing of a Race*,[7] in which he recounted those early events that moved him deeply and shaped his time. His story of the loss of the *John Bright* is full of Dickensian melodrama (remember, he owned a theatre), Victorian indignation, and Presbyterian guilt. His voice, however, is consistent with the press of the day. It is fitting, then, that it is through Higgins and the press that we begin our tale.

In December 1868, the small, English-registered barque, the *John Bright*, sailed into Port Gamble, Washington Territory. Windjammers and square-riggers from around the world came to Puget Sound and waited to load lumber from the new Pope and Talbot mill. Set on the leeward side of the Olympic Peninsula, with first-growth forests lining the shores of the Pacific Northwest, small, new milling operations and surrounding townsites were springing up in practically every sheltered cove or hidden bay of Puget Sound. Think of it. There were literally hundreds of sailing ships: barques, barkentines, brigs, brigantines, and the infamous west coast sealing schooners—forests of masts all eager to catch the next tide. Some were bound for San Francisco, which was still booming in the wake of the California gold rush of 1849. Others were bound for the Antipodes, Australia, South America, or the South Seas. Many would return, again and again, to the Pacific Northwest with cargoes of copra, sugar, tobacco, and rum.

Of those that did make regular visits, it is said that over half were lost to the sea. The stretch of coast between Oregon and the northern end of Vancouver Island is a most inhospitable place for *any* vessel, with or without an engine. For a ship powered only by its sails, the place is a nightmare. The American outer coast has few protective

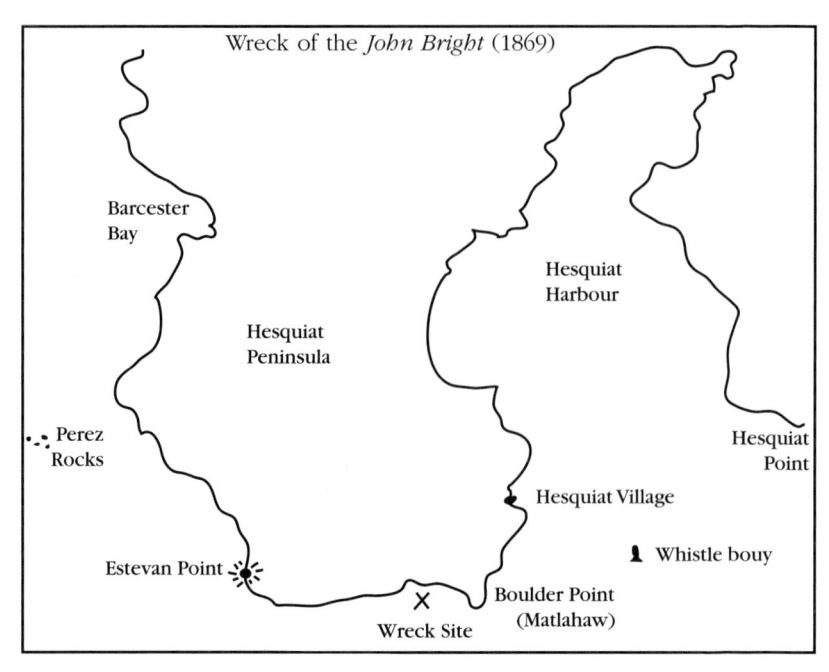

Wreck site of *John Bright*, Matlahaw Point, Hesquiat Peninsula. This peninsula is one of the most dangerous on the west coast. (Map reproduced with permission of the B.C. Underwater Archeological Society.)

harbours for an inbound vessel. The necessity of getting goods in, or out, of Puget Sound meant crossing notorious river bars, such as the infamous bar at the mouth of the Columbia River. Here, as in other such places, shallows, currents, ocean swells, wind (or the total absence of it) all converged. Until the end of the age of sail, a falling barometer, a falling tide, and a dropping wind would commit a prudent skipper to suffer days of yet another gruelling southeasterly in open water. In December 1890, Oliver Peterson, captain of the schooner *Lucy*, tried unsuccessfully for over three weeks to make it safely over the Umpqua Bar, only to be forced finally into Puget Sound, miles from his destination.[8] An imprudent skipper choosing to run in before a gale or, worse, in flat air, would be playing Russian roulette with the lives of his crew. However, once committed to crossing the bar, there was no turning back.

Further north, the entrance to the Strait of Juan de Fuca is, for a large part of the year, obscured by sea fog. When it is not, winter winds of hurricane force, and the varying current systems, combine to drive unwary sailing ships onto the reefs, cliffs, or beaches of Vancouver Island. With a compass, sextant, and captain's intuition as the only aids to navigation, even the most wary were often doomed.

The *John Bright* was a solid old barque that had plied the trade lanes of the world for some 20 years before putting into Puget Sound in December 1868. Lloyds Register of Shipping noted it as being constructed in Dumbarton, Scotland, in 1847. It was 126 feet long and displaced some 541 tons.[9] Its seams were caulked with felt, and its hull was sheathed with yellow metal. Built originally for the English traders Thomas and Company, it registered Beaumaris as its home port, with its main destination port reported as Buenos Aires. It was given twelve years on its initial survey and apparently had a refit in 1862. The *John Bright* was surveyed again in the mid-1860s and may well have been chartered out at that time to John Trevick and Captain Burgess of Valparaiso, Chile.[10]

Captain Burgess was a Welshman by birth, "as fine a man as one ever met with."[11] He was master on the current voyage to Port Gamble and would take the *John Bright*, full of lumber, home to Valparaiso. Burgess had with him his wife and their children. To care for the children the Burgesses had brought with them an English nursemaid named Beatrice Holden, "on whose cheeks the rosies and posies of her native land bloomed."[12]

The *John Bright* remained almost two months in Port Gamble. Higgins speculated that this was due to the troublesome loading facilities at the new mill. Nonetheless, Christmas must have been one round of visits after another for the affable Burgess and his young, Spanish-looking wife. According to Higgins, "While the bark was taking in cargo, the captain and his wife became well acquainted on shore, and through their geniality and hospitality soon grew to be general favorites."[13]

The nursemaid, it seems, didn't spend all her time minding the children. Only just seventeen, Beatrice Holden "had the lovely English complexion, bright blue eyes, and long hair of tawny hue. Pretty girls were scarce on the Sound at that time, and when the day came for the bark to go to sea this particular girl received no less than three offers of marriage."[14] Higgins notes that she gracefully declined all offers, intending to live and die on her own. However, should she change her mind, she said, "she would only marry an Englishman."[15] Such sweet purity must have swelled the heart of every Brit living in Victoria.

No picture of the *John Bright* on the inshore rocks at Hesquiat exists. Yet this picture of the *Soquel*, held fast on Sea Bird Rocks at the entrance to Pachena Bay, closely approximates the end of the *John Bright*.

The *John Bright* finally left Port Gamble, loaded with lumber, in early February 1869 and sailed smack into the teeth of a horrific winter gale. News of its loss reached Victoria in early March, when a local sealing skipper returning to port immediately filed a report with government officials. The *British Colonist* got wind of the report and, on March 13, printed the following headline and story:

Dreadful Marine Disaster on the West Coast
An English Bark and All hands lost Near Nootka Sound

> By the arrival of the schooner *Surprise*, Captain Christianson, from the West Coast of this Island, we receive intelligence of the loss of an English bark, supposed to be the *John Bright*, with all on board near Nootka Sound. Capt. Christianson thinks the bark was lost about the 8th. or 9th. of February, during a heavy gale which lasted two days. When first seen by the Captain, the wreck was lying on a rocky beach, some three miles South of Nootka Sound, and not far from an Indian village. She was lying on her beam-ends, the sea making a clean sweep over her, the foremast alone remaining intact.[16]

Some days later, Christenson was able to board the wreck.[17] The lumber it carried had floated off and lay scattered along the beach. The deckhouses were gone, and the vessel was stripped of all moveable gear. The *John Bright* had been seen initially by a local Native, who saw it the night before it came ashore. It was trying to beat off the coast but struck a reef a short distance from the beach early in the morning. Other local Natives reported to Christenson that "some of her people, living or dead, had been seen."[18]

Apparently Christenson had heard "contradictory stories" from the Natives regarding the bodies of those washed ashore, and he investigated further. He ascertained that two bodies had floated ashore from the wreck, one being that of a woman with long, flowing hair. A female body that Christenson said he actually saw was located well above the high-water mark, so he conjectured that the Natives had dragged it up the beach. Moreover, he reported that the woman's clothing had been stripped off, was carried away, and "now perhaps form[s] part of the apparel of a squaw."[19] With regard to this woman, "the flesh had nearly disappeared from the face and body, and it was impossible either to recognize the remains or discern marks of violence."[20] The other body Christenson did not see; nonetheless, he conjectured that it was even more disfigured than the first.

Christenson also noticed that the vessel's name-board was missing from the stern. He purchased, from the Natives on the scene, three rings and an accounts book that bore the ship's name. One ring was presumed to be a wedding ring; the other two were larger, with one bearing the engraved initials "P.M." Christenson related his suspicions of foul play in a report he filed with Governor Frederick Seymour, and he urged that a man-of-war be sent to the Native village of Hesquiat to investigate.[21] The *British Colonist*, having learned of the affair and always eager for a good story, published all the intelligence it could find—and then some. On March 15, the newspaper printed a further bit of news about the *John Bright*'s Chilean "owner," along with the statement that "an overcoat also recovered from the natives, is in the hands of the authorities."[22] It confidently reported that a man-of-war would soon be dispatched to the scene to investigate.

The two articles most likely penned by Higgins, who owned the *British Colonist* at the time, are full of innuendo, though as yet the perpetrators are unnamed. Captain Christenson had "suspicions." A body of a woman was found above the high-tide line. It had been stripped of clothing, as had the vessel itself. A second body was missing. The ship had had its name removed and had been looted; jewelry and clothing known to have been on board the *John Bright* had been found among the Natives. The catalyst of prejudice soon helped determine who was guilty. The Royal Navy would punish the wrongdoers quickly enough, and justice would be served. It took another report, a day later, concerning the likely involvement of innocent children, to make the unspoken become clear.

On March 16 the *British Colonist* found and interviewed someone directly connected with the doomed ship. It reported: "A man who assisted in loading the lost bark, *John Bright*, at Port Gamble, in January last, is in town, and states that the vessel had on board, in addition to her crew, a woman and two children ... supposed to be the Captain's family."[23] The article urged that there should not be the slightest room for indulging the hope that any of the barque's unfortunate passengers were alive: "All have undeniably found either a watery grave, or have fallen by the hands of the West Coast savages."[24]

That word "savages," the last of the article, was now out in the open. The die for retribution had been cast. Details of the innocent children's fate was unknown on March 16, but it struck a poignant chord in the minds of the citizens of Victoria. It reverberated throughout the community during the summer of 1869, as news of their fate was revealed. On April 30 the *British Colonist* reported that a shipwright, Neil Morrison of Port Ludlow, came forward claiming to have known Captain Burgess well. Morrison stated that the Welshman's wife was Chilean and that they had five children, two girls and three boys, the oldest boy being about twelve years of age.[25] If Morrison is right, then there were five, not two, children aboard the *John Bright*.

Though Governor Seymour was informed of the incident, he was not at all convinced of Native misdeeds. Possibly reflecting his personal opinion of the rogue sealing captain, the governor rejected Christenson's overtures outright. Moreover, Seymour did not think that intervention was necessary because, as Higgins wrote, he believed initially that all hands aboard the *John Bright* had perished at sea.

During this same time, Governor Seymour was embroiled in an argument with missionary-trader William Duncan of Metlakatla. Duncan, offering better prices, had lured the Tsimshian traders away from the HBC's more southerly post at Fort Simpson. That act of capitalist manipulation incurred the wrath of Natives around Fort Simpson because, of course, they lost the spin-off trade when the Tsimshian traders moved north.[26] In consequence, Duncan, along with other missionaries on the north coast, demanded a Royal Navy gunboat to protect their church settlements from disagreeable and angry Natives.[27] Gunboat protection, it seems, was being stretched thin.

Seymour was an experienced colonial envoy, well acquainted with the history of greed and avarice in the Empire's hinterlands. He had his own suspicions concerning the clamour coming from the coastal trading companies. He was an educated aristocrat and career diplomat; his wife was a gentle and naive English clergyman's daughter. He was a man most aware of ceremony, civility, and custom. He didn't like the aggressive, frontier mentality of self-made men and was cool to their demands. He seemed too able to find a sympathetic bond with outlying Native communities, visited them often, and approved of their highly stratified society. In contrast, he was guarded and ill at ease with the new egalitarian egoism of entrepreneurial Victoria. Seymour must have been fed up with the coastal traders, who "were forever demanding the presence of a warship, with one pretext or another, for their own protection."[28] Seymour had his own theory as to why the Natives were reportedly so often disgruntled, and this had to do with how they were treated by coastal traders. He was deaf to Christenson's rabble-rousing. Angry at the official inaction, Christenson returned to Hesquiat sometime during the first week of April, ostensibly to secure more convincing evidence to back his case. Of course, he found it. Yet as we shall soon see, Governor Seymour had definite grounds for his suspicions.

If Seymour was a passive conciliator, then James Christenson was an aggressive, self-taught, strong-minded opportunist. He was born in Denmark in 1840. In 1864, at the age of 24, Christenson sailed on the *King Oscar* from Liverpool to Victoria. There he jumped ship and, for a time, worked onshore at a trading station in Port San Juan on the southern outer coast of Vancouver Island.[29] That station is critical to our story, for it is where a friendship and a common motive were established among those particular seal traders who brought the *John Bright* tragedy to the attention of the public.

It must be remembered that in the 1830s, with the slaughter of the sea otter pretty well complete, coastal traders had turned their attention to the fur seal. On the north coast the Haida were the first Natives to respond to this new demand. In March of each year, with rifles and shotguns gained in earlier trade for the sea otter, they ventured out onto the sealing grounds of Dixon Entrance and Hecate Strait. There, they shot the seals as they migrated north. By 1869 the HBC post at Masset was doing a roaring business. As good as the Haida were, they were no match for the superior Nuu-chah-nulth seal hunters of Clayoquot Sound. The Clayoquot successfully hunted the seal on the shallows of the 40-mile-long La Perouse Bank off Barkley Sound.[30]

In 1864 the coastal trader William Spring, with his two schooners, the *Alert* and the *Surprise*, joined forces with Peter Francis, owner of the trading station at Port San Juan, where Christenson worked. The three formed a sealing company, and Christenson joined the *Alert* as mate, under Francis. Their plan was to tap into this whole new, untouched supply of fur seals on the outer coast of Vancouver Island. It wasn't long before Francis manned an out-station in Ucluelet. A Captain Carlton gained the *Alert,* and Christenson became skipper of the *Surprise*. Along the way, Christenson acquired a reputation for being a ruthless trader. Soon, all three were to play a part in the unfolding story.

At 28, James Christenson was a young, tough-minded, successful sealing skipper. In 1868 he seized on a plan to take the Clayoquot and their beloved canoes far offshore aboard the *Surprise* in order to catch the seals right in the middle of their feeding grounds. The catch would literally be taken from under the noses of his competitors. Four canoes and twelve Clayoquot were lowered from the deck of the *Surprise* into the Pacific some 30 miles offshore, and hunting began. Two of the canoes soon became lost in the fog. When a gale began two days later, Christenson left the lost canoes to the mercy of the open sea and headed for port with the remaining two canoes.[31] For this act Christenson became subject to the lasting enmity of the loyal Pacheenahts of Port San Juan, *not* for abandoning sailors on the open ocean, but for not taking *them* out to sea first. His ploy worked, but he incurred the wrath of the fur dealers in Victoria, who by 1868 were buying furs directly from Native traders. They had lost to the wily independent trader a cheap Native source of furs and would soon have to buy more expensive skins from the likes of him.

Christenson had set a new standard for Native exploitation. Others, such as his friend, Peter Francis, would copy his ways, and soon all was not well in Clayoquot Sound. Still others turned to whisky and violence to entice, or force, the Natives into a new, lucrative enterprise. In Victoria courts between 1865 and 1868, charges of violence towards Natives were often brought against sealing captains. Most cases were dismissed, but a general ill feeling towards sealers lingered.[32] No wonder Christenson wanted protection; no wonder Seymour was sceptical.

By March 31, after Christenson had left once again for Hesquiat, Captain Carleton of the sealing schooner *Alert* arrived in Victoria with a cargo of whale oil. He had been with the whaling party of Captain Roys in Badger Cove, near Hesquiat. Roys, in the steamer *Emma*, had killed three grey whales, but a towing line had parted and one had gotten away, only to be caught again by the local Natives who immediately appropriated it for their own use. It was during this time that Captain Carleton also visited the site of the *John Bright*. He brought to Victoria more news from the scene of the wreck.

Carleton reported that he had buried the body of a woman, the one that Christenson had previously seen. He noted that it lay on a bank about 30 yards above the high-water mark. Strangely, Christenson, for all his indignity, had not buried that body on his initial visit. Why not? The other body that Christenson had referred to, Carleton did not see. What he did see, however, was the broken wreck of one of the *John Bright*'s lifeboats, which, he claimed, Natives told him was full of bags of men's clothes. Carleton's story, published in the *British Colonist*, continued:

> The Indian who professed to have first discovered the wreck, and kept its existence a secret ten days, says that he found the woman lying dead in the very spot where Capt Carleton found the skeleton ... The Indians said that another boat came ashore near where the man's body was found; and that no other bodies were discovered. The natives here have any quantity of articles belonging to the wreck among them ... The Indians were greatly excited, being fearful of a visit from a man-of-war.[33]

Carleton went aboard the wrecked hull of the *John Bright*, which was still filled with lumber. It had, by then, been pushed ashore and was lying broadside to a still considerable surf. Carlton then set sail for Victoria with a few block-and-tackles, which, he said, he had retrieved from the wreck.

For the next three weeks there was nothing new to report, but by April 23, the Higgins-owned newspaper had decidedly changed. That day's headline set the new tone:

> ***Six more bodies of the Bark John Bright's people found
> with their heads cut off?
> They were without doubt murdered by the Indians.***

> Captain Peter Francis and his new sealing schooner *Reserve* had arrived in Victoria the morning of the 22nd., after a "boisterous" trip from Kyuquat. Fortunately, he reported that there was no word of further wrecks along the coast, but "sorrowful enough" news of the fate of those aboard the *John Bright*. The cause of the news is made most clear: Six more bodies have been found, and their position and appearance leave not the slightest room for doubt that they have been cruelly murdered by the Hesquaht Indians. Captain Christenson of the schooner *Surprise*, it will be remembered ... had visited the spot, passed over a long line of coast and discovered the fleshless remains of two human bodies, said by the Indians to have come ashore dead from the wreck. Upon his return to the West Coast, about two weeks ago, he visited the very same part of the coast over which he had gone on his previous visit and, to his horror and amazement, found the headless trunks of six dead men, who from their appearance had apparently been killed within a few days. Capt. Christenson's belief is that these men were alive when he first discovered the wreck and that they were secreted in the bush from the Indians; that one by one they came from their hiding places down to the beach to procure food to relieve their misery, and were ruthlessly slaughtered by the savages.[34]

Higgins obviously used this entry in his more perverse version of the story, which he penned at the turn of the century. At that time, he wrote:

> It was shown afterwards that the captain had been shot through the back while in the act of running away in the vain hope of escaping from the cruel savages, who had proved themselves to be less merciful than the wild waves. The other prisoners were thrown down and their heads removed while they piteously begged for mercy![35]

For Beatrice Holden, the lovely nursemaid to the missing children, Higgins would fashion a fate that played to the barely suppressed fears of his Victoria readers: "The pretty English maid was delivered up to the young men of the tribe, who dragged her into the bush. Her cries filled the air for hours, and when she was seen again by one of the native witnesses some hours later, the poor girl was dead, and her head had disappeared!"[36] Higgins the storyteller was not only a man of his time, he was also very much a man of the theatre.

More important to our unfolding story, however, is a letter from James Christenson himself. It was published April 23, 1869, on the same day, and in the same newspaper, as Peter Francis's report. This letter is critical to any search for the truth and so is worth reading in its entirety. It follows on page 133.[37]

By going public with these charges, Christenson precipitated such a public outcry that Governor Seymour's reticence was soundly condemned and swallowed up in a call for blood. The action that followed was a self-fulfilling prophecy. The high moral tone of the press is inescapable. "At the time the news of the disaster reached Victoria, the Governor was called upon by the press to send a gunboat down to the scene of the wreck, but no action was taken. We are even told that the Missionary from Barkley Sound made personal application to the same effect; but again nothing was done."[38] Years later, another missionary at Hesquiat, Father Brabant, would reveal quite a different story. However, for now, on the grounds of Christenson's new evidence, the press censured the government for its inaction.

For a week, the press was rife with indignation. The tone, which was one of horror, soon turned to outrage. "Possible Indian involvement" had become "lurking savages ruthlessly murdered the poor helpless creatures." The murders, as of the date of Christenson's letter, were believed to have occurred *after* Christenson's first visit and *after* his first call for intervention. The press accepted Christenson's account verbatim and pointed the finger of complicity towards the ruling oligarchy. "Had a gunboat been dispatched hence immediately after the first intimation of the affair received here, the lives of many might have been saved. Who is to blame for this? Who has the power of ordering a vessel round to the scene of the Catastrophe? Undoubtedly the Executive."[39] For the *Colonist*, omission had become commission, and censure had become "recall." The level of rhetoric, even today, remains alarming:

> A ship through stress of weather, is driven ashore a short distance from a city containing a populace possessing superior intelligence and enterprise compared with other British colonies. By superhuman efforts the ill-starred crew succeed in escaping from a watery grave to be slaughtered by savage brutes who perpetrate such horrors within a few miles of this very enlightened community.[40]

One winces now at the nineteenth-century view of what was considered "enlightened," especially when a blind eye was cast to the idea that ships could readily be tossed up onto beaches but bodies could not; that surf could readily break masts and legs, but heads could only be removed by Aboriginal depravity. The mindset had become frozen: "Indians" had become "savages," and they were to be erased from the land.

The hyperbole in the *British Colonist* continued:

> It cannot be from any want of disposition on the part of the people to do what is right, and the natural conclusion is, that those whose duty it is to look after such matters are neglectful or incapable. In charity we are deposed to accept the latter hypothesis, but that will not prevent the onus falling upon the community, and their only remedy lies in immediately petitioning for the removal of their ineffectual officers.[41]

In the interest of its own hidden agenda, the press struck deeply at an English taboo. Beheading was what the uncivilized French did; it was simply *not* done anymore—not in England, and certainly not here. Yet it was. The trader William G. Banfield was beheaded near Barkley Sound in 1864 (apparently for kicking a Native who had broken a knife).[42] Closer to home, along Victoria's Inner Harbour, the Songhees chief "King Freezy" once beheaded a Victoria citizen found to be trespassing on the nearby reserve. He gave the head to his companion to give to Governor Douglas.[43] To be sure, settlers were afraid, and the way to quell the source of that fear was with strong, decisive action.

By 1869 Higgins's *British Colonist* was soundly in favour of a democratically elected responsible government and fervently opposed to Governor Seymour's pro-British, anti-Confederationist agenda. The *John Bright* affair gave Higgins ammunition to build citizen fear of Native attacks. At the same time, it provided him with a pretext to further his own political views. By April 26, the two had become one:

Massacre of the Crew of the John Bright

> It would appear that the executive of this Colony, either in pursuance of orders from Downing Street, or in the exercise of his own will, is anxious to depopulate the country as fast as possible. Perhaps it is a part of Gov. Seymour's policy, if he has any, to show that Vancouver Island is but an incumbrance to Great Britain, and that in driving English settlers from it he is

Kuquaht, March 30th, 1869.

Dear Sir -

There is no doubt on my mind now as to the fate of the crew of the bark "John Bright," wrecked here in February last. The most of them, if not all, have been murdered by the Indians. The following are the additional facts ascertained. We arrived here yesterday at noon, and were informed by the Indians that six bodies were lying on the beach outside of the harbour. This

James Christenson

morning I took a canoe and went out to see them. We found five bodies near high water-mark not many yards apart, and buried them the best way we could. The two first ones were much decayed and had no heads, but appeared otherwise not disfigured. Of the others, two were skeletons; the fifth body was that of a big, stout man, not much decayed; it had a hole right through its back and no head; the sixth body had been already buried by the Indians at quite a distance from the rest, and they did not care to let me see it, but told me that the body was not injured a bit, only the head was not there. On my way out I landed at the village (Hesquiat) and walked through it to see what they had amongst them; but a crowd of scowling Indians soon collected around us and followed us wherever we went carrying knives under their blankets. But I had Ghwyer, Chief of Clayoquot, with me and therefore did not feel much alarmed about them doing me any harm. The Indians also told me that some of them had found the leg of a body yesterday with an india-rubber boot on, which they stripped off and left the leg. I looked for it to-day but could not find it anywhere. In conclusion I beg to state that if the government do not take any more notice of this affair than they have so far, I for one would beg to be excused from coming amongst the Indians on this coast after this trip.

Yours truly

J. Christenson.

doing good service. For most assuredly if such apathy as has been manifested in the case of the late Indian outrages is continued, there will be an end of any attempt at settlement on our shores whilst the Island remains nominally under the protection of the British flag.

This was yellow journalism at its best. It continued: "We are exposed to the attacks of savages, who are allowed to rob and murder white men trading upcoast, with impunity."[44] The *British Colonist* asserted: "The Indians are boasting far and wide that they can commit depredations with perfect security." Though unnamed, the author of the editorial had to be Higgins. Consider the following telling sentence: "Already there are murmurs which show that the settlers living in exposed districts would feel greater security living under a neighboring flag."[45] Suddenly, the *John Bright* affair had become part of the Annexation-Confederation debate. Any anti-American British subject living in Victoria at the time would naturally have been roused by Higgins's call for action. The rhetoric persisted:

> Gov. Seymour has allowed the British flag to be insulted and trampled upon by the savages of the West Coast. This alone is enough to call down upon him the hot indignation of every British subject in the colony ... not one single step has he taken to enquire into the matter, or to punish the wrong-doers. We can not admit the right of the apologists of Mr. Seymour to shelter him from blame, under the plea of imbecility.[46]

The article went on to say that Seymour's reticence caused "wholesale robbery and murder to occur almost within sound of the sunset gun in Esquimalt Harbor." It decried Seymour for not sending a gunboat sooner, and it noted: "The blood of the murdered victims calls for vengeance." Governor Seymour's behaviour over the affair was "disgraceful," and he was in "criminal neglect" of his duty. The rancour was only topped by the bitter irony of the editorial's conclusion: "As it is, a feeling of utter want of confidence in Her Majesty's representative in this colony is engendered, which it is very painful to contemplate."[47]

Did Higgins really have his finger on the pulse of Victorian opinion concerning the fate of those aboard the *John Bright*? Was the fear of so-called Native savagery so ingrained in the White culture of British Columbia that justice had become a pseudonym for revenge? Had the inherent sense of White superiority clouded all judgment completely?

No, not completely, as we shall see. Yet racism and genuine fear certainly existed among the White settlers. And Higgins's latest editorial inflamed those feelings. If its task was to stir a frightened, confused public and move a perceived recalcitrant government into action, then it was successful. I will let you be the judge of the double message inherent in Higgins's closing comment: "Unpleasant as it is to write in such terms of one in Mr. Seymour's position, we cannot, as journalists, neglect our duty, by failing to call public attention to the guilty party."[48]

Yes, the editorial did its job. Public attention was certainly aroused, as, on April 30, 1869, just four days after the editorial appeared, the *British Colonist* reported the following:

> We have been informed that our duty as white men is perfectly understood by some of our fellow citizens, such that a no. of 50 are prepared with military rifles and six-shooters to go up to the scene of the murders and wipe out the whole tribe of murderers ... It is the intention of the volunteers, if their plans would be carried out, that the Indian children belonging to the tribe should be brought down here and afforded Christian instruction.[49]

The self-deception remains chilling.

A day later, on May 1, there was a terse announcement in the *British Colonist*, reporting that HMS *Sparrowhawk*, with Governor Seymour himself aboard, would leave Esquimalt to investigate the alleged massacre connected with the wreck of the *John Bright*. The evidence of the rings, the overcoat, and the published testimony made it impossible for him to continue to deny that there were grounds for suspicion. The colonial government was forced to requisition a gunboat from the Royal Navy. At the last moment, Seymour opted to abandon the trip. He preferred to preserve himself from further criticism and, instead, to travel to Metlakatla and see the Reverend Duncan on the *Sparrowhawk* when it returned from Hesquiat. Five weeks later, he died from the prolonged effects of alcoholism.

When the gunboat HMS *Sparrowhawk* did finally leave for Hesquiat on May 3, it had aboard an impressive amount of firepower. First, there was a military detachment of Royal Marines that had been put together from the ranks of both the *Sparrowhawk* and *HMS Satellite*. Given the fear of violence engendered in the press, it was felt that a strong military deterrent was required just in case the investigations ashore proved dangerous. The civil authorities from the newly amalgamated colony of British Columbia included the Honourable H.M. Ball (magistrate for Cariboo West) and H.P.P. Crease (attorney-general of British Columbia). Interestingly, Captain James Christenson was also on board,[50] as interpreter and possible pilot.

The *Sparrowhawk* itself was impressive. It was wooden and, with the exception of its two very narrow smokestacks, was rigged as a sailing vessel. Its rig was somewhat like that of a modified barque, or "Jackass-Barque," with square-rigged topsails and fore-and-aft sails on each of three masts. Built in Limehouse, Port of London, in 1856, it was fitted with a 200-horsepower reciprocating steam engine, which drove a single screw. The *Sparrowhawk* was capable of eleven knots under power alone. At 181 feet overall, it reflected the latest in naval technology as well as the need for smaller, more manoeuvrable patrol vessels appropriate to this coastline. With four stout cannon, and a complement of 80 men, it was perfect for its west coast station.[51] Henry Wentworth Mist, its commander, was a serious, no-nonsense British career officer in the Royal Navy, who had joined the service as a sub-lieutenant in 1854. He took command of HMS *Sparrowhawk* in Esquimalt in 1868.[52] He carried with him, from Captain William Edge, the senior naval officer at Esquimalt, clear instructions: "Be active yet friendly, firm yet conciliatory."[53]

HMS *Sparrowhawk* first sailed for Barkley Sound to search for an interpreter. James Christenson was probably the only person on board who spoke Chinook, the patois used by the local traders and Natives. Without much challenge, Christenson could translate Native comments as he pleased. Not everyone aboard knew as much about Christenson as we do now. A suitable interpreter was not found in Barkley Sound, so the *Sparrowhawk* proceeded to Clayoquot Sound, where Christenson recruited his commercial ally Ghwyer. The feared Clayoquot chief, who helped him bury the bodies at Hesquiat on his second visit, was known to be a hereditary enemy of the people of that village.

It was blowing hard when the *Sparrowhawk* arrived at Hesquiat, so Mist took it to shelter at the head of Hesquiat Bay. Commander Mist's account of the landing the next morning in front of Hesquiat village itself differed from what was presented in the press on March 31. According to Mist, even with the detachment of Royal Marines, which

The Wreck of the *John Bright* 137

The *Sparrowhawk*, surrounded by its captain (top) and crew.

was drawn up in fighting order before the village, the Natives seemed "utterly unconcerned with our arrival, or at the landing of so large a force."⁵⁴ So much for the Native "fear" of a man-of-war. The story, as reported in the *British Colonist*, continued:

> On Wednesday morning the ship drops down and anchored off the village adjacent to the scene of the wreck, when a number of canoes came along-side, out of which several Indians were taken who were pointed out by Captain Christenson, as being like those concerned in the murder, or who might be rendered useful in the subsequent inquiries as witnesses. A large armed party was now formed, composed of marines of the *Sparrowhawk* and *Satellite*. Accompanied by Hon. Mr. Ball and the attorney general, with several officers, who landed and had an interview with the chiefs, they proceeded to search the ranches. Nothing very suspicious was discovered, however, and the whole party then marched round to the scene of the wreck. The beach was of the roughest and most disagreeable to travel over, and of such a wild and dangerous character towards the surf, that it seemed wholly impossible that anyone could escape from a wrecked ship by boat or otherwise.⁵⁵

All day Wednesday and Thursday Christenson pointed out to a working crew of the ship's company the burial sites he had erected on his second trip. It didn't take long to locate the makeshift graves of the others. The task of exhuming the bodies was supervised by the *Sparrowhawk*'s surgeon, Dr. Peter Comrie. The bodies had to be exhumed in order to determine how they had died. However, decomposition had already set in, and a cheerless job was made even more disagreeable by the awful stench. In all, eleven bodies were pulled from the shallow earth.⁵⁶

On Friday, a duly lawful inquest was convened aboard the *Sparrowhawk*, and a jury was empanelled to examine evidence, hear witnesses, and draw conclusions. The inquest began with an examination of the evidence gained from the exhumed remains of a very large man (the fifth body that Christenson had buried—the one "not much decayed") and that gained from the remains of the man with the so-called hole in his back. Evidence was also heard concerning the skeletal remains of the woman that Christenson stated he first found naked. It was Peter Comrie's job, as ship's surgeon, to ascertain whether the victims had died naturally and been beheaded in the surf or whether they had been victims of homicide: a difficult job, at best.

Matlahaw Point from the air. Huge boulders, some 15 feet high, ring the bay where the *John Bright* came ashore. It struck the inshore reef in the centre of the picture and spilled out its cargo of lumber and people among the boulders in the small bay. The oblong object at the bottom centre is a container from a modern-day container ship that also washed ashore in recent years.

Comrie's conclusions were most significant, so much so that he would later refuse to testify to any atrocities before the Grand Jury. For that refusal, he was almost cited for contempt of court by Chief Justice Needham. Comrie could find *no medical evidence* that indicated the bodies had been decapitated by human hands. In the medical officer's journal on the *Sparrowhawk,* Comrie wrote "that he believed that the gnawing of wild animals and the terrible pounding of the bodies in the surf on that rocky coast sufficiently accounted for their mutilated condition."[57] Comrie was angered that, in spite of his views, the suspicion of homicide lingered. Further witnesses were called.

Initially, the Natives of Hesquiat were co-operative witnesses and produced much that had been taken from the wreck. One Native submitted the *John Bright*'s supposed "boomboard"—an engraved board often attached to the lower spar (boom) of the scudding sails, bearing words of inspiration. Ironically, the inscription read *Neminen time, neminem laede*: "Fear none, injure none." Another asserted that, in the past, Whites had promised them that if they helped save lives from wrecks, rewards would be forthcoming. He then produced an old promissory note for ten blankets, which he claimed was ignored. Somebody wasn't keeping his promises.[58]

All through that weekend, the inquest continued. "One of the prisoners being duly impressed with the enormity of the crime of murder, stated that these two were murdered, and on further examination described their coming ashore alive and going to a ranch for a day and then being killed on the second."[59] Dr. Comrie's pathological evidence apparently wasn't enough, and from the evidence presented largely from the testimony of witnesses, the inquest returned a verdict of wilful murder.

What happened next was definitely *not* reported in the press, but news of it soon raised eyebrows in the Admiralty in London. Having rendered a verdict of murder, the inquest required a suspect, or suspects, to be brought to trial. However, the Natives of Hesquiat would not produce the accused. At this point, Captain Henry Wentworth Mist initiated a tactic that the Royal Navy had used at Fort Rupert and in Clayoquot Sound with devastating effect. He stated that if suspects were not brought forth, then violence would ensue. The threat produced nothing, so Mist instructed the Royal Marines to set fire to Native houses. He then ordered the *Sparrowhawk*'s cannons to destroy the huge, priceless Native canoes on the shore.

The *British Colonist* did not choose to mention Mist's act of aggression, nor did it choose to mention Dr. Comrie's explanation of the headless bodies. It chose, instead, to put the events in the following way: "On the return of the party on board the *Sparrowhawk* [presumably the torching party of Marines], the chief was requested to come off and send for the man that was accused. We heard quite a number of stories relating to the sad affair, all more or less possessing features of similarity. Several Indians were brought off before the chiefs were allowed to land suspected characters or witnesses."[60] As far as the *British Colonist* was concerned, the only possibly hostile act committed was that a few Native chiefs were held briefly on board the *Sparrowhawk* until those required were brought forth. On Comrie's medical opinion, there was complete silence.

From the eyewitness tone of the piece, it sounds as if there were a *British Colonist* reporter on board the *Sparrowhawk*. If there were, might it have been Higgins himself? To my knowledge, there is no record of such a representative, and the writer of the column was not named. I suspect that if Higgins had been an eyewitness, then he would surely have admitted it in *The Passing of a Race* and embellished Mist's action in his own forceful way. If another *British Colonist* reporter were present, then I am surprised at the short play he received. My guess is that Higgins is merely using a "you-are-there" style of journalism.

Back in Victoria, Captain Edge, Mist's superior officer in Esquimalt, stood behind his use of firepower against the village, as did the civil authorities, Judge Ball and the honourable attorney-general, H.P.P. Crease. Yet Mist's action resulted in a storm of diplomatic communiqués between Whitehall and Esquimalt. Edge wrote that Mist "acted with great good judgement." He supported the destruction of the Native canoes and the fiery punishment meted out to the Native population because "the whole tribe was implicated."[61] However, in London, the Lords of the Admiralty, amenable to the enlightened views of British prime minister Gladstone, promptly wrote the Colonial Office in British Columbia, suggesting that a more humanitarian policy for dealing with Indians should soon be in effect.[62]

All of this was kept from the general public in Victoria, which was merely told that HMS *Sparrowhawk* returned to Victoria on Wednesday, May 12, with "seven male Indian prisoners suspected of complicity in the murder of the *John Bright*'s crew."[63] They were also told that no trace of the children could be found and that no information regarding their fate was learned. It was hoped that the Natives held in custody would soon confess so that their fate could be determined. And with that, the trial of the decade was about to begin.

CHAPTER 9
Frocked and Righteous Men:
A Terrible Crime and Its Punishment

Beside us frocked and righteous men
Proclaimed their absolutes as laws.
They kept their purity of creed
By twisting facts that showed the flaws.

F.R. Scott [1]

In the spring of 1534, at the urging of the bishop of St. Malo, the king of France hired a young Breton seaman who was familiar with the old sailing routes of the offshore Atlantic fishery. His task was to sail for the New World and look for gold. What Jacques Cartier found in New Founde Land, in a vast river gulf full of white whales, and in the Baie des Chaleurs changed history completely. When he returned to France a year later with a cargo of beaver, bear, and otter pelts plus ten reluctant Iroquois, he had named the great river Rivière de Canada and the country La Nouvelle France.[2] What the captured Iroquois saw of Paris overwhelmed them completely.

In the spring of 1869, over 300 years later, a young British seaman took seven captured Hesquiat from a remote settlement on the western edge of nothing and plunged them into a colonial community already steeped in the values of the British Empire. Think of it. Like Cartier's Iroquois, Captain Mist's Hesquiat had likely never before left their local environs. When the seven were led off the *Sparrowhawk* at Esquimalt at 5:30 PM on Tuesday, May 12, 1869, some were in chains. None spoke English; all wore blankets (some undoubtedly of woven cedar). All had seen a White man and a white sailing ship; all were suspicious of them. But none had any idea whatsoever of what lay before him.

The Honourable Joseph Needham. With social forces against him, Judge Needham did try to run a fair trial.

The HMS *Sparrowhawk*'s surgeon, Dr. Comrie, whose reaction to Judge Needham's contempt of court order revealed a deeply rooted mistrust of the whole trial.

The seven were suddenly subject to the strange impressions of a bustling Victorian city—its bridges, hotels, gas-lamps, shops, churches, people, and manners. More startling was the pomp and ceremony that awaited them at the high Court of Assizes in Bastion Square. There, on May 27, they would come face to face with lawyers, a bailiff, a clerk, a sheriff, and the red robes and wig of Chief Justice Joseph Needham. For all intents and purposes, they might as well have been thrust into the Old Bailey in the City of London. The five Native witnesses and the two prisoners who found themselves before the earnest chief justice in Bastion Square soon also faced a jury of twenty White males chosen from a largely unsympathetic population.

If that was strange, consider that at the hearing for indictment, James Christenson, the sealing trader who first brought news of the wreck to Victoria and who claimed Native complicity in the murder of those aboard the *John Bright*, was sworn in to act as Chinook co-interpreter for those accused. As though this were not bad enough, Christenson's Clayoquot ally, Chief Ghwyer, was chosen to translate

Nuu-chah-nulth, which was unknown in Victoria and was the tribal language of the accused. The trouble was that Ghwyer, who was fluent in Nuu-chah-nulth and Chinook, was a Clayoquot chief who, due to historic inter-tribal conflicts, had reason to hate the Hesquiat.

The attorney-general of British Columbia, the Honourable H.P.P. Crease, appeared for the prosecution. No one appeared for the accused. James Christenson, under oath, interpreted the pleas of not guilty from the two prisoners, identified as Katkeena and John Anayitzaschist, when they were presented to the court. They faced, without counsel, the judge; the jury; the interpreters; plus fellow Hesquiat Cheecheepe, Nee-ta-kim, Hysietta, WeenenanaKince, and Klac-Kianish,[3] who would testify against them. The public gallery was also crowded with the good citizens of Victoria, most of whom undoubtedly had already made up their minds.

As counsel for the prosecution, BC Attorney-General Henry Pellew Crease showed precious little respect for justice during the trial.

The indictment hearings were a matter of accusation and counter-accusation. The *British Colonist* reported that Nee-ta-kim, a witness, testified (through Ghwyer and Christenson) that he saw "John shoot a man and woman. The woman had come ashore from the wreck and asked John to assist her; he complied and helped her over the rocks a short distance, when he threw her down, drew a pistol from beneath his blanket and shot her through the right side. She died soon after. The man who was killed was very weak and was crawling along on his hands and knees, when he was shot through the left shoulder and died almost immediately."[4]

Nee-ta-kim claimed John told him that he (John) saw Katkeena shoot the man. Both of the accused, he claimed, were on the beach together, but Katkeena did not see John fire a shot. This same witness testified that he saw the holes in the body of the dead man, who was further inshore than the woman. Yet another witness, Hysietta, claimed to have seen John at a potlatch held in one of the Hesquiat houses after the wreck. It was reported that there John had admitted his crime and that a man-of-war had come to take him to Victoria.[5]

Evidence presented included three rings and an elegant brooch containing a small photograph of a young, dark-haired woman of about eighteen years. It was said to be the captain's wife. The brooch was recovered from local Hesquiat. The implication was clear; simply having the jewelry established foul play. The Hesquiat, it seems, were not allowed the traditional rights of maritime salvage accorded to others who lived on the coast.

Dr. Comrie, in defiance of a subpoena issued by the court, had

Henry Wentworth Mist, captain of the *Sparrowhawk*. Tight-lipped about the affair and its aftermath, Mist remained through-out the whole trial the quintessential Royal Navy officer-bureaucrat.

left for Metlakatla in the *Sparrowhawk* with Governor Seymour. The *Sparrowhawk*'s convenient voyage north allowed him to extract himself from the proceedings. Chief Justice Needham, however, deemed that the case could not be completed until after Comrie's testimony, intimating that actions would be taken against the absent gentleman for contempt of court. With that the jury retired, to return shortly with its verdict. Three Hesquiat—Katkeena, John Anayitzaschist, and KlacKianish—would be indicted on charges of murder and would go to trial.

One further bizarre event clouded that day—an omen of the life-and-death struggle that awaited those charged. It was the publication of a letter in the *British Colonist* by Robert Burnaby, the foreman of the Grand Jury. He lambasted the government for its inaction and publicly praised the conduct of the interpreter, who was to be a star witness for the prosecution:

> *Victoria, May 27, 1869*
>
> The Grand Jury respectfully present their regret at the delay which appears to have occurred before active measures were taken on the part of the authorities in investigating the circumstances connected with the wreck of the "John Bright," by which valuable evidences may have been lost and additional loss of life incurred. Such supineness on the part of the Government having a tendency to weaken the influence, which should be at all times sustained over the native population—a period of nearly three months having elapsed from the time of the information being received before any steps were taken in the matter. The Grand Jury cannot but feel that it is essentially the duty of the Colonial Government to take special cognizance of such cases; and they further suggest that the Indians should be rewarded in all cases where they sucour and assist shipwrecked sailors.
>
> The Grand Jury desire further to express their recognition of the praiseworthy conduct of Capt. Christenson and those who assisted him, for the energetic steps taken by them in the matter, which they respectfully suggest should be substantially recognized by the Government also.
>
> *Robert Burnaby, Foreman* [6]

Given the role that the Grand Jury knew Christenson would play in the upcoming trial, Burnaby's letter, by today's standards, would be seen as out of order. Furthermore, was Burnaby really intimating that Christenson should be paid for bringing his allegations forward?

D.W. Higgins's *British Colonist* said nothing of procedural correctness but wasted no time in taking full advantage of Burnaby's letter to advocate its own agenda. In a well-placed editorial just below the letter, it was noted: "Executive inactivity and indolence receive a well deserved reprimand in the report of the Grand Jury submitted yesterday. The document is manly and temperate in tone, and represents popular sentiment thoroughly."[7] Mercifully, there were some in court who were of the quaint notion that justice must serve all. When James Christenson was sworn in as a prime witness for the prosecution the following day, four members of the Grand Jury argued that justice would be compromised by his dual function as interpreter. Chief Justice Needham did not replace the interpreter but, rather, suggested that the Court would judge whether Christenson's evidence was prejudiced by his second role.[8] The question of how Needham might make that assessment was not asked. However, Needham did at this point provide the accused with legal counsel.[9]

Under oath, Christenson detailed the nature of his "contradictory stories." He reported that he was on good terms with the "tribe" and with John Anayitzaschist but that, on the day he discovered the remains of what he believed to be a headless woman,[10] John had said to him that no bodies had come ashore. Subsequent visits resulted in his finding a total of five naked bodies, all without heads, which he testified were not there on the first visit. Christenson implied that the murders of this quintet had occurred after this first visit and that they were survivors of the wreck who were being held captive, possibly nearby, at the time of his first visit. He then provided the court with what today would be called hearsay evidence. In short, he conducted what amounted to a character assassination of John Anayitzaschist. At length he related how he believed Anayitzaschist had a bad name among the Hesquiat. The *British Colonist* reported as follows: "They say he is a bad Indian; politically he opposes the Chief; there are two parties in the tribe; he was a slave at Cape Flattery; the parties who believe in him call him their tyhee." The rest of Christenson's evidence corroborated Hysietta's initial brief testimony. John confessed his guilt to Christenson as well as to Nee-ta-kim. Christenson also took great pains to point out that, unlike other witnesses (such as the chief's brother), Nee-ta-kim was not mixed up in tribal quarrels.

Christenson had established that there were factions within the Hesquiat community, and he spelled out the nature of the village schism. Contradictory testimony, he explained, may be due to the fact that there were members of both factions in court. The real trouble was, of course, that Christenson, with Ghwyer, was doing all the interpreting. Counsel for the defence, Mr. Wood, did not recall Hesquiat witnesses at this time in order to establish the reality of the so-called internecine tribal conflict; rather, he seemed to have accepted Christenson's view without his clients' corroboration. He simply argued that John Anayitzaschist was perhaps a scapegoat for those more truly guilty.

The attorney-general wanted to press on with another witness and the trial proper, but Justice Needham wanted the medical evidence from the exhumations. He had not been amused when told by server

Frederick Williams that Dr. Comrie ignored the subpoena that he had been served just five minutes before the *Sparrowhawk* left for Metlakatla, the northern village of the missionary William Duncan. The *British Colonist* credited Chief Justice Needham, who "deemed the [new] witness entirely inadmissible until the medical evidence had been obtained. The life of an Indian, so far as justice was concerned, was equally valuable with that of a white man, and the life of the prisoner at the bar [Anayitzaschist] was in peril ... the non-attendance of the medical man who could have testified to the appearance of the bodies was inexcusable."[11] His Lordship postponed the case until all others before the Spring Assizes were heard, allowing time for Comrie, Governor Seymour, and the *Sparrowhawk* to return. Even then, there would be one more delay.

> **Colony of British Columbia Court Records**
> (GR2030, v. 2, p. 169)
>
> Part of Joseph Needham's recording of Katkeena's "confession."
>
> *I shot him but the water was running out of his mouth. I thought he would not live and I shot him.*
>
> Needham's response to Katkeena's "confession" was the death sentence.

The funeral service for Governor Seymour in Christ Church Cathedral on June 16, 1869, and subsequent time for respectful, if insincere, mourning interrupted the Spring Assizes. When they reconvened on June 22, Justice Needham had his man, Dr. Comrie, front and centre. Comrie justified his decision to go north, saying that he was attending the dying governor. Of course he was forgiven, and the charges of contempt against him were dropped. Chief Justice Needham's bench books of the case for the Crown are remarkably detailed and give further credibility to Comrie's conclusions. Comrie, it seemed, would also get his day in court.

First, however, the prisoner Katkeena was arraigned on the charge of the murder of the large male whose corpse had been found on the beach. When called upon to plead through Christenson, the interpreter, he was reported to have said: "I shot the man, as he was coming ashore from the wreck. I went to help him. He shook his head [gesturing denial?] at me and then I shot him."[12] Case closed. No questions asked.

No details given. The prisoner was removed; the sentence would be death.

A new jury was struck to try John Anayitzaschist, who was indicted for the murder of a female passenger of the wrecked *John Bright*. "In the most emphatic manner he pleaded not guilty."[13] Commander Mist testified as to the site of the wreck and noted the myriad of round boulders that covered the foreshore. Captain Henry Maynard Ball, as both magistrate and coroner, testified that he was with Dr. Comrie when the remains were exhumed. The magistrate further testified that the remains, by virtue of the size of the small detached skull, "might have been a Boy for all I know."[14]

When the only doctor to inspect the bodies was finally called, the reasons for his apparent reluctance to testify became more obvious. The citizens of Victoria were not going to like what they were about to hear. Dr. Comrie confirmed that the skeletal remains of a human being were disinterred from under a boulder on May 6, near Hole-in-the-Wall, just west of Matlahaw Point. The skeleton was in pieces and included seven ribs, two pieces of a thigh bone, and four small fragments of an arm. He commented that "some of the bones were gnawed slightly by some wild animal."[15] Though detached from the rest of the skeleton, "the first two bones of the spine were found attached to the skull. The lower jaw was found wanting. The bones of the skull were perfectly bare."[16] He added that a further close measurement of the skull led him to believe that the person "was not a European."[17] He concluded, by the hardness of the bones, the smallness of the skull, and the delicacy of the teeth, that the remains were those of a woman somewhere between 20 and 30 years old.[18] Comrie couldn't tell the height of the person, the time of death, or whether the skull fracture had occurred before or after death, though he did believe it was certainly the result of violence. He did say, however, that "the teeth of the upper jaw were complete."[19] He added, "The mere weight of the body falling on such boulders as I saw, might occasion the fracture."[20]

Upon cross-examination by Mr. Wood, Justice Needham noted that Dr. Comrie said again, "I think such a fracture very likely to occur from a fall on the boulders or having washed backwards and forwards against the boulders by the tide."[21] Dr. Comrie was very careful. He was not going to dismiss telling the defence attorney that the remains may have indeed been those of a Native and that the long black hair possibly, although not probably, belonged to a man.

So Dr. Comrie had examined a decomposing skeleton. He, like Mist, testified that the beach was full of dangerous boulders, where someone exhausted after having made it through the surf could have readily fallen unconscious, drowned, and been further dismembered by wave action. He could not, and would not, indicate foul play.

Nee-ta-kim was then called again. He testified that it was blowing hard and that he saw the *John Bright* twice, once sailing westward in a heavy gale before it struck the reef and once at noon when it was on the rocks. Noticing Katkeena along the beach, he (Nee-ta-kim) went towards the wreck. Katkeena, he testified, started running when he saw him. As Nee-ta-kim approached the wreck he saw two people, both in the rigging. Christenson translated for Justice Needham, who noted Nee-ta-kim's testimony:

> "I saw a man come down on the rigging and he seemed to me to jump into the water. After the man got into the water the woman came down the rigging and she also went overboard. I saw the man in the water turned over and over feet and head and then his feet in the breakers in the seas. The man got on shore on the dry rocks out of the breakers when Katkeena tried to get hold of him. Katkeena took the man by the arm, this was when he was up to dry ground but the man was not able to walk and was hanging on Katkeena's arm. Katkeena brought him half way between high water and the ground and shot him there."[22]

Nee-ta-kim next described the death of what was believed to be the woman whose skeletal remains were examined by Dr. Comrie.

> "The woman got into the sea, and the sea turned her over the same as the man and she could not swim. I saw the woman in the water and I saw her out of the water on the rocks. I know the prisoner he is called John. John went down and took her by her hand. John took her by the arms and hauled her up to the dry rocks. But she was in the same condition as the man and could not walk and leant heavily on John's arms and the salt water came out of her mouth. John brought her up as far as halfway between the rocks and the beach and he drew his pistol and shot her. When he left her she was on her hands and knees."[23]

At Matlahaw (Boulder) Point, during a winter gale, any ship caught amidst the boulders wouldn't stand a chance.

Nee-ta-kim then went to her and found that she was dead. Later that day he went aboard the wreck looking for clothes but found only lumber. Returning to the body later that day, he noted that the woman was dark and had her hair "tied up behind." She was wearing colourful clothing, a red and white patterned shirt, black jacket, black shoes, and a ring. Native friends had told him of her broken ribs, and Nee-ta-kim stated that he saw the same broken ribs through a hole in her shirt. It was established that she was shot in the ribs by a pistol that the prisoner John had hidden in his blanket. Nee-ta-kim stated that he didn't actually see John remove her clothing but did see him hanging them out to dry.

Cross-examined by Mr. Wood, Nee-ta-kim said he didn't actually see John shoot the woman, as he was some 40 yards behind and eastward of him. Nee-ta-kim said, however, that he did see John raise her arms and that he saw the smoke and heard the report of a pistol. Of course, he was too far away to intercede in the killing and felt that John would have killed her regardless. Nee-ta-kim did not supply a motive for John's alleged murder of the woman because Mr. Wood did not ask for one.

It was this story that Nee-ta-kim told "Mr. Charlie" (Captain Carleton)[24] when he arrived on the scene in the third week of March. He stated: "Charlie was the first white man I told about the matter. I told Charlie that there was a woman dead on the beach. Charlie had belonged to a schooner that comes to our place."²⁵ This was the body that the sea had washed away from where she was shot, and the same body that Carleton reportedly had buried under a boulder some two weeks after the wreck. Nee-ta-kim did establish that he was friends with John and that John was friends with the chiefs.

The witness WeenenanaKince put a whole different slant on the story. He, too, saw the ship at noon "a little to the West of Chickaloo [Matlahaw] point."²⁶ Hearing several shots, he saw John on the beach, who said that Katkeena had shot a White man. "I asked John who fired the other shot and John said I did. I shot the white woman and she was very cold. I don't think she was alive when I shot."²⁷ Fearing for his own life before the High Court, WeenenanaKince stated that he too went aboard the wreck and "got some jams, no clothes, nothing else."²⁸ He stated emphatically that he did not touch the body he saw after coming from the wreck, but he did say, "the mark in the woman's cheek was like a shot, but I did not examine it. I only saw the blood."²⁹ WeenenanaKince stated he knew John well, as he lived at Hesquiat: "The prisoner is a chief, but not a head chief."³⁰ Of the grand chief Taahnasin and his subordinate, he stated: "The prisoner has not quarreled with either of them."³¹

So two Hesquiat friends of John pointed him out as the murderer of the young woman who came ashore and was ostensibly shot. Yet both stated that the woman was shot in different places: the cheek and the chest. Dr. Comrie's careful examination of the presumed victim showed no bullet damage either to the upper jaw or the ribs. At the inquest on board the *Sparrowhawk*, the woman's clothes were neither procured as evidence nor examined for signs (such as bullet holes or powder burns) of foul play. Only WeenenanaKince offered a motive—that of mercy. Nee-ta-kim offered no motive. Both discounted James Christenson's testimony of John's involvement in a tribal power play. John Anayitzaschist fingered Katkeena, yet the latter had no motive whatsoever for committing the crime. There was a mix of contradictory and circumstantial evidence. One could fairly argue that if Judge Needham had been sitting in the Old Bailey listening to such testimony against three thugs from the London docks, he would have thrown the whole affair out of court as a silly farce. Why didn't he do this in his Victoria courtroom? For two reasons: (1) the persistence of the prosecution and

(2) the community expectation that the court would return a guilty verdict. And so a tragedy in the making continued.

Hysietta was recalled. He reiterated his testimony of hearing John's alleged confession at the potlatch, yet he added that all the chiefs were there (implying, once more, the improbability of tribal conflict). Katkeena, he testified, was not present. Cheecheepe seemed sympathetic to the accused. He testified that John "told me he shot the white woman, she was cold he said and he did not think that the woman was alive."[32] Cheecheepe corroborated WeenenanaKince's earlier statement concerning motive. When KlacKinish was called, the poor man didn't even know he was accused. He kept repeating, "I saw nothing" and denied that he had been promised a pardon if the prisoner were to be found guilty.

With regard to Christenson's translation, it is impossible to find specific fault with it. There was enough corroboration among some witnesses, as well as conflicting and uncertain opinions among others, to conclude that the interpreter and his aide, Chief Ghwyer, were not purposefully shaping the outcome through wilful manipulation of language. The overall effect of Christenson's final testimony for the Crown, however, cast the Hesquiat in a negative light. He stated once again that "when I first saw it the head [of the woman] was attached to the body."[33] Again, the implication of decapitation and foul play is clear. He correctly noted Carleton's act: "It was buried and a rock rolled over it at high tide."[34] Where Hesquiat witnesses claimed that John Anayitzaschist had lived in Hesquiat except for a period when he was held as a slave at Neah Bay, Christenson stated: "He lives apart from the village at times, sometimes with his woman, sometimes [for] two or three months."[35] Yet, under cross-examination, he conceded that "a Good lot of the Indians call him Chief, and he calls himself one."[36] In general, Christenson found the Hesquiat "reasonable" yet "untruthful."[37]

Initially, Christenson had found what he believed to be a female body still intact. Upon his return with Ghwyer some two weeks later, he found, to his horror, the mangled remains of White men scattered about. From this he determined that the murders had been committed recently and then concluded that all those who had reached shore had been massacred. Returning to Ucluelet, Christenson wrote the infamous letter that roused the ire of Victoria. Dr. Comrie, you will remember, disagreed strongly with Christenson's view.

The whole case boiled down to the problem of the missing bodies. If Christenson saw one on his first visit, then why did he not see the others? If the Natives killed them between his first and second visit, then why did they place them conveniently on the beach just before his return, when it would have been easier to destroy and hide them in any one of a thousand places? If the Natives were indeed hiding those who survived the terrible experience of the wreck, not to mention the pounding surf, surely that very act would have given at least one of them the courage to shout out or escape?

There were other unanswered questions. Why, for example, did John ostensibly shoot his victim under the arm and not in the head? If he was acting mercifully towards someone suffering from compound fractures caused by the surf, surely a shot to the head would be quicker and more humane. Katkeena might have done the same, yet he, too, was said to have shot his victim in the chest. Why were there no Native witnesses other than the local chiefs of Hesquiat, who were not asked to submit testimony on board the *Sparrowhawk* while it was in Hesquiat? Why did the initial investigation warrant so little time? Nee-ta-kim's testimony was key to the trial. Why did he so readily identify John and Katkeena as perpetrators when he had stated that John, at least, was a friend?

Christenson's story may be interpreted another way: the "massacre" was apocryphal. A massacre would enable Christenson to elicit regular naval protection from Natives that he and other unscrupulous traders had cheated and abused. There needed to be a verdict and due punishment to compensate for other regional "Native violence." There needed, in short, to be a massacre so that there could be an exorcism.

Part of the answer to the many questions surrounding the trial lies in the nature of fear itself and in the need for a guilty party. Throughout the trial, the press blamed and vilified those presumed guilty of murder. Reporters heard the same evidence as did Chief Justice Needham, yet they reported it with such bias that no degree of fairness was possible. Two particular examples of this type of reporting are worth noting. Nee-ta-kim testified, regarding John's role in the alleged murder, that "John brought her up as far as halfway between the rocks and the beach."[38] The press wrote: "The woman ... asked John to assist her; he complied and helped her over the rocks a short distance, when he threw her down."[39] The second example of journalistic bias is even more marked. When the brooch was simply submitted as evidence against the accused in court, the *British Colonist* reported as follows:

> The photograph contained in the brooch found upon the poor woman who lost her life by the *John Bright* tragedy, is that of a handsome young brunette of about 18 years, with a round, laughing face and coal-black eyes. Long black ringlets descend from her head and fall gracefully over the shoulders, while a narrow white collar encircles the small white neck and is secured by an elegant brooch. The portrait is said to be that of the Captain's wife, who was cruelly murdered by the Indians upon whom she relied for assistance.[40]

The pen is mightier than the sword, and the pen of the press had spoken. This trial was not just about murder; it was about race. It was about "innocence" despoiled by "savages," and about Victorian indignation and the demand for retribution. The press told the community what it should expect, and anything less was simply unacceptable.

By virtue of the circumstantial nature of the evidence given by two of the accused, indictments against them were quashed. That left John Anayitzaschist to take the fall. Following Christenson's testimony, at 6:30 PM on Wednesday, June 23, 1869, the jury retired to consider its verdict. Five minutes later it returned. Tersely, the *British Colonist* stated: "The prisoner wept when the verdict of the jury was announced, and [he] said he did not kill the woman. Anayitzaschist and Katkeena were then sentenced to death."[41]

The Aftermath

If the story had ended there, the denouement would have been understandable. But it did not. Thus far, the *John Bright* affair has alternated between drama and farce. The second act of the tale, like the first, is full of twists and ironies that highlight the poignancy of this travesty.

On July 6, a week after the verdict, a whisper of doubt raised its first, tentative voice. The *British Colonist* printed a report first published in the *Port Townsend Message*. In that paper, a Mr. J.G. Swan had made a startling statement regarding the same brooch that was submitted as evidence against the accused and made so much of by the Victoria press. The account caused the *British Colonist* to engage in some nifty footwork. Rather than choosing to comfort those facing the gallows, it chose to condemn an entire race:

> Mr. J.G. Swan [is] a gentleman who had many years' experience with the Indian tribes on Puget Sound and the West Coast of this island, and who understands their language thoroughly ... In conversation with Mr. Swan, a few days ago, he informed us that the brooch belonged to an Indian of the Nitinat tribe and that the portrait was that of a female relative of Mr. H.A. Webster, Indian Agent at Neah Bay!
>
> We mention this circumstance, not to discredit the evidence on which the Indians were convicted, but to show how untrustworthy is Indian evidence as a rule.[42]

The same column praised the "very nice discrimination" of the judge and jury in warranting their conviction. Two days later, on the heels of this announcement, came a bombshell. "The Barclay Sound Murderers Writ of Error Applied for and Refused," rang the headline.

Mr. Wood, counsel for the defence, perhaps having read the newspapers, decided to petition Chief Justice Begbie for a writ of error. He wanted Needham to argue before the infamous Begbie that the trial had committed three procedural errors and should, therefore, be declared a mistrial. These errors were: (1) the first jury had been allowed to go about at large without finding a verdict (Mr. Wood alluded here to the said jury's access to the press); (2) the Assizes had been adjourned for a prolonged period instead of proceeding contiguously; and (3) an irregular question had been asked Dr. Comrie. Wood could, and should, have pointed out further inherent weaknesses in procedure, such as Christenson's dual role and the lack of hard evidence. However, he did not. The reported reply of Chief Justice Begbie is amazing still: he declined to hear the application, saying he understood very well the motives that activated it and that he had lived sufficiently long on Vancouver Island to understand the people thoroughly.[43] Meek and tractable, Wood withdrew.

Higgins did not. With renewed vigour he thrust his pen deftly between the shoulder blades of the ever-malleable public. The immediate fate of a few Hesquiat now served an apparent higher cause. At the same time, perhaps the vociferous publisher was doing some soul-searching. The column ended with his familiar clarion call: "It is a source of deep regret to all that there is not in this Colony a Court of Appeal. The evil is one that Confederation will cure."[44]

Of the case, there were small leftover details that needed attention. The five witnesses had to be returned to Hesquiat, and on June 28, Attorney-General Crease asked Christenson if he would oblige and what fee he would charge. You can guess the response:

> To Hon. Attorney-General
>
> For not less than ten dollars a head. Cargo has to be displaced for the purpose. Will the Colonial Secretary let me know at once whether this will suit His Honour and whether I shall take them at once as I am about to start.
>
> James Christenson[45]

The very next day the colonial secretary, Philip Hankin, acting on behalf of the executive, agreed to the exorbitant fee. Obviously, Christenson did well through the trial, what with his salary as interpreter and his fee for transporting the Hesquiat back to their village. Even though he did not get the long-term gunboat protection he sought, his actions left an undying impression on coastal Natives.

John Anayitzaschist and Katkeena were to be hanged for the murder of two survivors of the wreck of the *John Bright*. They were not, however, to be hung in the local jail. A clear message had to be sent to other troublesome Natives. They were to be taken back to Hesquiat and hung before the entire assembled village, within sight of the wreck.

On Monday morning, July 26, 1869, while on single anchor in Constance Cove, Esquimalt, the *Sparrowhawk* was once again busily preparing for sea. By 12:40 PM it had watered up and fired its two boilers. Besides the two condemned men, the *Sparrowhawk* took on High Sheriff Elliot of Victoria; the Reverend Father Charles John Seghers; Mr. Lloyd Fisher, attendant and interpreter; the Victoria "bluejackets," consisting of some 15 police constables, to guard the prisoners and civil officials; several carpenters, who were to assemble the portable gallows; and a detachment of 20 Royal Marines to fly the flag of British sovereignty.

At 2:20 PM Captain Mist ordered anchors aweigh, and the *Sparrowhawk* steamed out of Esquimalt Harbour into the fog. Mist was most careful to follow the required course rounding Race Rocks. All that day, and into the small hours of Tuesday, the *Sparrowhawk* proceeded slowly through the fog and calm seas of the Strait of Juan de Fuca and the outer coast of Vancouver Island, sounding the fathoms as it went. At dawn it was stopped completely by dense fog. All morning it was trysails up, headsails down, trysails up, headsails down, as it steered northwest by west in fluky southeast winds. By noon its taffrail log showed it had proceeded 133 miles through the water. Mist noted in his log that Boulder Point bore 22 degrees true; either the fog momentarily must have lifted, or he was navigating solely by dead reckoning.

It was during this time that Father Seghers was said to have baptized the two condemned men. In the process, he gave his first thought to the idea of establishing a Roman Catholic mission at Hesquiat. His biographer, Sister Mary Mildred, in tracing his life with the west coast Natives, noted that, on Tuesday, July 27, the fog-bound *Sparrowhawk* had struck a rock near the point where the *John Bright* had foundered on its way into Hesquiat. She writes that Captain Mist

> ordered the steam engine to be started, but the ship would not budge. Then he called everyone on deck and ordered the crew to lower the lifeboats. Two pumps, in the meantime were put in place to bail the hold, but investigation showed that the boat had fortunately not taken any water. Finally, after prolonged efforts, they dislodged the vessel and continued on their way, having sustained no other damage than the bending of a few plates of copper sheathing.[46]

A dreaded tidal current had apparently caught the *Sparrowhawk* and carried it, as it had the *John Bright*, well beyond the open entrance to Hesquiat Harbour and into the rocks and reefs of Matlahaw Point.

The *Sparrowhawk*'s log reveals that Captain Mist was very circumspect about the whole affair. He noted that at about 2:00 PM he had lost the patent log line, as it had wrapped itself around the propeller. Without the taffrail log, Mist had no indicator of speed or distance travelled. In plain English, Mist had, for the moment, become lost in the fog off notorious Estevan Point. Mist continued: "At 2:25 PM, found ship amongst kelp, put helm down and reversed engines. On gaining sternway, turned ahead and steamed out southeast; least water 14 feet off Point Estevan."[47] Kelp grows over rocks and shallow water. The *Sparrowhawk*'s designed draft was eight feet, though it probably drew a foot more. Mist noted that, for a time, it was stopped dead before it could reverse engines. With a sounding of fourteen feet, it was very possible that it could have drifted over a shelf and bumped its bottom. The *Sparrowhawk* apparently either leaked or took on some water, as Mist noted in the log that he employed seamen "packing oakum as requisite."[48] Mist was a hair's-breadth away from disaster. Had the weather been as foul as it had been some six months previously, Higgins would have been beside himself with narrative possibilities. As it was, the Church of England's Henry Wentworth Mist must have felt like paying a brief visit to the Very Jesuit, Very Reverend, Charles Seghers. Once off, the dense fog prevented them from going south and entering Hesquiat Harbour proper. Wisely, they remained at sea, taking soundings hourly throughout the night.

On Wednesday morning the fog lifted slightly, and the *Sparrowhawk* entered Hesquiat Harbour, anchoring at 11:00 AM off a point near the head of the bay. The fog proved to be too thick to anchor off the village directly. Immediately, Sheriff Elliot was rowed ashore to find a suitable site for the hanging. Upon his return, Mist ordered the carpenters ashore to raise the gallows under the watchful eyes of Lieutenant Wright and the detachment of Royal Marines on loan from HMS *Satellite*. When the job was done, a guard was placed on shore to "keep the Indians from destroying [the] scaffold."[49] Not so strangely, the Hesquiat were nowhere in sight.[50] Mary Mildred noted that Father Seghers saw only one old Native who was fishing alone in his canoe. He was hailed and told to summon the villagers at once to witness the execution. Typically, "the old man listened attentively and politely, then quietly continued fishing."[51]

Suddenly, at midday on Wednesday, Natives appeared and drew alongside the gunboat. Strangely enough, friends, family, and others known to the prisoners were allowed on board. When a suitable crowd of Natives had gathered on the main deck, Captain Mist used the occasion to make a short presentation. The *British Colonist* painted a portrait of Native remorse and colonial puffery. It was reported that Mist addressed the Natives first, informing them of the nature of the proceedings and why the hangings were about to be undertaken. He then told them how further hangings could be prevented: "In the event of a vessel being again wrecked on the coast, should they shelter and protect the survivors and send them to Victoria, they would be rewarded for their trouble."[52] The *British Colonist* further reported that High Sheriff Elliot said "that the executions were intended to serve as a warning; that on this occasion only two men were to be punished, but on future occasions should any arise, the whole tribe would suffer."[53] Mary Mildred, in her later biography, suggested that the villagers appeared singularly unimpressed. She wrote that some, however, seemed more interested in the ship itself than in the fate of John and Katkeena. John tearfully recommended his wife and two children to the care of his brother, who seemed cool and diffident.[54] As the day passed, the *British Colonist* continued, both John and Katkeena appeared to appreciate their condition. "John told Mr. Fisher that he did not fear death, but he feared the effect of his execution upon his little daughter, whose heart would break when she heard that he was no more. Katkeena was reserved and said nothing."[55]

At 9:35 AM Thursday, four boats were lowered and the constables, civil officials, clergy, Mr. Fisher, the high sheriff, the Royal Marines, Captain Mist, the ship's doctor, and the condemned all went ashore. The tight-lipped Mist noted in his log that they were doing this only "to carry out the extreme penalty of the law on two Indians."[56] By 10:00 AM some 45 male Natives had gathered, so the brief proceedings quickly began. According to the *British Colonist*, "The guard were drawn up on either side of the scaffold, in front of which the Indian spectators were directed to gather." Father Seghers said a few words to the condemned men. Their hands were bound, and they were then led up the steps of the gallows to the platform and instructed to stand beside each other over the drop. The *British Colonist* reported that John Anayitzaschist addressed the gathered assembly, denouncing the chief of the tribe (who was present). A translation of what he said is not available. As the black hoods were placed over the prisoners' heads, and the nooses fitted securely about their necks, John Anayitzaschist began to mumble over and over in his native tongue. Suddenly, without warning, the bolt was sprung and the drop fell.

John Anayitzaschist died almost immediately, but the rope around Katkeena's neck did not draw tightly. He squirmed, gurgled, and choked, dangling grotesquely in space, until the executioner raced up the scaffold and jammed his foot downward against the knot, bringing an end to his suffering.[57] Most of the landing party returned to the ship. An hour later, the bodies were cut down, put in boxes, and handed over to the villagers for burial. At 11:40 AM, the *Sparrowhawk* weighed anchor and steamed out of sight.[58]

⚓ ⚓ ⚓ ⚓ ⚓

Back in Victoria a strongly worded editorial on the *John Bright* affair soon appeared in Higgins's paper. It was inspired by the return of the *Sparrowhawk* and details of the hangings that appeared in the *British Colonist* on July 31, 1869. It tried to counter the feelings of shame that some citizens were experiencing over the executions of the convicted murderers. Several reported that, considering that the Hesquiat had been ignorant of English law, the death penalty was too high a price to pay. Others felt that Katkeena and Anayitzaschist may have been made scapegoats for crimes not of their doing. Higgins came crashing down on such views. He argued that the evidence alone was enough to have convicted John and Katkeena, and he readily criticized what he believed to be an overly affected sensibility. For the *British Colonist*, the executions of Natives who indulged in violence were necessary in order to send all Natives a much-needed message. "No sane man who has read the evidence can doubt that the hands of these savages were stained with the blood of the poor, helpless survivors from the wreck of the bark; and how many other similar cold-blooded murders no one can tell."[59] The final, self-righteous blow read as follows:

> If we treat with savages we must act in a manner intelligible to them; it is absurd to suppose that our views of equity and justice can apply to people ignorant of the commonest sense of humanity. [There will] be time enough to treat them as we do ourselves, when we have educated them to realize the difference between harshness and mercy ... we must speak in a language they understand.[60]

For Higgins, the *British Colonist*, and many Victorians of the day, the appropriate language of British law and order was violence. Referring to the Royal Navy gunboat action against Native villages in Clayoquot Sound (for alleged acts of piracy against traders), the *British Colonist* downplayed the destructiveness of lawful White retaliation: "The only consequence in any case was [our] expenditure of much powder and bombs that probably knocked over a few wigwams." In nineteenth-century terms, and in a nineteenth-century context, justice had been both served and endorsed. Those of the Victorian period considered "Western civilization" far more important than other age-old cultures. The "great crime and its punishment," as the *John Bright* affair came to be known, was a product of nineteenth-century thinking, and most Victorians, if not all, were trapped in it. The extreme penalty had been paid, and the last act of this strange morality play was over.

However, the curtain was not yet down. Throughout the inquest and subsequent trial, not a word had been spoken about the fate of the children. No one, except High Sheriff Elliot, suggested that the decomposing body found on the beach could, in fact, have been a boy. But the suggestion was neither investigated nor linked to the Burgess's oldest child, a young lad of twelve. Two years passed. Then, on February 24, 1871, this headline appeared in the *British Colonist*:

A CAPTIVE GIRL
Among the Nitinahts Thrilling Incidents

> It was intimated in these columns a short time ago that the Ahousat Indians at Barclay Sound had a captive English girl in their possession, supposed to be one of the survivors of the *John Bright* disaster, nearly two years ago.[61]

The story of the tragedy in the surf at Hesquiat was recounted, and the suggestion was made that the captain's daughter, "a lovely girl of eight or nine years," was taken alive and retained by the same tribe that had murdered her parents. It was speculated that, fearing yet another investigation, the Hesquiat moved the child to a neighbouring Ahousat encampment in Clayoquot Sound.

> The Ahousat soon afterwards sold her to the Wyahts, opposite Cape Flattery. The Wyahts, however, soon learned that information of the white captive being in their possession had been communicated to Capt. Hays, at Neah Bay, in consequence of which, fearing investigation and rescue, they traded her away to the Nitinahts residing [sic] between Cape Flattery and Barclay Sound in exchange for an Indian slave.[62]

The trader, Captain Hays, had passed this news on to ex-U.S. consul Francis (no relation to Peter Francis, Christenson's employer), who was well known in Victoria. It was no doubt Francis who passed the story on to the press.

Again, the *Sparrowhawk* was dispatched across the Strait of Juan de Fuca to Neah Bay to investigate. It returned to Esquimalt with news that the girl in question was, in fact, a mixed-blood child who had been sold into slavery two years before the wreck of the *John Bright*. Still the story would not die. Some time later, two Natives from Neah Bay who had seen the child disputed that she was the mixed-blood that Captain Mist had reported. The two claimed adamantly that the child was indeed White, but they refused to travel over to Nitinaht to identify her, claiming they would be killed.[63] Again, details persisted. Members of the crew of the trading schooner *Forest King* came forward and swore that they, too, had seen a White girl among the Ahousat. She was, they claimed about twelve years old.

It was possible that she could have been one of the Burgess's two girls, if—and this is a very big if—she had made it through the surf that terrible day two years before. There is no record of anyone seeing a child on deck. Yet it is not entirely improbable that she might have been taken to safety from the ship itself some days after the *John Bright* washed up closer to that fateful shore and was boarded by various Natives. After the last sighting by those aboard the *Forest King*, it was said that some in Victoria conjectured that she had been shuttled from tribe to tribe (in order to avoid detection) until she was old enough to marry and "become Indian."[64]

The story of the children had hung over the *John Bright* affair from the beginning. At the narrative level, the fate of the children provided the story with a paradox that was both provocative and tantalizing. One could ponder images of cruelty, or one could ponder images of hope. If one pondered the latter, then one had to re-think the view that "savages" had no humanity. At best, the paradox was discomforting.

Those same stirrings of hope also caused some to ponder the sanity of the executions themselves. The story simply would not die, and people held different positions with regard to it. A few who had lived through the transitional period between early coastal trade and full-fledged White settlement on Vancouver Island believed that the *John Bright* affair had been a monstrous injustice right from the start. Chief among these people was Father Augustin Brabant.[65]

Soon after the Jesuit missionary Charles John Seghers gave his last prayer to Katkeena and John on July 29, 1869, he became the bishop of Vancouver Island. One of his first acts was to establish a Roman Catholic mission and school at Hesquiat. He gave that task to Father Augustin Brabant, who went to Hesquiat in 1874 and remained there for over 30 years. Not surprisingly, he saw Aboriginal culture through European lenses. Like Seghers, Brabant looked upon Natives as "superstitious

Hesquiat, seen here 25 years after the wreck of the *John Bright*, remained a remote Native village, its only constant European influence being the spiritual guidance offered by a lone missionary of the Roman Catholic Church, who used lumber salvaged from the *John Bright* to build his mission.

Missionary at Hesquiat for over 30 years, Father Augustin Brabant (left) had an inherent dislike of coastal traders, who often took advantage of Natives. He did not arrive at Hesquiat until after the trial, but he would hear much of the event over ensuing decades. Yet he remained silent about his misgivings for over a quarter of a century.

children" who had to be "saved" by Christianity. He, like other missionaries, rooted out their beliefs, their customs, and their religious and familial ceremonies with a zeal that was noted even amongst his peers. Almost single-handedly, Father Brabant destroyed a culture. Like, among others, John Meares, Judge Begbie, and William Duncan, Brabant, by sheer force of will, pushed his own view of humanity upon already besieged Aboriginals.

Brabant never believed that Katkeena and John Anayitzaschist were guilty of the crimes for which they were hung. Moreover, he believed that James Christenson was the real culprit.

Thirty Years Later

Father Brabant would hear many stories of village life, oral history, and west coast legend as he established his mission. Amazingly, though he would finally express himself 30 years after he first went to Hesquiat, there is no public record of him ever speaking out on the possible injustice done to those tried in 1869.

On March 7, 1904, Father Brabant wrote David Higgins a long letter upon hearing that the retired publisher planned to cover Native subjects in a forthcoming book. This letter, which was recently rediscovered in British Columbia's provincial archives, sheds a new light on the hearings. Brabant, with no personal stake in the original event, asked Higgins to refrain from publishing the popular story of the wreck of the *John Bright* in book form for the simple reason that it was not true. Brabant's letter speaks for itself:

> *7 August, 1904*
>
> *D.W. Higgins Victoria B.C.*
>
> *Dear Mr. Higgins -*
>
> *The account of your "Reminiscences" which you are giving in the "Colonist" is very interesting; and I am sure that most readers of the paper, like myself, always read every word printed under the initials of D.W.H. I have been disappointed though—and I am writing to you in order to tell you so—upon reading in the "Jesuit Weekly" 25 March— True tales of the Sea , and I sincerely hope that for the sake of truth and justice, when your Reminiscences appear in book form as everybody hopes and expects they will some time, you will leave out the account of the Wreck of the "John Bright" or materially correct it—Why? is it not a true account? To this I emphatically answer: No!* [66]

Brabant went on to explain that, for some 30 years, he had lived within two miles of the wreck of the *John Bright*. With his neighbours being Hesquiat who were friends and relatives of the accused, he had the time and the interest to find out everything he could about the matter. This was facilitated, he added, by his "speaking the language of the natives with more facilities which no one else has or ever had."[67] More than this, he wrote that he was given two further accounts of the affair by Bishop Seghers, "who visited the men in prison and was present at the hanging of two of them ... and also that of Capt. P. Francis, the employer of Capt. Christenson at the time."[68]

He confirmed the court testimony that there had been a southeasterly gale and that, due to the boulders and the surf, it would have been

Father Brabant's (right) attack on James Christenson, and his damning letter to D.W. Higgins (left) in 1904, didn't see the light of day.

impossible to make a landing from a shipwreck. The lifeboats, he wrote, "were found all broken up for miles along the shore."[69] For several days after the wreck, the letter continues, no bodies were found except that of a woman "whose face and forehead were badly bruised and who must have met her death by drowning or by being cast against the rocks."[70] He then disclosed a piece of information that could only have been gained had he read the trial transcripts, something he was not likely to have done. "Some bodies of men washed on shore after a week or ten days and having got entangled in the sea weed and kelp were all torn to pieces by the force of the waves—boots found with the leg in it torn from the trunk."[71] He confirmed this and, supporting Dr. Comrie's assessment of the *John Bright* corpses, told of similar carnage in the case of the *Malleville*, which he witnessed foundering off Sunday Rocks in October, 1882. He wrote:

> The argument was made [then] against the Indians because the bodies of the dead men were afterwards found above high water mark—it is a pity that there was nobody at the trial to state that such is, in all cases the practice of the Indians: any corpse [or even body of a wolf or other animal] floating close to shore is always pulled out of the sea, so that the fish on which the Indians live cannot pick at them.[72]

Next came the most damning revelation of all:

> During the night that the *J. Bright* came on shore Capt. James Christenson was not in Clayoquot Sound or anywhere else, he was right in his bunk in Hesquiat Harbour; and he was informed early in the morning that a ship was on shore and that white men were on board—this witness is alive this day: It was this party who carried the news to the Skipper—did he go out to her? Not much![73]
>
> He had a short conversation with a Hesquiat, who acted as cook on his schooner and ordered all sails hoisted and made for Kyuquot, 60 miles away—to his employers, [who] afterwards upbraided him for his conduct leaving a crew perhaps some of them alive, at least the cargo of a ship without trying to save anybody or anything of value. He simply remarked, "I was not going to expose myself to be killed by the Indians"—This was stated to me in 1874 by Capt. P. Francis. Francis, the employer of Christenson, who also made the statement that Pilot Christenson was for quite a time in dread of being arrested for not doing what, I believe, the law expects any Captain of a ship to do in case of meeting a wreck at sea or a vessel in distress —[74]
>
> Christenson was away five weeks at Kyuquot amid other tribes. Meanwhile Capt. Charles Colton [Carleton?] of the ship *Leonidas* had called at Hesquiat and visited the wreck of the *J. Bright*.—Having learned this Capt. Christenson on his return to Hesquiat also mustered courage to go out to the wreck, and brought to town a tale of cruelty, and barbarism, of which there is not a particle of truth.[75]

In his letter, Father Brabant, or someone else at a later time, had put a large "X" over this paragraph, in effect crossing it out. Then the words "this is not correct" were written through it diagonally. The handwriting seems not to be Brabant's. Could this have been Higgins's own reaction to Brabant's charges? In that we know Higgins had interviewed Captain Carleton on March 31, 1869, after his return to Victoria from Hesquiat, this is most likely the reason for the "X." Not surprisingly, much of the information corroborates the testimony given by Dr. Comrie and others during the trial. We must consider that Brabant had no particular grievance against Higgins or against Christenson himself (though he was undoubtedly dismayed by coastal whisky traders). If Higgins made the "X," did he also choose not to reply to Brabant's charges? There is no known record of any response. If someone else had seen the letter and made the notation, then we can only guess who it might have been. In his letter, Brabant continued, shifting his attack only slightly, and spoke about the accused:

168   Glyphs and Gallows

> *Katkeena and John Anayitzachist were hanged; Katkeena could have proved an alibi for he was in Nootka when the wreck occurred—the trouble was and is now in Indian cases before a Court of Justice—we cannot be sure of a reliable interpreter.*
>
> *I am very well acquainted with Pilot Christenson but in my mind his name is always associated with the wreck of the "John Bright" from which he cowardly sailed away—and with the wreck of the San Pedro which he ran on Brotchie Ledge—a fine ship—a loss to the owners of several hundred thousand dollars.*
>
> *Enjoyment of your usual good health*
>
> *I remain Sincerely yours*
> *A.J. Brabant* [76]

Father Brabant then went on to pen an extremely thorough report, ostensibly to set Higgins straight, on the wreck of the *John Bright*. In it, he detailed a more complete and, frankly, more believable story. He also advanced a plausible theory to explain the innocence of Katkeena and John Anayitzaschist.

Apparently, John was camping near a village off Sunday Rocks with his wife and two children some days before the wreck. In stating that individuals or blood families often left the main village of Hesquiat in winter and early spring to roam along the coast trapping and hunting deer and birds (or searching for wild clover roots), Brabant dispelled Christenson's charges that Anayitzaschist was not in Hesquiat much and, therefore, an enemy of the tribe. According to Brabant, John's brother had come to meet him and tell him of the wreck of the *John Bright* when John almost stumbled over the body of a dead woman among the rocks. As others approached the wreck, Anayitzaschist held the dead woman by her clothes in order to prevent her from being pulled out to sea by the falling tide. Meanwhile, amidst the excitement of the wreck, a canoe was dispatched to tell James Christenson, who was thought to still be at anchor in Hesquiat trading with the local Natives. As in his letter, Brabant repeated that Christenson promptly took off for Kyuquot without visiting the wreck at all.[77]

> After hearing this most unusual news the trading Captain immediately gave orders to his men to weigh the anchor. But

after sailing a short distance he ordered it about again—The Indians naturally expected him to go to the wreck. But no! He ordered sails up again, beat out of Hesquiat harbour and took his course for Kyuquot, sixty miles away.[79]

The evidence that Christenson presented in Victoria, Brabant claimed, was gained solely from northern Kwakwaka'wakw who resided at the different villages where he stopped to trade after leaving Hesquiat.[78] The Kwakwaka'wakw, who were hostile to the Hesquiat, took delight in making insinuations that grew into accusations of murder. Brabant was certain that James Christenson was never at the wreck.

Brabant's accusation of Christenson's cowardice places a chilling slant on the whole story. Did Christenson return to the wreck to cover his initial desertion of the survivors of the *John Bright*, as Brabant notes? Remember, he had already been accused of abandoning Native seal hunters in peril on the open sea. Or did his eagerness to regain stature among the White seal traders who had battled continually with Natives wise to the game of coastal trade prompt him to sacrifice what he must have thought were a few worthless Aboriginals? By embellishing the accusations, and placing himself in the centre of the action, Christenson could control the situation and make the story his own.

Brabant praised Seymour's view that the *John Bright* had been untimely abandoned by its crew, who, in consequence, perished among the murderous boulders and surf in the aftermath of the storm. Brabant also claimed to have known Ghwyer, the Clayoquot chief secured by Christenson as the interpreter for the inquest at Hesquiat. Having employed him, Brabant asserted, "he could not be relied upon to interpret anything which did not agree with his ideals, and as his tribes were the sworn enemies of the Hesquiats, it was more than probable that his 'interpretations' would be defective if not manifestly false."[80]

When, on the strength of Ghwyer's translations, John Anayitzaschist was accused by several "witnesses" and summoned aboard the *Sparrowhawk*, many of his friends and brothers became unnerved. Closing ranks, they went to rescue him but were frightened by Mist's threat of reprisal. Brabant continued: "Foolishly and as Savages, ignorant of the ways of the white men, will do, they decided to sacrifice a man called Katkeena expecting thereby to appease the threat, and thereby secure the release of their brother and Chief."[81]

Of Katkeena, Brabant had written: "This man Katkeena was a simpleton of inferior rank and considered so worthless that not one woman of his tribe would take him as a husband."[82] Brabant noted that he pleaded not guilty on board the *Sparrowhawk*, when the possibility of a charge of murder might be laid against him. (It will be remembered that, before Justice Needham and the Court of Assizes in Victoria, Ghwyer and Christenson have Katkeena pleading guilty.) Self-preservation, Brabant asserted, made Katkeena, in turn, point to John Anayitzaschist as the real culprit, as he had been the first on the spot after the wreck had occurred. "Katkeena could not possibly have been guilty of any misdeeds on this occasion for when the wreck took place and for two weeks later, he was living with friends in Friendly Cove, Nootka Sound."[83]

At this point in the proceedings, Brabant continued, there were only two suspects being held on the *Sparrowhawk*. After hearing that John was a prisoner and had been implicated in a great crime, "hastily a number of [his] friends, six or ten, went on board to see him off! But as no witnesses had as yet been secured by Mist, these men were detained on board and forcibly taken along to civilization."[84] These, of course, were the same five witnesses that, in Victoria, testified through Ghwyer and Christenson that Katkeena and John were guilty.

It is not known whether Higgins replied to Father Brabant's thoughtful letter and report. When *The Passing of a Race* came out early in 1905, Higgins's account of the *John Bright* affair was full of the same anti-Native invective and melodramatic distortions that Brabant had read a year before.

Someone else who doubted the guilt of the executed Hesquiat was the famous coastal hydrographer and place-name historian Captain John Walbran. Knowing the horrific weather of the coast, Walbran accepts Brabant's view that the Hesquiat could not have been responsible for the deaths of those aboard the *John Bright*, and he offers some additional information. He notes that a member of the *John Bright*'s crew had talked directly with Reverend Brabant, as he had left the ship before it set sail from Port Gamble. He was able to converse with Brabant because, Walbran claims, "he had charge of a store at Hesquiat."[85] Furthermore, this crew member supported the report that indicated that Captain Burgess had a Chilean wife, one child, and a servant girl with him, not the report of shipwright Neil Morrison, which indicated that there were five children aboard. The nagging question is, if Walbran is correct, then why did the sole remaining crew member of the *John Bright,* having lived with the Hesquiat after the disaster, choose to remain silent?

So "a great crime and its punishment" was laid to rest. Brabant's private accusations never saw the light of day, and the version that continues to surface periodically is much the same as the one that Higgins penned nearly 100 years ago. When James Christenson died on May 8, 1927, he was a famous man. An acknowledged maritime pioneer of heroic proportions, he was given the full treatment by the *Vancouver Province*. Recounting his exploits as a famous coastal pilot, the paper also noted his involvement in the *John Bright* affair: "Late in 1869, while on a trading trip Christenson heard that a British vessel had been wrecked at Hesquiat, a few miles from where he was in shelter during a storm. He sought out the wreck but found no survivors."[86] The column went on to declare that:

> Captain Christensen was wont to declare in his later years that the successful civilization of the West Coast Indians was due to the missionaries and to the honest treatment meted out to the tribes by the early traders. The missionaries ... were men of wonderful courage and high ideals, he said, and the traders who operated were careful to treat the natives fairly.[87]

Father Brabant and the Hesquiat would disagree.

Captain Henry Wentworth Mist retired from the Royal Navy on October 5, 1872, just three years after the *John Bright* affair. After an eighteen-year career at sea, he returned to England and obscurity.[88] Father Augustin Brabant remained at the mission school he founded at Hesquiat for 34 more years. In 1908 he was named Apostolic Administrator of the Diocese of Victoria. He died in 1912.[89]

After British Columbia joined Canada in 1871, the indefatigable D.W. Higgins sold his newspaper and turned to politics. He eventually served as the second Speaker of the British Columbia legislature. He sponsored Victoria's first theatre and fire department, and, of course, is recognized as a chronicler of his time. He died on his 83rd birthday in 1917.[90]

All of the characters in this morality play were either products, or victims, of nineteenth-century prejudice and its concomitant colonial mentality. It is only when we begin to see as human those who were victimized by these prejudices that we realize just how dangerous such culturally embedded racism can be. One way to recover a sense of our collective common humanity lies in the universal truths of art. And this is why the petroglyphs of Clo-oose are so important.

Chapter 10
The Motive for Metaphor

The obscure moon, lighting an obscure world
Of things that would never be quite expressed,
Where you yourself were never quite yourself,
And did not want, nor have to be.
                                                  Wallace Stevens[1]

I had been thinking about the petroglyphs since the first light of dawn. I hadn't slept well and had awoken several times during the night, thinking I had heard a strange moaning sound. On one occasion I shot up to hear what I thought were falling pots. What I heard for certain was the sound of the wind in the trees, the crashing of the surf upon the shore, and the unperturbed snoring of John in a nearby tent. What was only just visible through the inky blackness were some upturned pots and the strangely white crests of waves as they broke on the beach. With my flashlight I could discern the food bag still swinging high in a nearby tree. It was threatening rain, so I put on my fleece, zippered tight my tent door, and curled up once again in my sleeping bag. Was it the wind or a cougar that had knocked over the pots—or was it a Wasgo? I decided that the moaning was the sound the ocean made as it retreated, at the turn of the tide, from the hollows of the sea caves beneath the high cliffs close by. I went to sleep.

It was the roar of the primus that finally got me moving. By 7:00 AM we were eating a breakfast of oatmeal and dried fruit. With a cookie, and a lovely cup of hot tea in hand, I wandered over to the site. Emerging from the rich and abundant forest, the cove was hardly prepossessing. A thin dark band of rough, flat sandstone lay in a semicircular fashion between two small rock promontories. The whole uneven sandstone shelf was no more than 200 yards long from north to south and only 20 yards *across from the sea to the dark forest. It was honeycombed and, in various places, worn into smooth hollows. At the southern edge, a wall of devil's club, salmonberries, brambles, and salal made the approach to a short, low, rocky point exceedingly difficult at high tide. The slope of the sandstone shelf rose gently towards the northern end, becoming, finally, a high rugged rock promontory that jutted sharply out into the open sea only to curve back and close off the cove almost completely. Several natural faults cut deeply into the sandstone shelf, giving definition to areas of pockmarked rock and the smoother hollows, upon which the glyphs were drawn. We made our way out onto the more northerly point. Looking northwest from this longer, more accessible promontory, we watched as the Pacific Ocean rolled in across the infamous graveyard and, for as far as the eye could see, crashed against an open coast of cliffs and huge broken boulders.*

A great, deep, and narrow fissure split this northern projection almost in two, creating a long gap into which the ocean surged with every new wave. With each inward roaring swell, 20-foot towers of seawater were forced up through blowholes and cavities along the gap. The rock was black, wet, and dangerous. Being tired, I became momentarily mesmerized by a long white log that had been caught in the gap, and I watched it being rolled over and over as it was carried up and down the fissure with each incoming breaker. A fall here, and one would be carried out to sea or bashed to pieces by the endless surf. I thought of those on the John Bright *who had been caught in just such a murderous surf at Matlahaw Point and turned away.*

It was impossible to see beyond the southern promontory. There, low forest and more black jagged rocks consumed by sea-spray obscured the view. Inside the two rocky points was a small, very secluded cove, with an oval pebble beach. I stepped up to the second flattened area of rock, looked down, and examined closely an exquisite petroglyph of a two-masted brigantine—a common commercial trading vessel of the mid-nineteenth century. Once I recognized this first sailing-ship glyph, the whole site suddenly seemed to present itself to me. Beneath me lay wondrously carved shapes of birds and strange human figures. Suddenly, John let out a yell. He had found not only another huge sailing-ship glyph, this time a barque, but also a glyph of a ship he thought to be a paddlewheel steamer. In between the image of the brigantine and the

John Gellard makes a rubbing of the largest sailing-ship glyph.

Blowhole Beach, or Glyph Cove, seen here at low tide, is one of the most important petroglyph sites on the British Columbia coast. Cape Flattery is just visible on the horizon.

steamer lay a whole panorama of remarkable glyphs, the likes of which I had never seen before. They were little more than fifteen feet above high tide and were exposed to the driving westerly wind of the open sea. Excited as we were by our find, we eventually paused and reflected upon our isolation and this inhospitable setting. Ironically, we stood in a place where recent generations of an ancient people had come to record their history, yet, looking about, we concluded that this was not a place where one could live.

It was not just the condition of the glyphs that amazed me—they had not eroded away as I had expected—it was their stunning variety and complexity. Donning fleece jackets to ward off the incessant blasts of cold wind, we made an initial inventory. A quick first count revealed the following: five ships, at least six bird figures, three sea creatures, three human-like torsos with outstretched arms, several bodiless heads, and one very unusual glyph of a man sitting on a horse. There was also a vertical row of three human figures, the one closest to the sea being the largest female of the whole site. Two natural hollows in the rock had become two long, pointed breasts; a cleft, a disproportionately large vulva. Like the mounted figure, she surprised me completely.

From the perspective of the higher northern promontory, I again gazed over the whole site, knowing that drawings, photographs, and much thought would soon follow. What I needed now was a way to begin. As the day wore on, the wind died down and an eerie sunlight diffused through the sea fog to illuminate the enigmatic carvings. John prepared his camera; I sat above the glyphs on the edge of the northern promontory and studied the small cove intently.

The shape of the whole site intrigued me. Like anyone who has studied a variety of anthropological settings, I had learned to distinguish those strongly influenced by sexuality. More than one paleoanthropologist has written that caves and coves were symbolic of female entities.[2] Other such sites soon came to mind. The Pachena Point site, a day's hike north of where I sat, is full of small pecked divided ovals (universally recognized female symbols) along with a single fish. That site is in a cave. Another nearby site, at Cape Alava in Washington (just across the Strait of Juan de Fuca) contains a sailing-ship glyph. The carvers at that site were linguistically and culturally related to the Nuu-chah-nulth, and I wondered if the renderings at that site were somehow related to those at

Clo-oose. Some historic reports had conjectured that one of the Burgesses' children, a young teenage girl, had been secreted away from Hesquiat after the John Bright's *demise and had lived for a time with the Wyaht of Cape Flattery, near Alava. Any journey to Alava from Hesquiat would, of course, pass Clo-oose. Could she be a common link between the place where I stood and the Alava site? The same divided ovals abound there too. Yet at Alava, there is something more: the whole site is overlooked by a predominant phallic rock spire some 200 feet high.[3] This expression of sexuality is important in our interpretation of the sailing-ship glyphs of Clo-oose, as the undiscovered remains of the Burgesses' young nursemaid, the nineteen-year-old Beatrice Holden, and/or the fate of the young female children might well have had some special ritualistic significance within the Native community. Could they, as the* British Colonist *reported on February 24, 1871, have been turned into White slaves? And, this being the case, could their sexuality be figuring in the layout of the whole site? More likely, I pondered, the sexual nature of the site is related to the power of the shaman.*

Most fascinating about our discovery was the duality of the symbolism. The sailing-ship glyphs of Clo-oose are without precedent. Yet it is the sexuality of the site that is most predominant. The small cove is nearly enclosed. The beach is decidedly oval shaped. The pecked glyph nearest the sea is a fecund female. Nearby, a natural fissure creates a huge gouge into which the sea roars with resulting towering projections of water. As at Alava, the same natural male-female iconography seems to occur. Perhaps the whole site at Clo-oose ought to be understood as having sexual significance or, at least, a sexually symbolic subtext. If that is so, then the Clo-oose site is clearly some sort of sanctuary, as were such ancient sites as those among the Desana of the Amazon and the Tassili of South Africa.[4]

If the blowhole site of Clo-oose had been a sanctuary, then this would explain the plethora of glyphs located there. There are only one or two other glyph sites close by, one of which has an intriguing glyph that may be related to our story. Of that glyph I shall speak presently. However, the gender tension of the blowhole site is most dramatic, and its explicit and spectacular allusions to human sexual symbolism ought, I thought, to be kept in mind when I attempted to put the pieces together. I would return to the explicitly sexual nature of the cove shortly, but first I needed some first-hand history. I dug out my notebook and the information I had found on Robert Connell.

During the 1920s, Robert Connell was a feature writer with the Victoria Daily Times. *His articles, which appeared regularly in the Saturday edition of that paper, did much to bring the natural wonders of the Pacific Northwest to an eager and affluent Victoria population. Connell's gift for lively description, his informal tone, and his extensive knowledge of the flora and fauna of the area gained him a faithful readership. He urged restless, young, and able Victorians to venture out beyond the known confines of their tight little island community. His column ran beguiling stories such as "A Night in the Mount Rainier Forest Reserve" and "The Canyons of the Nisqually."[5] He, too, must have been enchanted by the juxtaposition of the pastoral and the wild. Connell had done a fair bit of tramping along this isolated Northwest Coast; the wonder he felt for this place poured out in his articles. Full of allure, his columns described in detail the lesser known areas of Washington and coastal British Columbia. He was among the first to awaken the twentieth-century tourist-adventurer.*

"Among the Rocks of Clo-oose" appeared in the Victoria Daily Times *on August 28, 1926. In it, Connell described a hiking trip to see what he called the "rock-drawings" and the unique dentalium fossils of Clo-oose. He had discovered that, besides petroglyphs, the San Lorenzo Formation, of which the Carmanah (Clo-oose) Rock is a part, contained the fossilized remains of a now extinct Toothshell. Long before the arrival of the Whites, these white, four-inch, glistening fossils were highly valued articles of exchange among the Aboriginals. Word of the glyphs must have been circulating informally in Victoria since the construction of the West Coast Life-Saving Trail in 1906, but who had actually seen them prior to Connell is open to conjecture. There is no doubt that Connell was completely captivated by the strange sailing-ship glyphs of Clo-oose. He was the first to publish information about them, and his drawings alerted others to their existence.*

Connell had been taken to the site by his friend, a Mr. Halket, who had first come across the sailing-ship glyphs in 1914. Upon closely examining the disconnected drawings incised into the soft flat stone with a "pointed tool," Connell noticed "a three-masted vessel under full sail and, recognizably like the old Hudson's Bay Company vessel, the

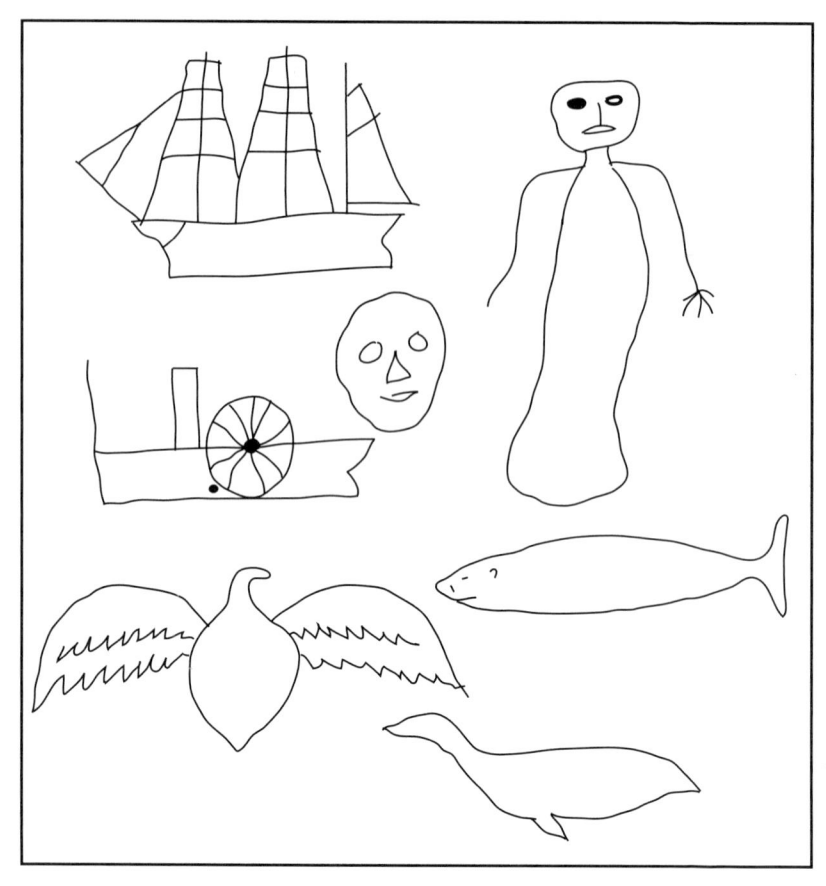

The *Victoria Daily Times* of September 4, 1926, printed samples of the "rock-drawings" at Clo-oose. Connell's copies of the glyphs were remarkably accurate, save for the bird figure.

Beaver, *a steamer with side-paddles."*[6] *He tried to fix the age of the glyphs at the site by figuring out the number of years the* Beaver *served on the coast and by the design of the sailing-ship glyphs themselves. He wrote: "I am inclined to think that fifty or sixty years is about their age, and that this is confirmed by the picture of the sailing-ship which in spite of a little weakness about the mizzen [after-most mast] is, I think a barque of the type which came to the front in the early sixties and was conspicuous among the fleet of vessels that came to the Columbia River for wheat and to other points on the coast for lumber, etc."*[7] *He felt that the artistic proportions of the barque, though carved only in outline, were "good."*

Below the nautical pieces Connell noted a "large figure of a woman in a 'white' dress of the older fashion since no trace of the feet is to be seen." Nearby he saw a "carved conventional face resembling that of the woman." An adjacent eagle with outstretched wings Connell saw as reminiscent of the United States national emblem. He didn't know what to make of the bird-seal combination or the whale that seemed like a shark, but he felt that "the Indian artists were thoroughly conventional in their interpretation of the forms familiar to them." For Connell, the glyphs were, indeed, works of art; but they were also thoroughly primitive. He seemed not to know enough of Native culture (almost no information was available) to attach the stylistic conventions to Aboriginal myth. Consequently, he thought that the sailing-ship glyphs allowed their creators to experiment in a newer, more free style. "When new objects presented themselves to their wonder and curiosity the freedom of art asserted itself and a more natural and truer style of rendering resulted. It is one of the ways, though not the greater, by which all the arts progress. Either by a new instinct into old things or by the response awakened by the appeal of new things to the senses, the shackles of old custom are broken and the spirit revives."[8] A Victorian by nature, and someone who thoroughly believed in the idea of progress, Connell nonetheless brought the sailing-ship glyphs before the members of an amazed public, giving them pause to reflect. On September 4, 1926, the Victoria Daily Times published eight reasonably accurate sketches that Robert Connell had made of a few of the glyphs that he had found at Clo-oose.

Two weeks later, a letter responding to the views of Connell's article was sent to a Mr. Goodfellow at the Times. That letter, while making a clear reference to D.W. Higgins's The Passing of a Race, not only summarized the details of the John Bright affair, but also offered a powerful interpretation of it. The author claimed that "there is no need to look for complete accuracy in the representations. There is however, plainly a barque, and a warship as the native might understand it, together with the corpse, mutilated, of a woman."[9] He suggested that the glyphs appear where they are because the artist may have fled to a safer haven further south and done penance before fleeing by inscribing the glyphs. Moreover, he suggested that the smaller trading barque, the Edwin, which came to grief in 1874 at exactly the same spot as did the John Bright, may be the subject of one of the glyphs. The letter was signed only with the initials D.H.

For the longest time I thought that D.H. must have been D.W. Higgins himself, stirring up the usual controversy. Yet the infamous David William Higgins had died some nine years before, on his 83rd birthday. He had two daughters and three sons, all of whom would have read their father's books. Perhaps one of them simply wanted to draw attention to what their father had written about the John Bright *affair and, consequently, used a nom de plume. In any case, the author of the letter to Mr. Goodfellow remains, for now, a mystery.*

When I gave up the Higgins idea, another, more tantalizing, theory soon began to take form. D.H.—H—who would have known of the glyphs, even before Connell, if not Halket himself? Things began to take shape. I tried to find Halket's first name. If it was "David" or "Donald," then we would have our man. I had no such luck, however, and the cryptic D.H. remained a mystery. Yet the idea of Mr. Halket writing this most portentous letter intrigued me. If he had been a trader at Clo-oose, then he would certainly have heard of the origins of the glyphs. Did he have something to hide in choosing anonymity? Why did he remain so silent?

There is a clear historical connection between the wreck of the John Bright *and the sailing-ship glyphs of Clo-oose. Was the mysterious D.H. merely elaborating upon a story he had himself heard from another, even more mysterious, source? Or, as Franz Boas wrote at the turn of the century, were portraying events such as this part of the purpose of Aboriginal rock art? It was with these concerns in mind that I set about to examine the glyphs of Clo-oose in earnest.*

The first task was to solve the timeline of the Clo-oose site. Were all the groupings done at the same time and, therefore, possibly related? Or were the glyphs unrelated, rendered at different times, and placed together only because of the scarcity of glyph sites or because of the sanctity of this particular one? Without serious anthropological study, it is not possible to answer such questions. Certainly, the glyphs are all of the same darkened colouration; there is no glyph with a visibly different patination. The depth of the grooves, and the degree of weathering, appears to be the same, at least for the three sailing-ship glyphs. Though some glyphs have faded to the point of total obscurity, none appears to have been carved more deeply than any other, and none (unlike the whale glyph at Degnan Bay) appears to have been re-pointed. Stylistically, the sailing ships are of a common period, as are the zoomorphic figures

The Motive for Metaphor 181

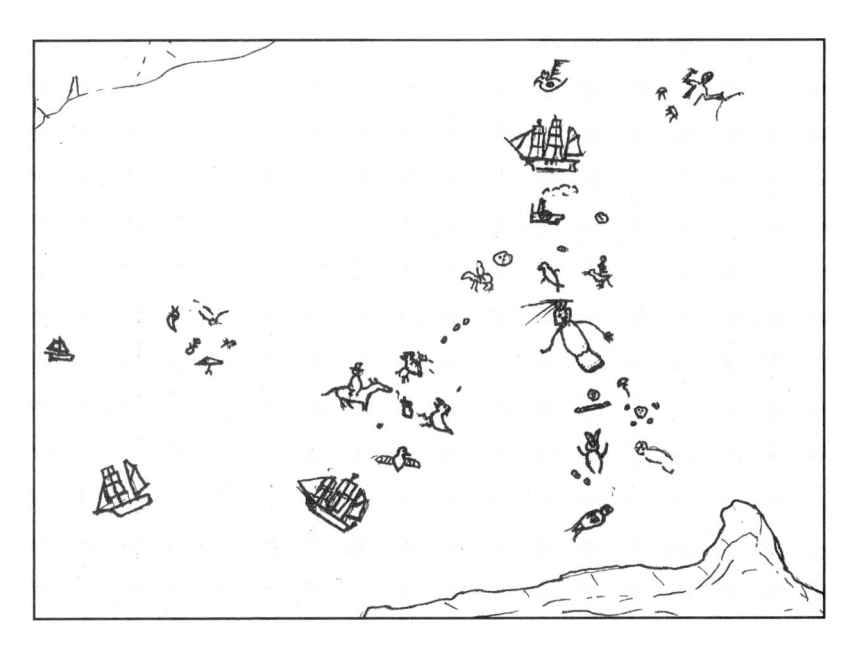

As best we could with our limited tools, we mapped the Clo-oose Blowhole site. (Author's map)

of sea creatures and birds. No depiction of any creature seems unique in relation to others of its kind. The only surrounding marks of a noticeably different style and age are thinner etched lines supplied by later visitors who wished to make their presence known by despoiling the glyphs and scratching a "Kilroy"-type signature on top of them.

For me, the many figures at the site seem to be constructed around common themes. There are the sailing-ship glyphs and the strange figure of a man on horseback—all clearly rendered during the nineteenth century. The sea creatures seem to surround the ship glyphs and appear to complement them. Bird figures, like the sea creatures, are positioned close to the ships. The human figures, two of whom are depicted near the sailing-ship glyphs, are torso-figures with arms upraised. One such figure is clearly depicted as being in the sea and is closely associated with fishes and other sea creatures. Only the three longitudinal human figures—a man and two women—seem out of place; yet two of the three have the same curvilinear outline, suggesting a common carver. This may be a projection, but, given the inter-relatedness of the figures, I believe that the site is some sort of a tableau.

The images themselves encompass an area little more than 40 by 15 feet and occupy two distinct groupings. The glyphs at the Clo-oose site have used every available smooth, flattened area of sandstone. All are surrounded by the same rock, which has become completely honeycombed, the result of small hard stones becoming trapped in hundreds of natural hollows and depressions. Over the millennia, the rising and falling of the tides has set the many different-sized hard stones to whirring about, drill-like, gradually wearing away perfectly natural, deeply incised circles. Many of the honeycombs are conjoined, some having worn into their neighbours. Such a honeycomb effect frames the glyphs, as well as sadly reminding us that this rock upon which they are drawn is certainly not permanent. The most southerly group begins at the very top of the sandstone shelf and runs the whole length of it in two separate natural terraces until it turns steeply to meet the small gravel beach.

The top glyphs of this set consist of two birds, one above the other. Each has outstretched wings, and both appear to be flying in different directions. One certainly looks like an eagle, though Connell's rendering of it is (like the White nineteenth-century paintings of Aboriginals) more

The Motive for Metaphor 183

Are the sexual figures depicted at the Clo-oose Hill site (pictured here) related to those at Blowhole Beach?

imagined than real. If the topmost bird serves the same function as does the Haida Eagle crest, then these two glyphs may serve to identify the site itself. The interior of each bird-figure is incised with the ever-present concentric circles, and graven all about them are many small vulva-like ovals.

Ten feet to the east of the lower bird, and located just above a sailing-ship glyph, is a torso-figure with raised arms. It, too, is surrounded by figures—these ones resembling jellyfish. The artist may have been working with a drowning motif, for the incised marks of the man's body clearly end at the waist, where the sea creatures abound. However, as the Native informant Annie York has pointed out with regard to the pictographs (rock paintings) of the Stein River Valley, such slash marks around a geometric shape may denote a particular aspect of time rather than sea creatures.[10]

Below the bird glyphs are the images of two ships, one a mid-nineteenth-century sailing ship and the other a paddlewheel steamer

184   Glyphs and Gallows

8' x 2.5'

4' x 2'

Author's map of Clo-oose Hill site.

very like the HBC *Beaver. Below the two ships there is a semicircle consisting of vulva-like ovals, birds, seals, and the strange jellyfish images. Two seals are graven vertically, one above and one below the figure of a "woman in a long dress." At least one authority on west coast art has suggested that the seal may be an ancient metaphor for a vulva, in which case their proximity to the female figure certainly has sexual connotations.*

Surrounding the female figure are numerous disembodied heads, two outstretched hands graven horizontally beneath the woman, and again, numerous small vulva-like ovals. Above her is a faint bird figure that appears to be carrying a small oval shape (a head?) upon one of its wings. In Northwest Coast cultures, bird images are associated with the transformation of body to soul. Everywhere there is the sense of movement.

Immediately below these figures is a series of three vertical human figures, the two most interesting of which are female. The top one has uplifted stick arms (with no hands) and two oblong-shaped projections coming from its head. This glyph seems to be unfinished at its lower extremities, the "dress" simply ending before the depiction of feet. Here the mysterious D.H. enters our story again. He suggested that this figure was of the woman in the "white dress of the older fashion" that Connell had described. If so, she may, in fact, be a depiction of poor Beatrice Holden, nursemaid to the Burgesses' children on board the John Bright.

Photo of fecund female at Clo-oose Blowhole site.

According to Higgins's version of the story, she was raped after coming ashore, and her body was never found. I do not believe Higgins's version of the story, nor do I accept that the woman in the so-called "European" dress is Beatrice Holden. For one thing, Native women were known to wear long dresses that covered their feet. For another, the dress is not hooped enough to be strictly European. But am I being too literal?

Maleness and femaleness seem to double and redouble about the site like the chorus of a Greek play. There are the female cove, the male geyser, strange stickmen, disembodied heads, and the woman in the dress. And there are the male and female whale and seal glyphs as well as the haunting presence of yet another very sexual, very powerful, and very large female. If this male-female reduplication is correct, then the whole site is screaming with sexual tension.

The large glyph of a fecund female is all sex. She has no arms, no projections of any kind, and no feet. She is simply a full-bodied female whose sexual anatomy—the large breasts and huge vulva—is part of the natural depressions in the sandstone shelf itself. Is she a microcosm of the blatant sexuality of the whole site? We can only guess at the psychological meaning of her appearance. If the images of the many birds are the harbingers of death, then the glyph of the fecund female figure could represent the abundance and proliferation of life.

Whether this female figure represents the cycle of life and death, the inherent fertility of the human species, or something more direct and more sinister related to the events of the John Bright *story, we will never know. It is possible, however, that this figure could be a self-conscious icon, drawing attention to the power of sexuality itself, as manifest in the wisdom of the shaman, who, indeed, may have been the carver herself. If the Clo-oose site is some sort of sanctuary, as I think it is, then this full-figured, sexually explicit female may have performed a direct role in the*

186   Glyphs and Gallows

We made diagrams of the sailing vessel and steamer glyphs photographed here. I believe the top glyph depicts the HMS *Sparrowhawk*. Below is the paddlewheeler I take to be the SS *Beaver*, which measured 90 cm by 65 cm high.

Seen here as a survey ship in the 1880s, the SS *Beaver* enjoyed a distinguished career before sinking off Stanley Park in Vancouver.

shamanic rites performed there. Several researchers have documented the strongly erotic element of gaining visionary power.[11] It is well known among Natives of the Northwest Coast that the singing of songs and the wearing of phallic symbols increases fertility and strengthens those who strive to prevail against the forces of destruction. Though not directly depicted, a shaman's knowledge of the John Bright affair could call for a powerful female image to sanctify its memory, to suggest something of fate, to create harmony with the promise of life, and/or to mark the site as important for the training of other artists and seers.

There is another set of glyphs graven into a smooth, slightly sloped terrace about ten feet north and slightly above the other two groupings. It is this group that I find the most amazing. There are three sailing ships depicted in this set: a large (four-foot) three-masted barque, a smaller (three-foot) two-masted brigantine, and (above it and off to the right) a small foot-long pinnace. The most astonishing feature of this set is located immediately above the rendering of the largest sailing ship. It is a deeply grooved glyph of a male figure, complete with a top hat, seated upon a horse.

Directly in front of this mounted figure are three large, open-mouthed, wingless, squawking birds. Two are almost as large as the

188   Glyphs and Gallows

Of all the sailing-ship glyphs, it is this one that is most likely to be a rendition of the *John Bright*.

mounted figure itself. All are depicted as being raised up, much like an angered rooster. All seem to be squawking at the figure on the horse. Between the large ship and the other glyphs in this particular location is yet another bird glyph with wings fully outstretched. This may be the glyph that Connell thought was reminiscent of the American national emblem.

In all, the blowhole site at Clo-oose is truly breathtaking. Most of the sailing-ship glyphs seemed to have been carved at about the same depth, and most are easily recognizable. Connell believed that the glyphs were relatively recent. Most are quite distinct, and only a few—the northernmost sailing ship and one of the female figures—have been defaced. It is difficult not to take the site as a tableau depicting the events that occurred at Hesquiat between 1869 and 1875. The water motif, replete with figures with upraised arms, is suggestive of those being caught in the surf. The bird-like figures, clearly affronted by the man on horseback, suggest anger and an out-of-body experience. Last, the design and detail of the pecked ships themselves do seem to fit the vessels known to have been involved in the John Bright *affair*. Looked at as a whole, this glyph site begs for an even closer examination than has hitherto been offered.

A well-known researcher once believed that the ships might be Captain Cook's Resolution or *Captain Barkley's* Loudoun *(disguised as the* Imperial

Eagle).[12] *In other words, she interprets the ships as belonging to the eighteenth, rather than to the nineteenth, century. Even if we accepted D.H.'s hypothesis that complete accuracy is not necessary, the clear outline of the three hulls, as well as the depiction of the sail-plan and rigging, discounts completely the idea that the sailing ships are renderings of eighteenth-century frigates, merchantmen, or naval ships of the line. The reason for this lies in the noticeably marked change in the hull design of nineteenth-century sailing ships.*

In 1653 the British Admiralty issued an order that all its vessels were to enter battles in a line.[13] *From this time, British naval readiness was rated by the number of guns a vessel could carry and use effectively in a "broadsides" encounter. Heavily armed vessels having over 50 guns were thought strong enough to fight in a line and, therefore, were called "ships of the line." Such armaments required a very specific hull and rig design. Soon most European sailing ships, right to the end of the eighteenth century, were beamy, with high, blunt-nosed, tumblehomed, rounded sterns. The high "castle-like" stern, leftover from the days of the old galleons, provided much room for several gun platforms, a galley, and officers quarters.*

Merchantmen, commercial ships of the same period, were lower in the water than the ships of the line (they carried only one complete gun deck), and the rounded stern lost its counter to become flat and square. Such vessels were called frigates. The shape of the castle-like quarterdeck (afterdeck) changed. By 1800, the rather boxy, high afterdeck was lowered slightly, and it began, not in an abrupt aft "castle," or cabin, but in a long sweeping curve from the mainmast. The result was a hull form that was much more graceful, with a lovely, almost scooped, sheer-line from bow to stern. Such refinements made for small, broad, and roomy ships, powerfully driven by large square sails on three masts.

James Cook's first ship, the Endeavour, *is a benchmark of progress. Originally, it was the* Earl of Pembroke—*an English east-coast, Whitby-built collier. In 1768 it was refitted and became the* Endeavour, *the prototype for the small, seaworthy, exploratory and trading barque of the period. Cook's later ships, the* Resolution *and the* Discovery *(the vessels that visited Nootka Sound), introduced further refinements to this stout little ship. The early three-masted barque had square sails set on huge yardarms on the forward and main masts, with the mizzenmast alone* being rigged with fore-and-aft sails. The Spanish and American ships that visited the west coast of Vancouver Island at the beginning of the nineteenth century were variations on either the East India trading frigate or the larger Spanish ships of the line.

The sailing-ship glyphs at Clo-oose do not depict any of the types described above. Artisans capable of rendering perfect concentric circles in stone, no matter how conventional their notions of what a sailing ship should look like, would not fail to notice the sweeping quarter-deck; the blunt, S-shaped bow; the flat stern; and the scooped sheer-line of such vessels. The ships incised into the stone, by virtue of the artistic rendering of the hull alone, are clearly not depictions of Cook's Resolution or Discovery, Barkley's Loudoun, Meares's Iphigenia, or any other British, Spanish, or American ships of the eighteenth century.

If accuracy, and Connell's observations on "fine proportions," are to count for anything, then the ships engraved on the rocks at Clo-oose are, indeed, of a much later period. The give-away is the clear "fan-tail" stern on the southernmost vessel (see Figure 1) and the unmistakable "r"-shaped clipper bow on each of the three large vessels depicted. Such features situate one of the ships (see Figure 2) in the same period as the large Blackwall frigates—the ships that began to be built at Blackwall on the Thames in 1837 and were used to carry emigrants and goods along the sea routes to China, India, and California. The third sailing-ship glyph (see Figure 3) is that of a small vessel rigged as a brigantine, or hermaphrodite brig, which has only two masts, with the foremast square-rigged (or full-rigged) and the mainmast fitted solely for fore-and-aft sails. Such a rig would give a ship superior windward performance due to the larger fore-and-aft sail on the mainmast—a development that was important to coastal traders in the later nineteenth century. From a distance, on a certain point of sail, such a rig could easily be mistaken for a topsail schooner. The fourth sailing-ship glyph (see Figure 4) is that of a gaff-rigged tender, or lifeboat—one that might go ashore to trade or embark upon other shorter forays, leaving the larger mother ship at anchor.

HMS Sparrowhawk had a definite "clipper" bow and a pronounced "fan-tail" stern. Though also a steam-driven auxiliary, it was still very much a sailing ship, and its two thin side-by-side funnels could easily be obscured by its sails. Under full sail, it would look like a barque, with

Figure 1

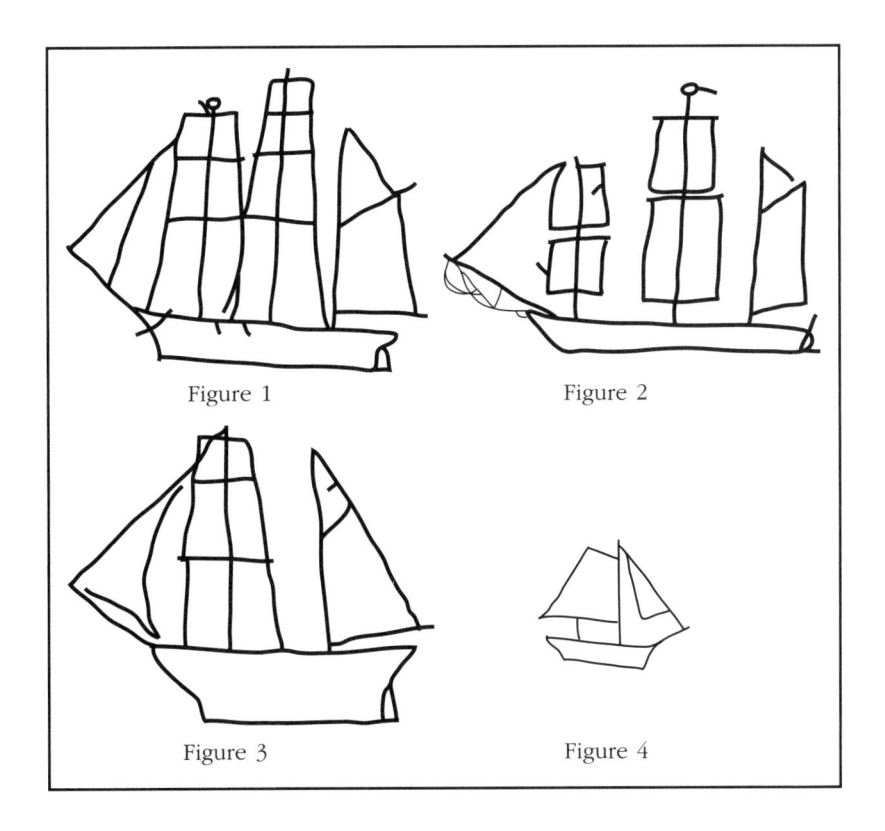

Figure 2

Figure 3

Figure 4

jibs set on its long bowsprit (as depicted in a glyph). So, is there anything in the rendering of the sailing-ship glyph in Figure 1 that marks it out as the HMS Sparrowhawk? *What distinguishes it from the vessels depicted in Figure 2 and Figure 3?*

Well, for one thing, below the Sparrowhawk *is a clear depiction of a side-paddlewheel steamer, a vessel much like the HBC's* Beaver *or HMS* Virago. *The glyph depicts a blunt and boxy vessel, more in keeping with the* Beaver *than with the more graceful* Virago *and its long bowsprit and sleeker lines. It is known that James Christenson, the instigator of the* John Bright *affair, travelled to Hesquiat aboard the* Sparrowhawk. *He was also, for a time, master of the* Beaver. *Both these facts would have been known to local Natives, especially those with higher status, such as shamans. Could this be an Aboriginal way of "naming" Christenson (and, for that matter, the* Sparrowhawk)? *If the site offers a recording of the troubles at Hesquiat, then would it be important for a Native artist to make some reference to one of the major figures? Would a reference* such as the parallel placement of the Beaver *and the* Sparrowhawk *be too cryptic, too esoteric, to be understood by anyone other than the carver? Is this a latter-day attempt at some sort of pictorial literacy? Something analogous to the rock "writings" of the Stein River Valley in the BC interior? Would such a reference even need to be understood by those who visited the site? Or was the depiction of generic ships message enough?*

The second sailing-ship glyph (Figure 2) is the most intriguing of the four, not so much for its lines, as for the glyphs that surround it and create its context. This glyph depicts yet another mid-nineteenth-century barque under full sail. With the fore- and mainmasts square-rigged, and the mizzen carrying one large fore-and-aft sail, this glyph of a barque is the largest of the whole group. Flags are depicted as flying from the top of the mainmast and the mizzenmast, though the prominently featured stern staff is rendered without a flag. Could this glyph be that of the John Bright *itself? It has no features that exclude other possibilities. It could, quite easily, be any one of literally hundreds of similar barques that entered and exited the Strait of Juan de Fuca with lumber and other goods until the last days of sail in the late nineteenth century. Natives all along the outer coast, from Neah Bay to Barkley Sound, would have seen many such ocean-going ships far offshore. These large vessels were not small coastal schooners, the latter being the sort of which James Christenson was master. They were, for the most part, full-rigged ships bound for ports well beyond the horizon. Unless the creators of these glyphs had travelled to White settlements and had seen such vessels up close, the detailed and accurate renderings at Clo-oose could not have been possible.*

The glyph in Figure 2 (which, for the moment, we shall consider to be a depiction of the John Bright*) shows a large, over-500-ton ship. It is a drawing of a big barque with the flat hull sheer-line so characteristic of the somewhat larger Blackwall frigates of its time. Proportionally, when set against the smaller vessels depicted in Figure 1 and Figure 3, it is drawn "correctly." Yet, unlike the other two, this particular rendering has a long bowsprit. Like the fore-and-aft spanker sail on the mizzenmast, a bowsprit on a vessel of the type engraved allows for even more sail to be added in front of the three masts. These sails would also be of the fore-and-aft type and would aid in a ship's windward ability. From the base of its long bowsprit there are more etchings of what may be furled spritsails* *(or the standing rigging, such as a bob-stay) used to secure the long bowsprit from the upward pull of the forestay and the tension of the headsails.*

There may, however, be another reason for the nautically intensive detail graven upon the bowsprit of the vessel we are scrutinizing. It could be a Native rendering of the John Bright*'s figurehead, that statue-like ornament at the stem of most nineteenth-century sailing ships. It protruded from the underside of the bowsprit and provided a support member for the sprit itself. The figurehead would also have a symbolic function, like the "eyes" at the bow of a Chinese junk. The ornate, often loosely clad, buxom female carving would "keep an eye out" for danger and remind the ship's company of home and hearth and love.*

We don't know if the John Bright *had a figurehead, as there no longer seem to be any line drawings to tell us. We do know that it had a boomboard, which would be hung near the bowsprit, with its Latin phrase, translated as "Fear none, injure none," belying the ship's future. So, is it the* John Bright? *Well, the scale is right; it is the largest vessel graven at the site. Its topmast pennants identify it as a merchantman. The detailing about the bowsprit and the "barque" rig itself are all right. However, without some sort of visual record, it seems that more certain identification is not possible. Yet the identity of this sailing-ship glyph need not be determined solely on its own terms. Let us consider the petroglyphs that are so closely associated with it.*

These glyphs depict the four birds that I have already briefly mentioned. They occur in a group about a foot above and behind the glyph of the ship in question. The three birds of interest are those that are graven in profile and are squawking like mad in front of a large image of a man wearing a top hat and seated upon a horse. Bird imagery pertaining to the eagle, the raven, the loon, and the owl abounds in Northwest Coast art. The eagle, which was often a clan crest, was a symbol of power and prestige; eagle down was a symbol of peace and friendship. Raven, the transformer, could do anything and had created things as they are. The Owl was often associated with death.[14] *Among the Kwakwaka'wakw, "a person who was soon to die heard the owl call his name." Among the Tsimshian, the owl was the shaman's helper.*[15]

Could these squawking birds be a symbolic representation of a cataclysmic change, of souls in flight, of death—perhaps caused by the

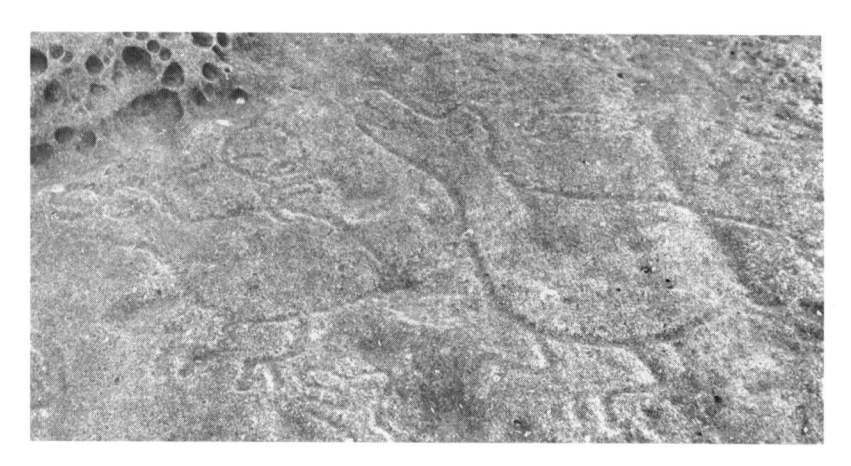

Bird figures at Clo-oose.

man facing them on the horse? The bird closest to the mounted figure seems to carry a small object (a child?) on its back. While images of death seem to occur throughout the site, as do images of sexuality, the birds themselves are full of life. Below the three outraged birds is yet another bird glyph, this one shown frontally, wings outstretched, as if in flight. If the bird may be likened to the Haida or Tlingit Thunderbird, then it is a hunter, the one who eats whales. If it is a hawk figure, then it is a messenger, a go-between, a symbol of process. Hawks initiate the act of transformation.[16] Seen in this light, the bird glyphs may be interpreted as having to do with change, death, hunting, and/or power. Is the winged bird portrayed in the glyph in the act of changing sailors to souls? No wonder the birds are squawking at the figure on a horse. If, however, the winged bird is akin to the Haida eagle and is a crest figure, then something very strong is taking possession of something else.

The clearly top-hatted glyph is unique and is a rendering of a high-status White official. We do know that the high sheriff of Victoria, Mr. Elliot, attended the hangings at Hesquiat. We also know that a sizable contingent of Royal Marines was present. Yet try as I might, I could not find out if the marines were equipped with horses. Since they were commandeered from the naval base at Esquimalt and were permanently stationed aboard HMS Satellite, *the presence of horses seems doubtful. However, the* Sparrowhawk *also had aboard a contingent of Victoria bluecoats, who were known to be outfitted with horses. Captain Mist makes no mention of horses in the* Sparrowhawk's *log. If aboard, they*

Top-hatted figure on horseback.

would have had a most uncomfortable time. No one connected with the Sparrowhawk's *fateful investigation mentions horses. And certainly, a White man on horseback would be extremely rare at Hesquiat, or even at Clo-oose, as getting there on such a beast would be impossible.*

However, the figure on horseback, like the sailing-ship glyphs themselves, may be symbolic. Both are emissaries from the outside world—emissaries that signalled the end of a way of life for Native peoples on this northern coast. It is possible that the artist (a person of high status) had visited Victoria and, seeing uniformed men on horseback for the first time, recreated their image to symbolize a man powerful enough to authorize something so rare as an on-site Native hanging. Again, the possibility that this figure represents the construction of a new icon standing for something hitherto unknown (such as absolute human authority) looms very large.

It has been suggested that the fourth sailing-ship glyph (Figure 3) is the American trading ship the Edwin, *which came ashore in December 1874 at exactly the same point where the* John Bright *had been wrecked five years earlier. The story of the* Edwin *parallels that of the* John Bright *and deserves a brief mention.*

The Edwin *was smaller (404 tons) than the* John Bright. *Loaded with 300,000 feet of lumber at Utsalady in Puget Sound before stopping at Victoria, it was outbound for Australia when it left its Royal Roads*

It is impossible to confirm that these glyphs represent specific ships. However, this two-masted brigantine may be the *Edwin*.

anchorage on December 1, 1874. Again, all was normal until it cleared Cape Flattery at the end of the Strait of Juan de Fuca and entered the open Pacific Ocean. A winter gale broached the Edwin *several times, and, with its pumps not working, it was soon doomed. The* Edwin's *master, Samuel Hughes, brought his wife and two children from below and placed them in a small deckhouse, only to see it washed away into the sea at the height of the storm with his family inside.*

The Edwin's *nine remaining crew members clambered to the top of the masts and survived there for three nights and two days, living off condensed milk and canned peas scavenged from their flooded vessel, which was slowly sinking beneath them. When the* Edwin *hit the rocks at Matlahaw Point on December 7, it broke up. This time, however, perhaps because of the stunning 1869 hangings and Captain Mist's prior afternoon injunction to help shipwrecked sailors, many of the crew of the* Edwin, *still clinging to the rigging, were physically saved by Natives who took some life-threatening risks. As D.H. wrote in his letter, "This time the natives acted with great humility, and rendered every assistance."*[17] *It seems that James Christenson learned something about humility from the* John Bright *affair because on December 19, with his*

The Motive for Metaphor 197

Torso-figure surrounded by "jellyfish."

new schooner the Alert, *he took the survivors of the* Edwin *to Victoria. Interestingly, the lumber from the* Edwin *was collected by the local Natives to build Father Brabant's first mission at Hesquiat.*

This glyph, if it is indeed a depiction of the Edwin, is unadorned. Only a small gaff-rigged ship's tender hovers above it, in much the same location as are the birds with regard to the sailing-ship glyph shown in Figure 2. Is this small lifeboat enough to link such a vessel to a rescue? How would one visually depict the idea of rescue? A small boat standing by seems eminently logical. Yet I can think of other logical expressions for the same thing. The trouble is, art is not necessarily logical.

There is one more mystery connected with the Edwin. It was a three-masted barque, and the vessel drawn is rigged as a two-masted brig. However, here, too, the plot thickens. Prior to its coming ashore, Captain Hughes "ordered her mizzen mast to be cut down,"[18] presumably to prevent further loss and injury from falling debris, as the vessel shuddered and rolled with every crashing wave. That being the case, the Edwin would have had only two masts visible to the artists and other Natives as it came ashore.

One other glyph may have connections to the *John Bright story, but it is not one that appears at the blowhole site; rather, it is located about half a mile south of Clo-oose. That glyph can be found beneath an inaccessible cliff face just above a particularly dangerous flat stretch of sandstone bedrock that floods completely at high tide, leaving one trapped by the rising sea. It is not the whales carved into the rock at this small site that capture the attention, but the strange single figure of a human holding what appears to be a decapitated "trophy head."[19] If this glyph is linked to those beheaded in the John Bright *affair*, then why is it not to be found at the Clo-oose site itself? In truth, most of the available smooth sandstone at the site is covered with fish glyphs, which brings us back to where we began: the question of time.

It is difficult to know from a cursory, visual examination whether the figure-holding-a-trophy-head glyph was graven long before, or soon after, the petroglyphs at the Clo-oose site. We know that raids were common among the Nitinaht, as they were among the Clayoquot, the Moachat, and the Kwakwaka'wakw. The impetus behind such raids might be to gain slaves, to gain goods, or to effect vengeance for past crimes.[20] Like the head glyph at Fort Rupert (at least according to Boas), this lone figure could record just such a raiding encounter rather than the John Bright *affair*. I am about to shut the door on the latter possibility when memory intrudes again. One of the missing White children in the John Bright *story*, a young girl of about 12 years old, was, according to Native rumour, sold by the Hesquiat to the Ahousat of Clayoquot Sound some time after the wreck. The Ahousat, in turn, sold her to the Wyaht, who, fearing detection, traded her to the Nitinaht of Clo-oose.[21] If this is true, then could she have offered her version of the tragedy to an artist or chief at Clo-oose? Could she or her nursemaid be rendered as one of the women at the site?

What we have in the sailing-ship glyphs of Clo-oose is a sweeping panorama of life on the west coast of Vancouver Island during the last half of the nineteenth century. Here, ships of the White traders collided with a way of life that was centuries old. The glyphs reveal an image of Western civilization (the top-hatted rider) surrounded by seemingly infuriated Native religious icons. With the passage of time, and the deaths of those who might have carried some memory of the glyph site, it is now practically impossible to say what lies buried in the strange rock messages of Clo-oose. At the very least, the site is full of the effects of the collision of two cultures.

In the end, I have been excited by the patterns that have emerged in the petroglyphs of Clo-oose. I have been caught between the tantalizing *possibilities of the symbolic and the minimalist expression of the literal. In one moment, I saw the Clo-oose site as one great visual poem or song, full of metaphorical connections to an event that marked a change of life for the coastal peoples of British Columbia. In the next moment I saw no connections at all, just primitive isolated etchings on a lonely shore, carved by artists who saw cataclysmic change all about them. When convinced that nothing about the* John Bright *affair was depicted in the petroglyphs of Clo-oose, I suddenly came across some history, some pattern, that gave me cause to reconsider. I did not find an image of a set of gallows or an image of a "real" Victorian woman in a hooped skirt. What I did find was a plethora of metaphorical images and symbols that took me to places I did not know I wanted to go.*

Soon after the John Bright *affair, things changed on the coast. The Colony of British Columbia joined Confederation, and the Royal Navy no longer sent its gunboats to intimidate worrisome Aboriginals. Settlement occurred, law and order prevailed, the potlatch and the totem poles were taken away. Disease forced a good many Natives to sanitoria, and Native children were sent to the residential schools run by Roman Catholic and Anglican missionaries. Families were disconsolate. The soul of a race was broken, and the moss-wet forest slowly reclaimed the longhouses and the welcome figures of a once proud people. A whole culture was literally on the brink of being wiped out completely. And then, from the very edge of oblivion, the elders began to retell their stories. It was these bits of remembered tales, called up from a desperate soul's interior like images forced onto stone, that would enable everything to begin again.*

The motive for metaphor is the motive to create a story: it is the artistic drive. The impulse to use symbols is connected to our desire to create something to which we can become emotionally attached. Symbols, like relationships, involve us with deeply human attributes. Raven and Bear can speak to us directly. I can smile at the glyph of a seal, with its curious smiling head poking just above the water, and I am filled with wonder at the image of a bird carrying a small child or a bodiless head. A symbol is at once concrete, palpable, and sensual—like a rose. At the same time, it reaches beyond itself to convey an idea of beauty, of fragility, and of transience. The great thing about art is that it continually forces us to see new sets of resemblances. Those long-gone artists who created the petroglyphs at Clo-oose used two sets of symbols—their own and those of nineteenth-century Western Europeans—in order to depict a vignette that was firmly grounded in their point of view. Like the carvers of the Rosetta Stone, they wisely used sets of metaphors and imaginative icons against materialist images of nineteenth-century commercial technology. Unlike the Rosetta Stone, however, the petroglyphs of Clo-oose do not use one set of images to explicate the other; the petroglyphs of Clo-oose are stunning because they incorporate one set of images into the other. Like a series of lap dissolves in modern film, we are drawn to ponder one story while at the same time being faced with the jarring reality of another. The Native images carved into the sandstone shelves at Clo-oose are much more imagistic than are the red ochre inscriptions on the rock walls of the lower Stein Valley but they are related. They are rich metaphors of the interior world of Native spirituality and history, and they have been juxtaposed with metaphors of European conquest. As such, they are eloquent indeed.

It is impossible to completely crack the codes of the sailing-ship glyphs of Clo-oose because the meaning of the Native spiritual images cast upon the rocks on that lonely shore has died with those to whom it was relevant. Our interpretations are approximations born of respect for the images themselves and of a renewed feeling for the time. We are left to ponder one significant story born of cultural collision. The petroglyphs of Clo-oose have served us well. They have, like any great code, prompted us to express, and urged us to remember, what might otherwise have been ignored. They have brought some light to an obscure world.

EPILOGUE
Revelation and Desecration

I knew that I had to go back to see the petroglyphs of Clo-oose one more time. For years I had felt compelled to chase down minute, dispersed facts as I tried to recreate a context for the sailing-ship images, only to brood for hours over their interpretation. Now I ached for a dose of fresh air, for the stirrings I had felt on that wild and desolate coast as I breathed in the implications of the larger interplay before me—the forces of an implacable nature relentlessly eradicating the cultural imprints of humankind. It had been six years since my last visit, and I was curious to see what winter gales and summer hikers had done to the glyphs themselves. More pragmatically, I wanted to verify that both my impressions and deductions concerning the sailing-ship shapes had stood the test of time. And, as a final gesture, I wished to map the site carefully, take more photographs, search for other pertinent glyph locations, and bring a sense of closure to the self-imposed task with which I had lived.

What I didn't relish about this return journey was the prospect of another difficult hike down the West Coast Trail. With extra camera gear, and the wait for the crossing at the Nitinat River, it would take at least three days—and that was if the weather held—just to reach Clo-oose. Then there was the long hike out. In all, counting travel time to Bamfield, I needed ten days. I called my old friend and colleague John Gellard, who had accompanied me on the first trip. His response was sure and immediate: "Let's go!"

When we first hiked the West Coast Trail, we simply reported our destination to park wardens at Bamfield as a safety measure, and off we went. Since then, the growing reputation of the West Coast Trail has lured hikers from all over the world, and the desire to protect the habitat has led to visitor restrictions. Reservations are now a necessity and a permit must be purchased, all in the name of conservation. Between

Bamfield

1971 and 1986, the number of hikers on the trail increased fivefold to over 10,000 annually, and it became apparent that flora, fauna, and cultural artifacts were feeling the effects. Now the number of people allowed to undertake the hike is restricted to about 4,000 per year. By the time I committed to this 1999 journey to the Clo-oose area, the West Coast Trail regulator's dance card was booked solid for the summer.

I knew that we had only one other option. This time it was not important that we hike the trail itself. We had already done that and now simply needed to get to Clo-oose. Research, not recreation, was the motivation here. With manuscript in hand, I told my tale of the John Bright *tragedy and the petroglyphs of Clo-oose to Canadian Coast Guard officials in Vancouver. With an abiding interest in west coast maritime history and the clear understanding that I would have to adapt to their schedule, Coast Guard officials responded to my plight. As a part of their regular patrol of the coast, they offered me a lift from Bamfield to Clo-oose. The trip was on!*

The logging road that skirted the south shore of Vancouver Island's longest fjord had changed little since our last trip to Bamfield. Though it had been recently graded and was smoother, fully loaded logging trucks still barrelled towards the mill at Port Alberni, lurching regularly across a non-existent centre line, sliding sideways towards us in the loose gravel curves. More than once, the dust they kicked up, like sea fog, stopped us dead in our tracks. On the many single-lane log bridges, we found that we were no match for these weighty leviathans. My life passed before me more than once as we rounded sharp curves and crossed ravines. I longed for the opportunity to choose death at sea. Gale force winds screamed up Alberni Inlet, a portent of adventures ahead that made my frivolous death wish nearly come true.

On paper the plan was simple. We were to be dropped off at the south side of the Nitinat River by a Coast Guard rescue zodiac,[1] thus reducing our hiking time from days to mere hours. Yet the day we arrived in Bamfield, a strong northwesterly gale kept the Coast Guard busy responding to several maritime incidents. Their priorities, along with the weather itself, made our disembarkation impossible. We waited, very thankful not to be on the open sea. Overnight the storm subsided. When coxswain Don Amos and rescue specialist Ian McKenzie picked us up early the next morning, John and I expectantly climbed aboard the open zodiac. Little did we know that we would soon see and feel the aftermath of the storm on the "Graveyard of the Pacific."

The ocean swells, left over from the previous day's wind, hit us as soon as we left Bamfield Inlet. The same roller-coaster seas that were yesterday's huge breakers had caused one particular incident that we were to witness directly. Don Amos had mentioned the need for a brief detour to a nearby island. Over the roar of the engines, Ian explained that a small wooden sloop had been driven onto the rocks on one of the Deer Island Group at the southern extremity of Barkley Sound. The vessel, a home-built craft, was the Krilyatii Korolyeva *(Russian for "Winged Queen"). Its skipper and lone occupant, who had miraculously survived the wreck, was a small, bearded, articulate man who had a slight accent. His cargo was as simple as his voyage was ambitious: he intended to take 400 English bibles across the north Pacific to his faraway Russian homeland. Engineless, the* Krilyatii Korolyeva *was poorly designed, inadequately rigged, and completely ill-suited to face the perils of a savage northern ocean. This latter-day Don Quixote nonetheless appeared healthy and had already begun to unload his vessel. He confidently asserted that he would repair his small sloop and continue his fated journey.*

After building his craft in Tofino, this eccentric seafarer had defied Coast Guard warnings and set out at the storm's height for the Kamchatka Peninsula, thousands of nautical miles due west. Unable to beat offshore,

An inauspicious beginning for a voyage across the North Pacific, the *Krilyatii Korolyeva* is wrecked in Barkley Sound after only one day.

the vessel was pushed south by the gale into Barkley Sound, fortunately coming to rest only a few miles from the Bamfield Coast Guard Station.

As I surveyed this scene and took in the resilience of this stranded sailor, I was struck by the level of courtesy the Coast Guard crew exhibited. They neither lectured the hapless mariner on his prospects nor undermined his intent to remain on the barren inshore island with his beloved, broken vessel. They simply stated that they would look in on him the next day.

Later, the rescue specialist explained that it was not the intent of the Canadian Coast Guard to destroy a person's dreams but only see to it that they neither turned to folly nor endangered the lives of those who might later be called upon to effect a rescue. As we headed south I thought how little had changed on this cruel sea since the days of James Cook and John Meares and, later, the crew of the John Bright *and men like Father Brabant. Visionaries and missionaries of all sorts, with wild schemes and grand dreams, were still drawn here to land's edge, intent upon affecting the destiny of this desolate and unforgiving shore.*

At 40 knots, we seemed to fly by Tsusiat Falls, a historic landmark for mariners on the outer mid-coast. Cetaceans lolled in the glassy rolling sea, while great strands of bull kelp testified to the dangers of reefs that lurked just beneath the surface. We slammed across the standing waves that marked the Nitinat River sandbar only to find ourselves in the company of an enterprising grey whale yards from the beach. This massive creature hovered patiently, his huge mouth open to the rich harvest of food caught in the river's strong outflow current. Carefully we inched by one of his huge, barnacled flukes, which poked high above the water. He seemed only vaguely aware of us as the powerful zodiac entered the full outflow stream of the Nitinat Narrows between Tsuquanah and Whyac Points.

Don Amos steered the zodiac towards the southern shore, where we were deposited at the trailhead and made arrangements (always allowing for the vagaries of the weather) for possible future pick-up times. Even though it was summer, we had prepared to be self-sufficient for many days, knowing both the magnitude of storm possibilities and the frequency of Pacific low pressure troughs. Once unloaded, the Coast Guard duo, radio crackling, zoomed away towards the narrows as quickly as it had arrived. Soon all was silent. The search for the petroglyphs of Clo-oose had begun in earnest once again.

Although parts of the trail had been changed and upgraded, it didn't take long to find the site. We had carefully noted the hiking time from the Nitinat River on our first sortie. When we broke through the salal at the targeted hour, I felt the same apprehension about the glyphs that I had known years before. I was to be both surprised and disappointed at what I would find.

I pushed back the last of the undergrowth, stepped out onto the grey rock, and took that long breath. The small cove was even more beguiling than I remembered it. This time we had arrived at extreme low tide, and from my vantage point at the edge of the forest, some 40 feet above the ocean, the curved shape of the cove was dramatic and distinct. The two rock promontories stood like sentinels, completely exposed, while a series of swells assaulted a cragged surge channel to my right. First came the roar and then the whoosh as smooth, shiny pebbles were rolled across the small beach. The place was a virtual echo gallery, as the frothing surf eroded sea caves on the pockmarked promontories while the incessant thunder of the tidal surges reverberated throughout the cove. This awesome sound intermingled with the soft grating of the pebbles and the lesser sound of broken waves being spent up the beach. With blue Cape Flattery on the Olympic Peninsula just visible on the distant horizon, and sea spray gleaming iridescent in the afternoon sun, the small cove had become

This recent wreck of the motorboat *Defiance* occurred at the eastern end of Stanley Beach, less than 100 yards from the Clo-oose petroglyph site. It was uncanny, but the idea of shipwreck would simply not go away.

a cathedral of changing colours and symphonic movements. I stood, more convinced than ever that this place was a sanctuary, a sacred place where artisans could work sheltered from the full fury of the ocean, yet within ear-shot of its mesmerizing and meditative tones.

As I stood above the beauty, images appeared. I recalled the dramatic photos of Edward Curtis, showing burly Nuu-chah-nulth harpooners ready for the hunt. The Nitinaht band's nearby village of Whyac (meaning "lookout") was strategically placed for these once-famous Aboriginal whalers. Both the annual grey whale migration and the salmon run up the Nitinat River created an environment that accommodated a people who, like their more northern Hesquiat cousins, were at home on the sea.

My eyes turned to the glyphs, and I must admit to a sense of instant disappointment as I watched a group of hikers descend on them. I had anticipated solitude. As I rested above the cove, I tried to visualize the events that had occurred in this area over a century ago, when Hesquiat people were shanghaied and taken offshore by whalers and sealers following in the footsteps of James Christenson.

The Nitinaht, like the Hesquiat, were known to have rescued shipwrecked mariners during this same period, and they often transported them to Victoria in their long canoes. Potlatches were often held at nearby Agate Beach when the Makah visited from across the Strait of Juan de

Fuca.[2] *All these events and rituals were recorded in the strange petroglyphs of Clo-oose—the whales, seals, sailing ships, and other images of astonishment and taboo, were, thankfully, still visible. I would later walk to Clo-oose and talk with Fiona Chambers, who had lived there in the 1970s. She might remember her parents' stories of the pioneer Logan family and, therefore, be able to shed more light on the tentative link between the petroglyphs of Clo-oose and the wreck of the* John Bright. *For now, what needed my attention were the glyphs themselves.*

What became immediately apparent was that certain glyphs had eroded far more than had others. The most southerly set, containing the three longitudinal full human figures, seemed to have suffered the most. This particular part of the sandstone shelf was the softest of the whole site, and those figures inscribed in an area with a slight downhill slope suffered the combined effects of weathering and of run-off. Most noticeably affected was the bottom image of the full-breasted woman, which had been abraded around a natural vulva-form depression. Winter rains had found a natural channel here and washed away the patinated surface of the rock, exposing soft yellow sandstone. Soon her outline would be eroded away completely. The rest of the site seemed remarkably intact, although many of the images had certainly faded.

One aspect of the cove that I had tried to ignore on my first visit now screamed for attention. The site had been desecrated by graffiti, some of it dating from as early as 1901. T.E. Swanson left his name in 1915, while Jennie Andrews carved her name more deeply than others among the sacred stones in November 1927. In 1935, beside an exquisite set of three small killer whales, "F.M." and "E.L" declared their everlasting love in a valentine heart. And so it progressed up until the present day, when more modern images as well as mute initials and stronger signatures linger to deface the site. A Mickey Mouse head continues to mock the sanctity of a magical bird figure, while fake whale and bird figures demean the originals.

Things might have been worse. In 1911 a Victoria real estate firm promoted the idea of establishing a seaside resort (to be called Stanley Beach) just yards from the petroglyph site. The plan called for a huge pier, like that of Brighton, England, or Santa Monica, California, and the Inlet Queen, *filled with prospective investors, made its way to Clo-oose. Mercifully, the First World War stopped the gambit, and, fittingly, the*

Inlet Queen *sank while crossing the Nitinat Bar a year later.*[3] *However, some bad ideas just won't go away. In 1999 there is once again a strong rumour around Victoria that Stanley Beach Resort will rise.*

I descended to the beach, where a group of five hikers from Germany, along with their Canadian guide, was wandering willy-nilly over the glyphs, heedless of where they trod. The guide knew little about petroglyphs and less about this particular site, but seemed eager to gain any information I might have. More naive than negligent, the hikers were totally unaware of the cultural significance of these ancient images upon which they were standing. Possibly sensing my angst, they soon ambled away, to become more absorbed by the tide pools and rock formations carved by the surging sea.

I still find myself torn between the options of isolating the petroglyphs in order to keep them from being desecrated and of displaying them in order to build awareness. Certainly, the most obvious example of the latter is Petroglyph Provincial Park, south of Nanaimo. However, as I write, this pathetic attempt to celebrate an Aboriginal art form lies overgrown and under-maintained. As I stood in the cove near Clo-oose, I realized that these international travellers, like countless others before them, had just experienced a poor, even dismissive, introduction to the strong Native culture that once existed proudly on this wild coast. Every year, private guiding companies, capitalizing upon the popularity of the West Coast Trail, lead a lot of curious, sophisticated people along these 55 magnificent miles. I knew that a thousand ill-informed hikers with ill-placed hiking boots could do more damage to the wonderful petroglyphs of Clo-oose in a single season than could decades of wind and rain. I made my feelings about the human erosion of the glyphs known to the sympathetic guide, but the need for a long-term plan remains.

Left to ourselves, John and I set about mapping and photographing the site in much greater detail than we had done previously. What became apparent over the course of two days was that there truly were far more glyphs here than we had originally documented. In addition to the three major human figures I had first described, adjacent to the sexually explicit woman glyph was the faded outline of the one Halket had described in his 1920s Daily Times *article. The glyph had depicted a woman, a "European, with a long dress." No doubt time was quickly eliminating this glyph. We discovered, too, that there were in fact three images of*

Seventy years of reclamation, and the Logan house at Stanley Beach near Clo-oose is almost gone.

men upon horseback, not just the striking one with the top hat. Next we discovered a whole new shelf of sea and bird creatures that were stylistically very different from the seals and whales that surrounded the human figures we knew so well. They appeared to be more highly abstract figures and, alas, were almost completely obliterated. They were easy to miss, lying in a honeycombed hollow beyond where we first looked. They were obviously carved by an earlier generation of artisans.

On our second day at the site, we hiked towards Clo-oose to talk with Fiona Chambers, a woman who had lived here as a teenager and who might have learned something of its early days. Barely ten minutes south of the magnificent little cove, along the base of 80-foot sea cliffs that would be awash at high tide, was a plethora of orca images and a huge, rotund bird figure unlike anything I'd seen at Clo-oose. Beside these were the face-to-face images of two people copulating.[4] Were these figures somehow linked to the strange pendulum-breasted woman so dominantly portrayed in the protected cove? Did these blatantly sexual petroglyph images help trigger the graffiti expressions of love and self? Were they a response to a timeless and more universal acknowledgement of human sexuality pathetically acting out against the void? If that were the case, then perhaps these sexual forms were an attempt to control a tribal unit through a combination of sublimation and titillation.

Near the killer whale images, and within sight of the rusted anchor of the barquentine Skagit which had been wrecked against these same cliffs in October 1906, we sought to reacquaint ourselves with the glyph of the man holding a severed head. This time, perhaps because of the light, or the rising tide, or the many long cracks in the rock shelf, we failed to find it, and I was reminded of the fickle nature of treasure hunting, no matter how immovable the treasure.

Yet this glyph is most important in the John Bright story. Its close association with the killer whale figures is highly suggestive of a relationship between the two. The torso with the upraised arms, surrounded by jellyfish-like figures at the Clo-oose blowhole site, and the mention of the decapitated heads of those survivors found at Hesquiat, do seem to parallel Admiralty accounts of testimony given at the first inquest. Though many other shipwrecks, as mentioned, occurred at Clo-oose and at Hesquiat during this period, none but that of the John Bright were linked in any way with severed heads.

A glyph of a man holding a severed head, adjacent to sailing-ship glyphs, sea creatures, and human figures depicted as being in the sea, is certainly provocative. Its location some 300 yards south of the blowhole site may have more to do with the availability of useable rock than with anything else. Just as daunting, however, is the knowledge that slaving raids did occur among coastal Natives during the period of the John Bright tragedy, and decapitations and displays of trophy heads were not uncommon. The association of this particular glyph with a plethora of images of marine life will not let the John Bright tragedy go away.

At Clo-oose, Fiona could tell us nothing about the glyphs, although she mentioned the Logan family, whose rotting cabin above the glyph site was slowly being reclaimed by the forest. I recalled how, six years earlier, the cabin had provided us with some hope that we would find water nearby and had become the backdrop for our tents by the sea. Subsequently, that cabin also provided new information that I thought might unravel the mystery of the glyphs of men on horseback.

Born a Scot, David Logan emigrated to Vancouver Island from California and worked in the Dunsmuir Coal Mines near Nanaimo. In 1899 he met a Mr. Groves of Victoria, who had been the first European to

Revelation and Desecration   211

Though it looks idyllic from the air on a clear day, Clo-oose is the graveyard of many dreams. In the 1890s smallpox decimated 80 percent of the Nitinaht village located here. Those who survived were later recruited to join Victoria's sealing fleet. During prohibition the treacherous waters became a haven for coastal rumrunners.

In the 1930s, only seven White families remained from the time of earlier settlement at Clo-oose. Forty years later, only two buildings were occupied, and nature seemed to be relentlessly reclaiming the shoreline.

settle in the Clo-oose area. *Groves had brought a herd of cattle to grazing lands beside the Cheewhat River, located a half-mile from Clo-oose. Groves was leaving for Australia and needed a caretaker for the cattle. Logan and his new wife Sarah took the job, moved to Clo-oose, built a house above the petroglyph cove, opened a store, became postmaster and justice of the peace, and continued the enterprise of cattle raising.*[5]

Here, and at other sites to the north, the ranching industry was doomed to failure. Still, I had to consider whether the horsemen images at Clo-oose may have depicted this cattle enterprise rather than having any relevance to the John Bright tragedy. It certainly cast doubt on the whole John Bright connection. However, one major fact saved the credibility of the John Bright theory. The abrasion marks of the horsemen glyphs, in depth and width and shape, were surely of the same era as were the carved outlines of the sailing-ship and steamboat (Beaver) glyphs nearby. By 1880, the Beaver's illustrious career on the outer coast of Vancouver Island was finished. By 1888, well before there were any cattle near Clo-oose, it had sunk off Prospect Point near Vancouver. Hence, the glyph of the Beaver at Clo-oose must have been carved at a much earlier time. Between 1862 and 1870, the HBC vessel was secured by the Royal Navy and acted as a survey vessel on the outer coast. In 1869, the year of the John Bright shipwreck, HMS Beaver surveyed the *northern coast of Vancouver Island.*[6] *Was the artisan who carved the Beaver the same one who carved the sailing-ship and horsemen glyphs? If so, then the mounted men could well have been the constables involved in the* John Bright *hangings.*

Around our campfire that night, other alternatives to my thesis presented themselves. I knew that two men drowned when the Skagit hit the cliffs near Clo-oose in 1906. David Logan helped rescue the survivors. Could the drowning-man glyph at Clo-oose, still plainly visible, have been carved so late? It seemed unlikely. The Native villages of Wah-Kah-Sett, Qua-Ma-Doa, and Tsuquadra, just south of Clo-oose, were all wiped out in the smallpox epidemic at the end of the last century.[7] *Those left at Clo-oose and environs had moved inland. Only one, Klawana Charlie, still lived there when David Logan arrived. Was any Native shaman left in these parts to carve these later images? As a million stars filled the skies overhead, my mind buzzed with possibilities.*

I was able, some two weeks later, to secure a flight up to Hesquiat in a Coast Guard helicopter that was bound for the lighthouse at Estevan Point. I wanted to walk the boulder-strewn shore at nearby Matlahaw Point, where the John Bright *had come to grief. Returning from Kyuquot, we flew south across Nootka Sound below the sea fog, barely 50 feet above the whitecapped, rolling sea, towards a distant invisible tower at the end of Hesquiat Peninsula. The lighthouse at the northern end of the peninsula is well placed. Estevan Point juts eight miles into the open Pacific Ocean from its connected land mass and should rightly be called a cape because of its notorious reputation among mariners. Like Cape Cook or Cape Scott further north, Estevan Point is known for its sudden squalls and treacherous offshore rocky ledges. At the southern tip of this perilous peninsula lay Matlahaw Point and the remains of the* John Bright.

From the wary security of my airborne vantage point, I could see why, in 1774, Juan Perez had cut his anchor cables in the face of yet another storm and left the place in a hurry. Below me, obscured by rain and fog and groundswell, were numerous jagged rocks, at once awash and invisible in the dark, heaving ocean. Directly ahead, we saw nothing, though the radio beacon from Estevan lighthouse was strong and sure and the global positioning system (GPS) placed us still at one and a half miles offshore. We flew confidently and silently on.

Fog made it impossible for us to land at Matlahaw Point, but as we flew south after leaving the lighthouse, pilot Glenn Diachuk assured me he could get me in for a very close look. When Matlahaw Point came into view, I had a deja-vu experience. The ocean itself had flung a myriad of huge, round, dark boulders up from the depths to just this particular point. I was truly amazed at this geographic anomaly, and we hovered as I shot rolls of film. It was exactly as Dr. Comrie and Captain Mist had described it. Hundreds of perfectly round boulders were strewn everywhere, from the clearly visible underwater ledge where the John Bright had first struck, to the small, indented, rocky bay where Captain Burgess, perhaps some of their children, and Beatrice Holden met their horrific and untimely ends. I had read that just inside Matlahaw Point, upon one of the foreshore boulders in the bay where the John Bright came to rest, was a petroglyph. I ached to see it, but understood that, this time, it was not to be.

In the final analysis, I had not found the categorical truths I sought to shore up the theory that the John Bright massacre was represented in the petroglyphs at Clo-oose. There was no irrefutable evidence that solved the issue once and for all. Yet the John Bright connection remains plausible.

What I did find on my trip back to see the glyphs was a heightened appreciation for the site itself. Because it contains so much of that violent period of first contact, it is unique. European settlers, perhaps with more ignorance than malice, steamrolled over Aboriginal peoples, desecrating their entire cultures. If the John Bright story is not directly tied to the images graven in stone at Clo-oose, then it is certainly indirectly tied to them. Think of the hundreds of sailing ships that came to grief on this rugged coast during the colonial period. The petroglyphs of Clo-oose, as art, evoke these memories, intensity, and compassion. These stones and their stories must be preserved.

But how? What is the answer? Given my vocation, I believe that the answer, as always, lies in education. More recent editions of The West Coast Trail, the Sierra Club's popular guidebook, have deleted any significant reference to the sailing-ship glyphs of Clo-oose. One guide even suggests that hikers should not leave the trail on Dididaht reserve land. But prohibition and restriction are not the answer. Those who hike the West Coat Trail will stumble onto the beaches near Clo-oose, just because they are beaches. There, they will trip over the sailing-ship glyphs.

At best, they will briefly ponder them before walking over them; at worst, they will further despoil them with more mindless graffiti.

This is not good enough. If the federal government, through its National Parks Service, invites the world to experience the West Coast Trail, then I believe it has an obligation to raise public consciousness about the rock art of First Nations peoples. It would not take much to erect a proper presentation of the site, relating something of the Nu-chah-nulth peoples, their petroglyphs, and the roles such images may have played in their ancient society. Whether the story of the John Bright deserves a place here, I will leave to others to decide.

⚓ ⚓ ⚓ ⚓ ⚓

Sea otters caught crabs before us on the dock as we awaited our pick-up at Nitinat Narrows. Dall porpoises romped beside us in the waves on the way back to Bamfield, while a string of marbled murrelets easily overtook us, their sleek bodies flying mere inches above the water. These living things are protected from humankind's insatiable hunger to destroy. Can we not give equal protection to an art form that speaks so eloquently to us of a sophisticated and vibrant Aboriginal culture?

Appendix

The original text of D.W. Higgins's account of the *John Bright* tragedy, as published in his second book, *The Passing of a Race*, in 1904, is contained in the following ten pages.

"Every little while the sharp crack of a musket or rifle would be heard."

A GREAT CRIME AND ITS PUNISHMENT.

"For murder, though it have no tongue, will speak with most miraculous organ."
—*Hamlet.*

"How many lives do you think the Indian whisky manufacturers at Victoria destroyed, directly or indirectly, by their traffic?" I was asked the other day. I replied that the number would be difficult to estimate; but when I say that the western and southern shores of the harbor, as far as F. S. Barnard's residence on the one side, and as far as the gas works on the other, were thickly populated by members of the northern tribes who had moved to Victoria for commercial purposes, and that the Songish village, which now contains only some ninety natives of all ages and both sexes, numbered at the very least 4,000 souls, some idea of the terrible inroads that were made upon the tribes may be conceived. A rough census taken in 1859 gave a native population in and about Victoria of 8,500. In July, 1858, the Songish tribe were visited by the Mackah tribe, who inhabited the country in the vicinity of Neah Bay, Washington Territory. The visiting war-canoes numbered 210, with an average of twelve

178   *THE PASSING OF A RACE.*

Indians to a canoe. The Mackah tribe, in common with the Songish and other tribes along the island and mainland coasts, have nearly all disappeared. Of the great Hydahs, the Tsimpseans, the Bella Bellas, the Bella Coolas, the Nootkas, the Clayoquots, the Stickeens, and the Chilcats, only miserable remnants are to be found. The Hudson's Bay Company's records show that both coasts were studded here and there with thickly populated villages. Previous to 1858 there must have been 150,000 Indians on the island and mainland coasts. Twelve years afterwards the number throughout the entire province was computed at 140,000. How many of this smaller number now exist I do not know; but I venture to say that between 1858 and 1870 at least 100,000 natives perished directly from the use of alcoholic stimulants supplied them by illicit vendors. It is a bold statement to make, but I feel confident that I am under rather than over the mark. What an appalling record the manufacturers and their agents and abettors have faced in the other world—for they are all dead, and, with their victims, have been judged. For lucre they poisoned a vast army of their fellow beings. It was just such men our Saviour had in his eye when he put the great question to the listening Jews: "What shall it profit a man if he gain the whole world yet lose his own soul?" An ocean of penitent tears would not quench the flames to which they are condemned. If my readers imagine that the Indians

A GREAT CRIME AND ITS PUNISHMENT. 179

were the only sufferers from the effects of the whisky trade, the brief story I am about to relate will undeceive them.

* * *

In the month of December, 1868, there sailed into the harbor of Port Discovery, Washington Territory, a handsome English bark, named the *John Bright* in honor of one of Britain's greatest statesmen and orators. The captain, who was named Burgess, was part owner, and on board were his pretty young wife and baby boy, and an English nurse maid, on whose cheeks the " rosies and posies " of her native land bloomed. The vessel was a long time in loading, the facilities for quick dispatch being poor. While the bark was taking in cargo, the captain and his wife became well acquainted on shore, and through their geniality and hospitality soon grew to be general favorites. The nursemaid was about seventeen. Her name was Beatrice Holden. She had the lovely English complexion, bright blue eyes, and long hair of tawny hue. Pretty girls were scarce on the Sound at that time, and when the day came for the bark to go to sea this particular girl received no less than three offers of marriage. She declined all with merry laughter, remarking that she intended to live and die an old maid; but should she change her mind she would only marry an Englishman. The vessel sailed away, and passed out of the straits into the open sea early in the month of March, 1869. She was bound for Aus-

180   THE PASSING OF A RACE.

tralia. The weather was boisterous, and the bark was unable to keep off shore. After a gallant struggle she was cast away on the island coast at a point about fourteen miles north of Clayoquot Sound.

* * *

Captain Christenson (now one of the Nanaimo pilots) commanded at that time the trading schooner *Surprise*, owned by William Spring. The schooner was making one of her customary voyages at the time, and word reaching the captain that a vessel had gone ashore, he sailed at once for the scene of the wreck. He was some days in getting to the spot, and by that time the wreck was complete, the vessel lying broadside on the shore, and the sea making a clean breach over her. The captain saw the chiefs of the tribe, and they told him that all hands were lost in the surf. They showed him the remains of a woman (the captain's wife) with long hair lying on the beach, and Captain Christenson buried the body. He searched, but found no other remains. From some word a native let fall and from the evasive answers of the Indians generally, Captain Christenson suspected that there had been foul play. He wrote at once to Victoria of the wreck, adding that he believed some of the ship's company got ashore alive, and that they had been either murdered by the Indians or were held in captivity at some place well back from the shore.

A GREAT CRIME AND ITS PUNISHMENT. 181

Mr. Seymour, who was then Governor, was told of the captain's suspicions, and was asked to send a war vessel to the scene. He declined to act, expressing the belief that all hands had perished. Three weeks passed and nothing was done. Captain Christenson could not rest easy, and despairing of government assistance, at great personal risk he again visited the scene of the wreck. He walked along the shore—the very shore over which he had walked three weeks before—and to his horror discovered other bodies of white men lying above high-water mark. The remains had been frightfully mangled. In every case the head was missing, having been cut off to preclude the possibility of identification. In some instances an arm or leg was missing. The fast-decaying bodies had been stripped of all clothing, and no trace was ever found of the baby. The captain again wrote, and the facts were laid before the Governor, whose dilatory course caused the massacre. H.M.S. *Sparrowhawk* was directed to proceed to the coast.

* * *

The party landed at the nearest safe harbor to the scene of the wreck, and the shore was searched. Nine dead bodies, decapitated and mangled in the manner I have stated, were found. It was shown afterwards that the captain had been shot through the back while in the act of running away in the vain hope of escaping from the cruel savages, who had proved themselves to be less merciful

182   THE PASSING OF A RACE.

than the wild waves. The other prisoners were thrown down and their heads removed while they piteously begged for mercy!

* * *

The natives were questioned, and at first denied all knowledge of how the bodies came there. But when confronted with Christenson's evidence they confessed that the entire ship's company got safely ashore. The Indians were drunk, and in a dangerous mood. The captain's wife and one seaman were killed the first day. The pretty English maid was delivered up to the young men of the tribe, who dragged her into the bush. Her cries filled the air for hours, and when she was seen again by one of the native witnesses some hours later, the poor girl was dead, and her head had disappeared! Her body was not found by the officers, although a diligent search was instituted, for her sad fate appealed to the hearts of the officials and stirred their indignation, and they desired to give her remains a Christian burial. The witnesses further disclosed the fact that the captain and the rest of the survivors were secreted in the bush, and were alive and within a few hundred yards of Christenson when he first reached the scene. They saw him, too, and were threatened with instant death if they dared to make an outcry. After Christenson's departure the tribe waited several days, fearing the warships would come, and they hesitated to murder the survivors. At last the savages pretended they had secured

A GREAT CRIME AND ITS PUNISHMENT. 183

passage for the men on a liquor schooner that had just discharged her cargo and was sailing for Victoria. They lured the poor people to the shore, where they were cruelly massacred, and their bodies left where they fell.

* * *

Several Indians were seized and brought to Victoria. They were tried, and two of the number were convicted. The culprits were taken to the scene of their crime in the *Sparrowhawk,* and in the presence of the whole tribe were hanged. The scaffold was left standing as a warning to other evil-disposed Indians who might be inclined to ill-treat other crews that should be cast on their shore.

* * *

The lesson proved salutary. A year or two later the bark *Edwin,* owned and commanded by Captain S. A. Hughes, dropped anchor in Royal Roads. The captain had his wife and two bright little boys, aged seven and nine years, on board. Accompanied by his wife and children, Captain Hughes came ashore at Victoria and did some shopping. In the evening he set sail for California with a cargo of lumber. Three days later the bark encountered a severe gale. The sails split as if made of paper, and soon the vessel was being swept towards the rocky shore. Every effort was made to keep her off, but in vain. She struck nearly in the identical spot where the *John Bright* laid her bones. Mrs. Hughes, the two children and two seamen were swept overboard, and

184   THE PASSING OF A RACE.

drowned almost immediately. Captain Hughes and the remainder of the crew managed to reach the shore, landing almost at the foot of the scaffold on which the murderers were hanged. The Indians received them with kindness and hospitality, and showered favors upon the men. To those who had no clothes they contributed from their own scanty store. Captain Christenson brought the shipwrecked men to Victoria in the *Surprise*. Captain Hughes landed without a penny in his pockets or an acquaintance in the town. To a reporter he said:

"I never was in such a fix before in all my life. Ten days ago I had a wife and two children, was the owner of a neat little clipper bark, and had $5,000 in my cabin. I didn't owe a cent to anyone. To-day," he added, and his eyes filled with tears and his lips quivered, "I am destitute of wife and children and money, and am thrown on the world a beggar. A man had better be dead. How I wish the sea had swallowed me up, too!"

"Cheer up," said the reporter, "there are plenty of men here who will aid you."

"That's just it," he replied, "I don't want to accept favors from anyone. And yet I've seen the day when I was able to help, and did help, a shipwrecked crew."

"When was that?" was asked.

"It was in the mid-Atlantic," he replied. "The ship *Aquilla* was flying signals of distress. I hailed her, and was told that the ship was sinking. I

A GREAT CRIME AND ITS PUNISHMENT. 185

stood by and took off Captain Sayward and all his men, and carried them to New York. The United States Congress voted me this gold watch and chain."

He drew the watch from his pocket and, opening the case, showed an inscription which ran something like this:

"Presented to Captain S. A. Hughes, of the British bark *Gertrude,* as a mark of appreciation for his gallant conduct in saving the lives of Captain Sayward and the crew of the American ship *Aquilla.*"

It did not take many minutes for the information to pass from mouth to mouth that the man who had saved the life of one of Victoria's best-known citizens was in need of assistance, and the best that could be had was not deemed too good for Captain Hughes.

It is worthy of remark that never since the lesson taught the tribes on the West Coast have shipwrecked people been molested. In fact, the natives have been ever foremost in saving life, and in some instances have rescued and brought crews to Victoria.

* * *

The *Sparrowhawk* remained on the station several years, and, if I mistake not, was sold out of the navy when last here. In 1870, Governor Seymour, who was very ill, was ordered to take a sea voyage, and the *Sparrowhawk* was selected for the purpose. He embarked with Sir Joseph Trutch

186   *THE PASSING OF A RACE.*

and several other officials. The ship went direct to Bella Coola. The Governor was confined to his room all the way up the coast and showed signs of slight mental aberration. His body-servant was named Colston, and the night on which the *Sparrowhawk* arrived at Bella Coola he was left on duty in the Governor's room, with instructions to give him a tablespoonful of a certain medicine contained in a quart bottle every hour. In the dead hours of the night Colston dozed, and dreamed that he was derelict in a small boat without oars or sail. The water lapped the side of the boat, and tossed it from billow to billow. He was ahungered and athirst, for he had been a long time afloat. Mechanically he reached out his hand to grasp the bottle that contained the Governor's medicine. It was not there. His hand swept an empty shelf. He awoke with a start, and heard a strange gurgling sound that proceeded from the Governor's bed. He sprang forward just as His Excellency, who had drained the last drop of medicine from the bottle, sank into a state of insensibility. The ship was aroused and every effort made to save the Governor's life. But he never rallied or spoke again, and when the early sun rose to resume its daily course Governor Seymour had crossed to the other shore. The remains were brought to Esquimalt and buried in the Naval Cemetery, where a neat monument marks the last resting-place of the only Governor of British Columbia who died whilst in office.

Endnotes

Chapter 1

1. Miriam Waddington, "Canadians," in *The Oxford Anthology of Canadian Literature*, ed. Robert Weaver and William Toye (Toronto: Oxford University Press, 1973), 505.
2. A.P. Okladnikov, "The Petroglyphs of Siberia," in *Scientific American* 221, no. 2 (August 1969), 80. This is an absolutely fascinating early article in which Okladnikov argues that the dominance of the mask motif in Amur rock art is related to the use of masks in initiation rites by tribes of the Pacific and the American Northwest (see, especially, page 80).
3. Mary and Ted Bentley, *Gabriola: Petroglyph Island* (Victoria: Sono Nis, 1981), 80.
4. Ibid.
5. Beth and Ray Hill, *Indian Petroglyphs of the Pacific Northwest* (Seattle: University of Washington Press, 1975).
6. Those authors included, among others, Wayne Suttles, Ed Meade, Beth Hill, and Doris Lundy.
7. Peter Pitseolak, *People From Our Side* (Edmonton: Hurtig, 1975), 133.
8. Pudlo Pudlat, *Pudlo: Thirty Years of Drawing* (Ottawa: National Gallery of Canada, 1976), 94.
9. "D.H." to Mr. Goodfellow, in the *Victoria Daily Times*, 18 September 1926.

Chapter 2

1. Hubert Evans, *Mostly Coast People* (Madeira Park, BC: Harbour, 1992.), 15.
2. Barbara Efrat, "Linguistic Acculturation on the West Coast of Vancouver Island," in *Sound Heritage*, vol. 7, no. 1, ed. W.J. Langlois (Victoria: Aural History, Provincial Archives of BC (PABC), 1978), 92.
3. Ruth Kirk, *Wisdom of the Elders* (Vancouver: Douglas and McIntyre, 1986), 17.
4. Efrat, "Linguistic Acculturation," 92.
5. Francisco Morales Padron, "Galleons, Pirates, Pearls, and Straits," in *To the Totem Shore: The Spanish Presence on the Northwest Coast* (Vancouver: Ediciones El Viso, Pavilion of Spain, Expo 1986), 47. It was perhaps here, too, that the Natives received the two infamous spoons that James Cook would notice four years later.
6. Barbara Efrat and W.J. Langlois, "The Meeting of Captain Cook and Chief Maquinna," in *Sound Heritage: Voices from British Columbia*, ed. Saeko Usukawa (Vancouver: Douglas and McIntyre, 1984), 19. In 1805 John Jewitt, captured carpenter of the vessel *Boston*, noted "mamalni" as "mamethlee" in his journal.
7. Ibid.

8. Ibid., 17.
9. John Sendey, *The Nootkan Indian: A Pictorial* (Port Alberni: Alberni Valley Museum, 1977), 38.
10. Ibid., 17.
11. Ibid., 67.
12. Barbara Efrat and W.J. Langlois, ed. *Nu-tka: Captain Cook and the Spanish Explorers on the Coast* (Victoria: Aural History, PABC, 1978), 92.
13. The eighteen tribes identified by Brabant as having a common language were: Checkleset, Kyuquot, Ehatisat, Nuchatlat, Muchalat, Moachat, Hesquiat, Ahousat, Kelsemat, Clayoquot, Ucluelet, Toquat, Uchucklisat, Hopachisat, Tsishaat, Ohiat, Nitinaht, and Pachenat. Cited in Charles Lillard, ed., *Mission to Nootka* (Sidney, BC: Gray's, 1977.), 116. Today, there are fifteen officially recognized bands and several dialects. The neighbouring Makah people of Washington are thought to be blood relatives of the Nuu-chah-nulth, and they share not only a related language, but also common cultural ties.
14. E.N. Anderson, ed., *Bird of Paradox: The Unpublished Writings of Wilson Duff* (Surrey, BC: Hancock, 1996), 30. Nuu-chah-nulth, Nitinaht, and Makah are southern "Wakashan" languages. They are related to a northern language family spoken from Kitimat to Bute Inlet on the mainland. George Vancouver, who was with Cook on his first voyage to Tahiti and New Zealand, later recorded that "Wakash" means "good" or "hurrah" — in retrospect, a fine name for an "extended family" of inter-related tongues. Wakashan is said to be a part of Kwakwala (Southern Kwakwaka'wakw), but it is currently believed to be unrelated to Haida, Tsimshian, or Wet'suwet'en.
15. Thomas Vaughan, "Russian, French, British and American Incursions into the Spanish Lake," in Morales Padron, *To the Totem Shore*, 24.
16. Ibid., 29.
17. Daniel Conner and Lorraine Miller, *Master Mariner: Capt. James Cook and the Peoples of the Pacific* (Vancouver: Douglas and McIntyre, 1978), 22.
18. Barry Gough, "Nootka Sound in James Cook's Pacific World," in Efrat and Langlois, *Nu-tka,* 31.
19. G.P.V. Akrigg and Helen B. Akrigg, *British Columbia Chronicle: 1778-1846.* (Vancouver: Discovery, 1975), 39.
20. Vaughan, "Incursions into the Spanish Lake," 29.
21. Robin Fisher, *Contact and Conflict: Indian-European Relations in British Columbia, 1774-1890* (Vancouver: UBC Press, 1992), 3.
22. Akrigg and Akrigg, *British Columbia Chronicle*, 43.
23. Margaret Ormsby, *British Columbia: A History* (Toronto: Macmillan, 1985), 13.
24. James Colnet, "A Voyage to the South Atlantic and round Cape Horn into the Pacific Ocean," in *The Remarkable World of Frances Barkley, 1769-1845*, ed. Beth Hill (Sidney, BC: Gray's, 1978), 35.
25. Ibid., 31.
26. George Dixon, "A Voyage around the World, but more Particularly to the North-West Coast of America," in Hill, *The Remarkable World of Frances Barkley*, 31.
27. Ibid., 33. The somewhat naive Captain Barkley, however, did believe

Mackay when he stated that during his many side-trips to King George's Sound, he had come to the conclusion that the area was not part of North America but, rather, a chain of detached islands. Had Mackay seen or been told something that led him to reach the conclusion some six years before Vancouver?

28. Ormsby, *British Columbia*, 14.
29. John Hopper, *Indian Wars in the Old Pacific Northwest* (Burnaby: Artaman, 1996), 49.
30. Ibid., 14.
31. George Woodcock, *British Columbia: A History of the Province* (Vancouver: Douglas and McIntyre, 1990), 33. Earlier in 1787, John Cox had turned up in Macao.
32. James Gibson, "Bostonians and Muscovites on the Northwest Coast, 1788-1841," in *British Columbia: Historical Readings*, ed. Peter Ward and Robert McDonald (Vancouver: Douglas and McIntyre, 1981), 67.
33. Ibid.
34. During the summer of 1786, John Hanna, captain of the *Sea Otter*, tried to recover a stolen chisel (an increasingly valuable item of trade) by ordering a broadside to be fired into a nearby Native canoe. This resulted in the deaths of over 20 men, women, and children, including several chiefs. See Hilary Stewart, *The Adventures and Sufferings of John Jewitt* (Vancouver: Douglas and McIntyre, 1995), 21. In 1789, one of Martinez's men shot and killed Callicum, the second-highest-ranking chief in Yuquot. It was all a terrible mistake. The Yuquot had sided with the British when Martinez seized the *Iphigenia* and the *Argonaut*, and they were hurling abuse, and other things from their canoes, at Martinez's ship. Martinez stupidly shot his pistol into the air to drive the Natives away. An eager young crewman heard what he believed to be a signal and opened fire. The Natives were aghast at the death of their chief. News, rumour, and Native revulsion spread like wildfire. See George Woodcock, *Peoples of the Coast* (Edmonton: Hurtig, 1977), 98.
35. Akrigg and Akrigg, *British Columbia Chronicle*, 50.
36. Ibid., 53.
37. Christon Archer, "The Transient Presence," in Ward and McDonald, *British Columbia*, 62. Soon after, Colnet lost his mind completely and attempted suicide.
38. James Gibson, "The Maritime Fur Trade," in Ward and McDonald, *British Columbia*, 71.
39. Ibid.
40. Ibid., 72.
41. Robin Fisher, "Indian Control of the Maritime Fur Trade and the Northwest Coast," in Ward and McDonald, *British Columbia*, 106. Fisher and others believe that the hostility on the coast between trader and Aboriginal was not as widespread as was once believed. Though there was certainly plunder, this was not, he argues, simply a series of wanton, reckless acts but, rather, a carefully orchestrated game of moves and counter-moves. To be sure, wholesale unrestrained violence would have ruined what was a very good thing for both parties.

42. Fraud was not unheard-of among Aboriginal traders. Cook noted that Natives sometimes substituted water for oil in the containers that they traded. Ships' pewter plates were eagerly traded away for a night with a Moachat slave woman. Such White behaviour earned the lasting enmity of coastal Aboriginals. See Akrigg and Akrigg, *British Columbia Chronicle*, 25.
43. Ibid.
44. John Walbran, *British Columbia Coast Names, 1592-1906* (Vancouver: Douglas, 1971), 280.
45. Ibid., 281.
46. Wilson Duff, *The Indian History of British Columbia*, vol. 1, *The Impact of the White Man* (Victoria: Provincial Museum of Natural History and Anthropology, 1964), 8.
47. Barbara Efrat and W.J. Langlois, "The Contact Period as Recorded by Indian Oral Traditions," in Efrat and Langlois, *Nu-tka*, 60.
48. Ibid., 61.
49. Stewart, *John R. Jewitt*, 181-2.
50. Ward and McDonald, *British Columbia*, 75.
51. Ibid.
52. Ibid.
53. Woodcock, *British Columbia*, 59.
54. Gibson. "Bostonians and Muscovites," 87.
55. Ward and McDonald, *British Columbia*, 89.

Chapter 3
1. F.R. Scott, "Union," in *Canadian Anthology*, ed. Carl Klinck and Reginald Watters (Toronto: Gate, 1974), 262
2. Somehow the name of trader William Banfield's namesake community was corrupted to "Bamfield" in the late nineteenth century. Banfield was thought to have been murdered under mysterious circumstances in late 1862 near Clayoquot Sound.
3. Fred Rogers, *Shipwrecks of British Columbia* (Vancouver: Douglas and McIntyre, 1973), 114.
4. Robert Connell, *Victoria Daily Times*, 28 August 1926.
5. Ibid.

Chapter 4
1. *The Complete Works of William Shakespeare* (New York: Avenel, 1975), 1,065.
2. Were it not for the HBC having a firm presence in New Caledonia and establishing prudent management and fair treatment of interior Natives, it is very likely that the British would have completely lost their influence in that region. The idea of a "British" Columbia would then surely have died, allowing for a burgeoning United States to establish sovereignty over this northern region of the Pacific Northwest.
3. Jean Barman, *The West Beyond the West* (Toronto: University of Toronto Press, 1991), 59.
4. Terry Reksten, *More English than the English: A Very Social History of*

Endnotes 231

     Victoria (Victoria: Orca, 1986), 71.
5. George Bowering, *Bowering's B.C.: A Swashbuckling History* (Toronto: Viking, 1996), 148.
6. Harry Gregson, *A History of Victoria* (Victoria: Observer, 1970), 45.
7. Ibid.
8. Bowering. *Bowering's B.C.*, 147.
9. PRO, Medical Officer's Journals, no. 152, HMS *Sparrowhawk*, 1869, in G.P.V. Akrigg and Helen B. Akrigg, *British Columbia Chronicle, 1847-1871* (Vancouver: Discovery, 1977), 376.
10. Ibid.
11. Charles Lillard, *Seven Shillings a Year: A History of Vancouver Island* (Ganges: Horsdal and Schubart, 1986), 157.
12. Ibid., 156.
13. Reksten, *More English,* ix.
14. Irene Edwards, *Short Portage to Lillooet* (Mission: Cold Stream, 1985), 81.
15. Derek Pethick and Susan Baumgarten, *British Columbia Recalled* (Saanichton: Hancock, 1974).
16. Edwards, *Short Portage*, 80.
17. Margaret Ormsby, *British Columbia: A History* (Toronto: Macmillan, 1958), 167.
18. Ibid.
19. Bowering, *Bowering's B.C.,* 140.
20. Akrigg and Akrigg, *British Columbia Chronicle*, 253.
21. *Colonist*, 19 September 1862, in Akrigg and Akrigg, *British Columbia Chronicle,* 257.
22. Ibid.
23. *Colonist*, 13 January 1863.
24. B.A. McKelvie, "Tales of Conflict," *Vancouver Daily Province*, 1949, 68.
25. Reksten, *More English,* 47.
26. Akrigg and Akrigg, *British Columbia Chronicle*, 300.
27. T.W. Paterson, *British Columbia: The Pioneer Years* (Langley, BC: Stagecoach, 1977), 108. The haul was over $30,000 in gold coins, gold dust, currency, and silver, and it was probably an inside job.
28. Bowering, *Bowering's B.C.,* 118.
29. Michael Kluckner, *Victoria: The Way It Was* (Vancouver: Whitecap, 1986), 54.
30. Akrigg and Akrigg, *British Columbia Chronicle,* 405. These findings were based upon the 1871 census documented in the Langevin Report, but the listing of Victoria's businesses in 1869 would not have differed much.
31. Robert Kendrick, "Amor de Cosmos and Confederation," in *British Columbia And Confederation,* ed. George Shelton (Victoria: University of Victoria Press, 1967), 69.
32. De Cosmos, *British Colonist,* 11 December 1858.
33. Ibid., 18 December 1858.
34. H. Keith Ralston, ed., *Dictionary of Canadian Biography,* vol. 3 (Toronto: University of Toronto Press, 1976), 240.
35. Ibid., 479.
36. D.W. Higgins, *Victoria Weekly Chronicle*, 18 July 1865, in P.B.Waite, *The*

Life and Times of Confederation (Toronto: University of Toronto Press, 1962), 158.
37. British Colonist Weekly, 30 April 1867, in H. Hernstein, L. Hughes, and R. Kirbyson, Challenge and Survival (Toronto: Prentice-Hall, 1970), 224.
38. Olive Fairholm, "John Robson and Confederation," in Shelton, British Columbia and Confederation, 110.
39. Brian Smith, "The Confederation Delegation," in Shelton, British Columbia and Confederation, 198.
40. Kluckner, Victoria, 52.
41. Ibid., 32.

Chapter 5

1. "Dead reckoning" is a term used by sailors when estimating position. It is a navigational procedure, commonly used in the seventeenth century, that assesses a ship's position through the careful recording of compass course direction, speed, and known speed of current or drift. It is thought to be a corruption of the term "deduced reckoning."
2. Margaret Avison, "Snow," in Theme and Image, ed. Carol Gillanders (Toronto: Copp Clark Pitman, 1976), 42.
3. Wayne Suttles, Coast Salish Essays (Seattle: University of Washington Press, 1987), 48.
4. Ibid.
5. Ibid., 30.
6. Ibid.
7. Russell Harper, ed. Paul Kane's Frontier (Toronto: University of Toronto Press, 1971), 5.
8. Ibid., 304.
9. Ibid., 150.
10. Ibid.
11. Paintings are Norway House and Battle of I-ch-nue.
12. Ibid., 146. The painting is called Captain Bolger, Governor of Assiniboia, and the Chiefs and Warriors of the Chippewa Tribe at Red Lake. It was painted in 1823 and represents a meticulous style of watercolour. The Reverend John West of the Hudson's Bay Company was obviously taken with the docile and child-like renderings of the Aboriginals.

Chapter 6

1. Margaret Ormsby, British Columbia: A History (Toronto: Macmillan, 1958), 229. HMS Sparrowhawk was at the Nass River and, later, in May 1869, at Skidegate with Governor Seymour just before he died.
2. "Distribution of the Royal Navy, 1861-1874," Parliamentary Papers, Appendix C, in Barry Gough, The Royal Navy and the Northwest Coast of North America (Vancouver: UBC Press, 1971), 248.
3. G.P.V. Akrigg and Helen B. Akrigg, British Columbia Chronicle: 1778-1846 (Vancouver: Discovery, 1975), 119.
4. Ibid., 157.
5. From "Journal of a Voyage on the North West Coast of North America during the years 1811, 1812, 1813, 1814," in Akrigg and Akrigg, British

Columbia Chronicle, 160.
6. Ormsby, British Columbia, 68.
7. Gough, Royal Navy, 37.
8. Ibid., 42-43.
9. Akrigg and Akrigg, British Columbia Chronicle, 234.
10. Ibid.
11. Gough, Royal Navy, 67.
12. Ibid., 66.
13. Ibid., 69.
14. Don't you love it? After all the ballyhooing for protection from the HBC, the *Beaver* was away on a trading cruise. See Barry Gough, *Gunboat Frontier* (Vancouver: UBC Press, 1984), 70.
15. Ibid., 81.
16. The armaments of the ships listed are from "List by Types and Classes of British Warships on the Northwest Coast of North America or in British Columbia waters, 1778-1914," in Gough, *Royal Navy*, 259-66.
17. Ibid., 76.
18. Ibid., 79.
19. The term is Barry Gough's.
20. In conversation with Rodger Touchie of Heritage House.
21. Jean Barman, *The West Beyond the West* (Toronto: University of Toronto Press, 1991), 74.
22. Akrigg and Akrigg, *British Columbia Chronicle*, 76.
23. Fred V. Longstaff, *Esquimalt Naval Base* (Victoria: Victoria Book and Stationery, 1941), 17.
24. Ibid., 20.
25. Ibid., 19.
26. John Walbran, *British Columbia Coast Names* (Ottawa: Douglas, 1971), 406. I believe that this was the same Dickens who would later join the North-West Mounted Police.
27. Gough, *Royal Navy*, 133.
28. Ibid., 137.
29. Ibid., 147.
30. Akrigg and Akrigg, *British Columbia Chronicle*, 42, 43. Blanshard had picked up "tic douleroux" in the tropics and was taking morphine for the pain, which sapped his energy. However, the animosity between him and Douglas reached its zenith when the former publicly rebuked the latter in court for exceeding his executive power. After such a public condemnation, no citizen in Victoria with HBC connections would buy land from the disagreeable Blanshard.
31. James K. Smith, *Wilderness of Fortune* (Vancouver: Douglas and McIntyre, 1983), 107.
32. Barman, *The West Beyond the West*, 76.
33. Akrigg and Akrigg, *British Columbia Chronicle*, 173-74.
34. Ibid., 159.
35. Gough, *Royal Navy*, 161. Gough's detailed analysis of the stand-off between Governor Douglas and the Royal Navy is first class. Hornby left the *Tribune* moments before the *Massachusetts* arrived, leaving a young first-lieutenant,

David Boyle, in charge. He returned after meeting with the American military commander, Captain Pickett, and, just minutes before Boyle was to open fire on the *Massachusetts,* Hornby countermanded Douglas's order. Had Boyle fired the first shot, or had Hornby not arrived when he did, we surely would have gone to war over the "Pig War."
36. Gough, *Gunboat Frontier,* 125.
37. William Cronon, "Telling Tales of Canvas," in *Discovered Lands, Invented Pasts: Transforming Visions of the American West,* ed. Brian W. Dippe (New Haven: Yale University Press, 1992), 86.
38. Gough, *Gunboat Frontier,* 43.
39. Ibid.
40. Ibid., 3 (photographic inserts).
41. Ibid., 29.
42. Ibid.
43. Ibid., 61.
44. John Hopper, *Indian Wars in the Old Pacific Northwest* (Burnaby: Artaman, 1996), 64.
45. Gough, *Gunboat Frontier,* 119.
46. *British Colonist,* 17 October 1864.
47. Gough, *Gunboat Frontier,* 83.
48. Ibid., 123.
49. Robin Fisher, *Contact and Conflict: Indian-European Relations in British Columbia, 1774-1890* (Vancouver: UBC Press, 1992), 68.
50. Gerrard Steckler, S.J. *Charles Seghers, Priest and Bishop in the Pacific Northwest, 1839-1886* (Fairfield, Washington: Ye Galleon, 1986), 77.

Chapter 7

1. Margaret Atwood, "Colouring the World," in *The Oxford Book of Canadian Verse* ed. Margaret Atwood (Toronto: Oxford University Press), 355.
2. Edward Meade, *Indian Rock Carvings of the Pacific Northwest* (Sidney: Gray's, 1971), 12.
3. Ibid., 11. Even the site now virtually in front of the Lekwiltok village on Quadra Island was said to have been carved by "Spirit People" long before the villagers' presence.
4. Joy Inglis, *Spirit in the Stone* (Victoria: Horsdal and Schubart, 1998.) Part 1 of her book contains many references to Native respondents, elders, and carvers who passed on a wealth of information about the origin of the glyphs.
5. Beth and Ray Hill, *Indian Petroglyphs of the Northwest Coast,* (Seattle: University of Washington Press, 1975), 21.
6. James Keyser, *Indian Rock Art of the Columbia Plateau* (Seattle: University of Washington Press, 1992), 20.
7. Ibid.
8. Ibid., 19.
9. Ann McMurdo, "Excavation of a Petroglyph Site on Protection Island, British Columbia," in Inglis, *Spirit in the Stone,* 9.
10. Meade, *Indian Rock Carvings,* 10.
11. Francis Shepard, "Sea Level Change in the Past 6,000 years," *Science* 5

(1964): 374, cited in Hill, *Indian Petroglyphs*, 23.
12. Ibid.
13. From a conversation with Beth Hill in her home in Victoria in March 1992.
14. Hill, *Indian Petroglyphs*, 22.
15. Inglis, *Spirit in the Stone*, 8.
16. Knut Fladmark, *Prehistory of British Columbia* (Ottawa: National Museums of Canada, 1986), 78.
17. Keith Davis, "Modernism and the Quest for Primacy," in *Marks in Place: Contemporary Responses to Rock Art*, ed. Linda Conner (Albuquerque: University of New Mexico Press, 1988), 125.
18. E.N. Anderson, ed., *Bird of Paradox: The Unpublished Writings of Wilson Duff* (Surrey, BC: Hancock, 1996), 56.
19. Dorothy Kennedy and Randy Bouchard, *Sliammon Life, Sliammon Lands* (Vancouver: Talon, 1983), 51. This is an abridged version of the story.
20. Keyser, *Indian Rock Art*, 92.
21. George MacDonald, "Cosmic Equations in Northwest Coast Indian Art," in *The World Is as Sharp as a Knife: An Anthology in Honour of Wilson Duff*, ed. Donald Abbott (Victoria: British Columbia Provincial Museum, 1981), 227.
22. Hill, *Indian Petroglyphs*, 36.
23. Wilson Duff, "Levels of Meaning in Haida Art," in Anderson, *Bird of Paradox*, 177.
24. Inglis, *Spirit in the Stone*, 23.
25. Hill, *Indian Petroglyphs*, 270.
26. Claude Lévi-Strauss, *The Way of the Masks* (Vancouver: Douglas and McIntrye, 1982), 20.
27. Hill, *Indian Petroglyphs*, 285.
28. Ibid., 274.
29. Abbott, *The World Is as Sharp as a Knife*. Duff's three essays are on pages 95, 152, and 201, respectively.
30. Ibid., 209.
31. Anderson. *Bird of Paradox*, 92.
32. Ibid.
33. Ibid.
34. Ibid., 101.

Chapter 8

1. Epigraph to Mary di Michele, "The Moon And the Salt Flats," in *The New Oxford Book of Canadian Verse*, ed. Margaret Atwood (Toronto: Oxford University Press, 1982), 405.
2. Captain Thomas McKenzie, "Shipwrecked Sailors Got Short Shrift in Early Days on Coast," *British Colonist*, 1 April 1934.
3. Peter Kemp, ed. *The Oxford Companion to Ships and the Sea* (London: Oxford University Press, 1976), 319. The Dutchman was Captain Vanderdecken, who, with profanity on his lips and pride in his heart, made the error of trying to sail his full-rigged ship around the Cape of Good Hope in a howling gale. The vessel was wrecked, and its crew perished. The vessel and its men were then forced to sail their luminous

ship through the afterlife, always at the same spot. The German legend recounts that the ship was without a helmsman and that the captain was forced to play dice with the devil for his soul. If a sailor caught sight of the ship at sea, then his own shipwreck was imminent. Many variations of the story exist.
4. Ibid., 531. The *Mary Celeste* was abandoned at sea, between the Azores and Portugal, on December 4, 1872. The brigantine, bound from New York to Genoa, was found in good order, with an intact cargo. The crew of ten, who had suddenly and mysteriously left the ship for no apparent reason, was never found.
5. David W. Higgins, *The Passing of a Race* (Toronto: Briggs, 1905), 177.
6. In 1878, Higgins, with his cane, assaulted Robert Holloway, the editor of the *Standard*, in front of Victoria's Supreme Court, ostensibly over an article that had been critical of his family. He was fined five shillings. See Michael Kluckner, *Victoria: The Way It Was* (Vancouver: Whitecap, 1981), 49.
7. *The Mystic Spring* was first published in 1904 by William Briggs (Toronto), while *The Passing of a Race* was first published in 1905 by Briggs. Both of these books have long been out of print. However Higgins's writings are available in the book *Tales of a Pioneer Journalist* (Surrey, BC: Heritage House, 1996), a selection of Higgins's writings from his two original books combined with archival illustrations. Higgins's account "The *John Bright* Massacre" appears on pages 132-135.
8. John Gibbs, *West Coast Windjammers* (New York: Bonanza, 1968), 16.
9. David W. Griffiths, "The John Bright: Historical Background," in *Status Report on the Historic Shipwrecks of Clayoquot and Nootka Sound* (Vancouver: Underwater Archeological Society of British Columbia, 1982), 62. At the time of its loss, the *British Colonist* (15 March 1869) notes the *John Bright* as weighing 456 tons.
10. Ibid.
11. Comment by Port Ludlow shipwright Neil Morrison, an assumed friend of Burgess, in "The Lost Bark, John Bright," *British Colonist*, 30 April 1869.
12. Higgins, "A Great Crime and its Punishment," in *The Passing of a Race*, 179. This story was reprinted in *Tales of a Pioneer Journalist* and in Appendix A of this volume.
13. Ibid., 179.
14. Ibid.
15. Ibid.
16. *British Colonist*, 13 March 1869.
17. The *British Colonist* spells Christenson's name "Christianson." However, most sources, including his grandson, who wrote of the *John Bright* affair, spell his name "Christenson." Christenson himself uses this spelling in a letter to the *British Colonist*, 23 April 1869. It is this spelling that I have adopted.
18. *British Colonist*, 13 March 1869.
19. Ibid.
20. Ibid.
21. T.W. Paterson, "Christenson's Persistence Uncovered Hesquiat Murders,"

Daily Colonist, 15 December 1974.
22. *British Colonist*. 15 March 1869.
23. Ibid., 16 March 1869.
24. Ibid.
25. Ibid., 30 April 1869.
26. Peter Murray, *The Vagabond Fleet* (Victoria: Sono Nis, 1988), 15.
27. B.A. McKelvie, "Massacre at Nootka Sound," in the *Province Magazine*, 27 October 1956.
28. Paterson, "Christenson's Persistence."
29. Murray, *The Vagabond Fleet*, 16.
30. Ibid., 15.
31. Ibid., 17. They made it ashore safely themselves.
32. Ibid., 17-18.
33. *British Colonist*, 31 March 1869.
34. Ibid., 23 April 1869.
35. Higgins, *The Passing of a Race*, 182.
36. Ibid.
37. *British Colonist*, 23 April 1869.
38. Ibid.
39. Ibid., 24 April 1869.
40. Ibid.
41. Ibid.
42. Cecil Clark, "The Lost Children of Hesquiat Bay," *British Colonist*, 6 December 1959.
43. Ibid., 8.
44. *British Colonist*, 26 April 1869.
45. Ibid.
46. Ibid.
47. Ibid.
48. Ibid.
49. Ibid., 30 April 1869.
50. Ibid., 12 May 1869.
51. Antony Preston and John Major, "The Genealogy of the Gunboat Navy," in *Send A Gunboat* (London: Longman's, 1967), 199.
52. Unpublished correspondence with Liza Verity, Archivist, National Maritime Museum, Greenwich, 23 November 1998.
53. Barry Gough, *Gunboat Frontier* (Vancouver: UBC Press, 1984), 126.
54. Ibid.
55. *British Colonist*, 12 May 1869.
56. The press reported the exhumation of eleven bodies; Gough reports eight bodies, "some decapitated," with six more unaccounted for. See Gough, *Gunboat Frontier*, 126.
57. G.P.V. Akrigg and Helen B. Akrigg, *British Columbia Chronicle* (Vancouver: Discovery, 1977), 372.
58. Gough, *Gunboat Frontier*, 126.
59. *British Colonist*, 12 May 1869.
60. Ibid.
61. Gough, *Gunboat Frontier*, 127.

62. Ibid.
63. *British Colonist*, 12 May 1869.

Chapter 9

1. F. R. Scott, "Eclipses," in D.G. Jones, *Butterfly on Rock* (Toronto: University of Toronto Press, 1976), 83.
2. June Callwood, *Portrait of Canada* (Toronto: Paperjacks, 1981), 6.
3. Joseph Needham, Bench Books of the Trial of John Anayitzaschist, PABC, B9802, vol. 2. I am taking the spelling of the Native names from these bench books. Other spellings have appeared.
4. *British Colonist*, 28 May 1869.
5. Ibid.
6. Ibid.
7. Ibid.
8. Ibid., 29 May 1869.
9. Ibid.
10. Christenson based that opinion solely on the long hair that lay beside the skeleton and upon the smallness of the nearby unattached skull. See *British Colonist*, 29 May 1869.
11. Ibid., 29 May 1869.
12. *British Colonist*, 23 June 1869.
13. Ibid.
14. Needham, Bench Books, 173.
15. Ibid., 179.
16. Ibid.
17. Ibid., 181.
18. Ibid.
19. Ibid., 179
20. Ibid., 183.
21. Ibid., 185.
22. Needham, Bench Books, 191.
23. Ibid.
24. Mr. Charlie had to have been Captain Carleton because had he been Captain Christenson, Nee-ta-kim would have identified him as the interpreter in court. Carleton did regularly visit Hesquiat from the sealing and trading base at Kyuquot.
25. Needham, Bench Books, 203.
26. Ibid., 205.
27. Ibid., 207.
28. Ibid., 209.
29. Ibid.
30. Ibid., 211.
31. Ibid.
32. Ibid., 217.
33. Ibid., 225.
34. Ibid.
35. Ibid.
36. Ibid.

37. Ibid.
38. Ibid., 191.
39. *British Colonist*, 28 May 1869.
40. Ibid., 29 May 1869.
41. Ibid., 23 June 1869.
42. Ibid., 6 July 1869.
43. Ibid., 8 July 1869.
44. Ibid.
45. W.J. Christenson, "The West Coast Massacre," *Daily Colonist*, Sunday, 15 October 1950.
46. Mary Mildred. S.S.A., *The Apostle of Alaska: The Life of the Most Rev. Charles Seghers* (Paterson, NJ: St. Anthony Guild, 1943), 84.
47. Henry Wentworth Mist, Log of HMS *Sparrowhawk*. PABC ADM/53/10023, 27 July 1869.
48. Ibid.
49. Ibid., 28 July 1869.
50. *British Colonist*, 31 July 1869.
51. Mildred, *Apostle of Alaska*, 86.
52. *British Colonist*, 31 July 1869.
53. Ibid.
54. Mildred, *Apostle of Alaska*, 86.
55. *British Colonist*, 31 July 1869.
56. Mist, Log, 29 July 1869.
57. *British Colonist*, 31 July 1869.
58. Mist, Log, 29 July 1869.
59. *British Colonist*, 31 July 1869.
60. Ibid.
61. Ibid., 24 February 1871.
62. Ibid.
63. Cecil Clark, "The Lost Children of Hesquiat Bay," *Daily Colonist*, 6 December 1959.
64. Ibid.
65. Other doubters included Captain John Walbran, famous coastal hydrographer and place-name historian. He summarized an alternate viewpoint: "They [the Natives of Hesquiat] say the bodies were washed on shore and mangled by the surf dashing them among the rocks and boulders, and that all the Indians did was to remove the bodies above high water mark so that the fish, the Indian's great source of food, could not feed on the bodies. The Indians also say the executed men were the victims of an interpreter's mistakes, false accusations of hostile tribes, and too credulous white people." In *British Columbia Coast Names, 1592 - 1906* (Vancouver: Douglas, 1977), 242.
66. Augustin Brabant, letter to D.W. Higgins, 7 August 1904, PABC ED. B 72.4
67. Ibid., 38.
68. Ibid.
69. Ibid.
70. Ibid.
71. Ibid.

72. Ibid., 39.
73. Ibid.
74. Ibid., 40.
75. Ibid.
76. Ibid.
77. A. J. Brabant, unpublished report to D.W. Higgins, *On the John Bright*, PABC ED. 72.4, p. 42.
78. Ibid., 45.
79. Ibid., 44.
80. Ibid., 47.
81. Ibid., 48.
82. Ibid.
83. Ibid.
84. Ibid.
85. Walbran, *British Columbia Coast Names*, 241.
86. *Vancouver Province*, 9 May 1927.
87. Ibid.
88. Unpublished correspondence with Liza Verity, Archivist, National Maritime Museum, Greenwich, 23 November 1998.
89. Charles Lillard, ed., *Mission to Nootka* (Sidney, BC: Gray's, 1977), frontispiece.
90. *Daily Colonist*, 20 July 1958.

Chapter 10

1. Wallace Stevens, "The Motive for Metaphor," in *Theme and Image,* Book 2, ed. Carol Gillanders (Toronto: Copp Clark Pitman, 1966), 73.
2. Mario Rispoli, *The Caves of Lascaux* (New York: Abrams, 1986), 81.
3. Beth and Ray Hill, *Indian Petroglyphs of the Pacific Northwest* (Seattle: University of Washington Press, 1975), 262.
4. Joan M. Vastokas and Romas K. Vastokas, *Sacred Art of the Algonkians: A Study of the Peterborough Petroglyphs* (Peterborough: Mansard, 1973), 81. Vastokas reports that the anthropologist Reichel-Dolmatoff believed that the worldview of the Desana included a system that was filled with vaginal and phallic symbolism and that this was related to the power of the shaman.
5. *Victoria Daily Times,* 28 August and 4 September 1926.
6. Robert Connell, "Among the Rocks of Clo-oose," *Victoria Daily Times*, 28 August 1926.
7. Ibid.
8. Ibid.
9. D.H. to Goodfellow, 18 September 1926, unpublished letter.
10. Annie York, et al., *They Write Their Dreams on the Rocks Forever* (Vancouver: Douglas and McIntyre, 1994)
11. Vastokas and Vastokas, *Sacred Art of the Algonkians*, 86.
12. Beth Hill, *Moonrakers* (Victoria: Horsdal and Schubart, 1997), 44.
13. Bjorn Lanstrom, *The Ship* (New York: Doubleday, 1961), 162.
14. Hilary Sterwart, *Looking at Art of the Northwest Coast* (Vancouver: Douglas and McIntyre, 1979), 54, 55, 63, and 64.
15. Ibid.

16. Wilson Duff, *Images Stone B.C.: Thirty Centuries of Northwest Coast Indian Sculpture* (Saanichton: Hancock, 1975), 104.
17. D.H. to Goodfellow, 18 September 1926.
18. David W. Griffiths, "Edwin," in unpublished report of the Archeological Society of British Columbia, 1984.
19. Ibid.
20. Hill, *Moonrakers,* 25. Beth and Ray Hill first visited this site in 1973 in preparation for writing their monumental work on the petroglyphs of the Pacific Northwest.
21. Ruth Kirk, *Wisdom of the Elders: Native Traditions on the Northwest Coast* (Vancouver: Douglas and McIntyre, 1986), 144.

Epilogue

1. The Coast Guard vessel that took us to the mouth of the Nitinat River was a 20-foot, hard-bottomed, 733 Hurricane Zodiac inflatable powered by twin 90-horsepower outboards. The coxswain and rescue specialist were outfitted with survival suits, helmets, and neoprene masks, and they sat on motorbike-like padded seats, one behind the other. The Zodiac was equipped with rescue gear and differential GPS, and was constantly in touch via VHF with the Bamfield and Tofino Coast Guard Radio. The crew had brought survival suits for us, told us where to sit, and cautioned us to hang on.
2. R.E. Wells, *There's a Landing Today* (Victoria: Sono Nis, 1988), 23-5.
3. George Nicholson, *Vancouver Island's West Coast* (Victoria: Nicholson, 1965), 155.
4. Such copulating figures are common on the south coast and are found on Gabriola Island and in other places. They may have to do with sexual taboos that only the shaman carvers could vent, or they may have been related symbolically to "Mother Earth" metaphors inherent in Native cosmology.
5. Nicholson, *Vancouver Island's West Coast,* 287.
6. Derek Pethick, *S.S. Beaver: The Ship that Saved the West* (Vancouver: Mitchell, 1970), 80-3.
7. Wells, *There's a Landing,* 24.

Selected Bibliography

Archaeology

Bonnichsen, R., and K. Turnmire, eds. "Clovis Origins and Adaptations." In *Centre for the Study of the First Americans*. Corvallis: Oregon State University, 1991.

Cole, Douglas. *Captured Heritage: The Scramble for Northwest Coast Artifacts*. Vancouver/Seattle: Douglas and McIntyre/University of Washington Press, 1985.

Davis, S.D. "Prehistory of Southeastern Alaska." In *Handbook of North American Indians*. Vol. 7: *Northwest Coast*. Ed. W. Suttles. Washington: Smithsonian, 1990.

Denton, G.H., and T.J. Hughes, eds. *The Last Great Ice Sheets*. New York: Wiley, 1981.

Dewhirst, J. "The Indigenous Archaeology of Yuquot, A Nootkan Outside Village. Vol. 1: *The Yuquot Project*." Ed. W.J. Folan and J. Dewhirst. In *Canada National Historic Parks and Sites Branch History and Archaeology* 39, Ottawa, 1980.

Dixon, E.J. "The Pleistocene Prehistory of Arctic North America." In Colloque 17, IX Congres, Union Internationale des Sciences Prehistoriques et Protohistoriques, Nice, 1976.

Drucker, Philip. *Archaeological Survey of the Northern Northwest Coast*. Bureau of American Ethnology, Bulletin 133, 1943.

Dumond, D.E. "The Archaeology of Alaska and the Peopling of America." *Science* 209, 29 (1980): 984-91.

Fladmark, Knut. *Prehistory of British Columbia*. Ottawa: National Museum of Man, National Museums of Canada, 1986.

Griffiths, David W. "The John Bright: Historical Background." In *Status Report on the Historic Shipwrecks of Clayoquot and Nootka Sound*. Vancouver: Underwater Archeological Society of British Columbia, 1982.

Kirk, Ruth, with Richard D. Daugherty. *Hunters of the Whale: An Adventure in Northwest Coast Archaeology*. New York: Morrow, 1974.

Smith, Harlan I. *Archaeology of the Gulf of Georgia and Puget Sound*. American Museum of Natural History, vol. 4, part 6, 1907.

Stewart, Hilary. *Indian Artifacts of the Northwest Coast*. Seattle: University of Washington Press, 1976.

History

Akrigg, G.P.V., and H.B. Akrigg. *1001 British Columbia Place Names*. Vancouver: Discovery, 1969.

———. *British Columbia Chronicle*, 1778-1846. Vancouver: Discovery, 1975.

———. *British Columbia Chronicle*, 1874-1871. Vancouver: Discovery, 1977.

Selected Bibliography 243

Anderson, Bern. *Surveyor of the Sea*. Seattle: University of Washington Press, 1960.
Bancroft, Hubert H. *History of the Northwest Coast*. Vol. 1. San Francisco: Bancroft and Company, 1884.
Barman, Jean. *The West Beyond the West*. Toronto: University of Toronto Press, 1991.
Bowering, George. *Bowering's B.C.: A Swashbuckling History*. Toronto: Viking, 1996.
Brabant, Augustin. Unpublished letter to D.W. Higgins, 7 August 1904. In PABC ED B 72.4.
———. *The Wreck of the John Bright*. Unpublished report. In PABC ED. 72.4.
Callwood, June. *Portrait of Canada*. Toronto: Paperjacks, 1981.
Cook, James. *The Journals of Captain James Cook*. Ed. J.C. Beaglehole. 3 vols. Cambridge: Hakluyt Society, 1967.
Dawson, Will. *Coastal Cruising*. Vancouver: Mitchell, 1973.
Duff, Wilson. *The Indian History of British Columbia*. Vol. 1, *The Impact of the White Man*. Memoir no. 5. Victoria: Provincial Museum of British Columbia, 1964.
Edwards, Irene. *Short Portage to Lillooet*. Mission: Cold Stream, 1985.
Evans, Hubert. *Mostly Coast People*. Madeira Park, BC: Harbour, 1992.
Fisher, Robin. *Contact and Conflict: Indian-European Relations in British Columbia, 1774-1890*. Vancouver: UBC Press, 1977.
Forester, Joseph E. *Fishing: British Columbia's Fishing History*. Saanichton, BC: Hancock, 1975.
Gibbs, John. *West Coast Windjammers*. New York: Bonanza, 1968.
Gough, Barry. *The Royal Navy and the Northwest Coast of North America*. Vancouver: UBC Press, 1971.
———. *Gunboat Frontier*. Vancouver: UBC Press, 1984.
Greene, Ruth. *Personality Ships of British Columbia*. Vancouver: Marine Tapestry, 1969.
Gregson, Harry. *A History of Victoria*. Victoria: Observer, 1970.
Herstein, H., L. Hughes, and R. Kirbyson. *Challenge and Survival*. Scarborough: Prentice-Hall, 1970.
Higgins, D.W. *The Passing of a Race*. Toronto: Briggs, 1905.
———. *Tales of a Pioneer Journalist*. Surrey, BC: Heritage, 1996.
Hill, Beth. *The Remarkable World of Frances Barkley, 1769-1845*. Sidney, BC: Gray's, 1978.
Hopper, John. *Indian Wars in the Old Pacific Northwest*. Burnaby: Artaman, 1996.
Howay, F.W. *Voyages of the Columbia*. Boston: Massachusetts Historical Society, 1941.
Kluckner, Michael. *Victoria: The Way It Was*. Vancouver: Whitecap, 1981.
La Violette, F.E. *The Struggle for Survival: Indian Cultures and the Protestant Ethic in British Columbia*. 2nd ed. Toronto: University of Toronto Press, 1973.
Lillard, Charles, ed. *Mission to Nootka*. Sidney, BC: Gray's, 1977.
Lillard, Charles. *Seven Shillings A Year: A History of Vancouver Island*. Ganges: Horsdal and Schubart, 1986.

Longstaff, Fred V. *Esquimalt Naval Base*. Victoria: Victoria Book and Stationery, 1941.
Mayne, Richard C. *Four Years in British Columbia and Vancouver Island*. London: John Murray, 1862.
McCurdy, H.W. *The H.W. McCurdy Marine History of the Pacific Northwest*. Ed. Gordon Newell. Seattle: Superior, 1977.
McKelvie, B.A. *Tales of Conflict*. Surrey, BC: Heritage, 1985.
Mildred, Mary. *The Apostle of Alaska: The Life of the Most Reverend Charles Seghers*. Paterson, NJ: St. Anthony Guild, 1943.
Morales Padron, Francisco. *To the Totem Shore: The Spanish Presence on the Northwest Coast*. Vancouver: Ediciones El Viso, Expo 1986, Pavilion of Spain, 1986.
Murray, Peter. *The Vagabond Fleet*. Victoria: Sono Nis, 1988.
Ormsby, Margaret. *British Columbia: A History*. Toronto: Macmillan, 1985.
Paterson, T.W. *British Columbia: The Pioneer Years*. Langley, BC: Stagecoach, 1977.
Preston, Antony, and John Major. *Send A Gunboat*. London: Longman's, 1967.
Ralston, H. Keith, ed., *The Dictionary of Canadian Biography*. Vol. 3. Toronto: University of Toronto Press, 1976.
Reksten, Terry. *More English than the English: A Very Social History of Victoria*. Victoria: Orca, 1986.
Shelton, George, ed. *British Columbia and Confederation*. Victoria: University of Victoria Press, 1967.
Smith, James K. *Wilderness of Fortune*. Vancouver: Douglas and McIntyre, 1983.
Vancouver, George. *A Voyage of Discovery*. Vol. 1. London: G.G. and J. Robinson, 1798.

Ethnography

Anderson, E.N. ed. *Bird of Paradox: The Unpublished Writings of Wilson Duff*. Surrey, BC: Hancock, 1996.
Arima, Eugene Y. *The West Coast (Nootka) People*. Special Publication no. 6. Victoria: British Columbia Provincial Museum, 1983.
Barnett, Homer G. *The Coast Salish of British Columbia*. Eugene: University of Oregon Press, 1955.
Boas, Franz. *Primitive Art*. New York: Dover, 1955.
Boas, Franz, and George Hunt. *Kwakiutl Texts*. Second series. Publications of the Jesup North Pacific Expedition, vol. 10. Leiden: Brill, 1906.
—. *Kwakiutl Tales*. Vol. 2. New York: Columbia University Press, 1970.
De Laguna, Frederica. "Obituary on Mungo Martin." *American Anthropologist* 65, 4 (1963).
Drucker, Philip. *The Northern and Central Nootkan Tribes*. U.S. Bureau of American Ethnology, Bulletin 144. Washington, DC: U.S. Bureau of American Ethnology, 1951.
Efrat, Barbara. "Linguistic Acculturation on the West Coast of Vancouver Island." In *Sound Heritage*, vol. 7, no. 1, ed. W.J. Langlois. Victoria: Provincial Archives of British Columbia, 1978.
Gunther, Erna. *Indian Life on the Northwest Coast of North America as Seen by the Early Explorers and Fur Traders during the Last Decade of the Eighteenth Century*. Chicago: University of Chicago Press, 1972.

Haeggert, Dorothy. *Children of the First People.* Vancouver: Arsenal Pulp, 1983.
Hawthorn, Audrey E. *People of the Potlatch.* Vancouver: UBC Press, 1956.
Hill-Tout, C. "Notes of the Prehistoric Races of British Columbia and their Monuments." In *British Columbia Mining Record,* 1899.
Jewitt, John R. *The Adventures and Sufferings of John R. Jewitt, Captive among the Nootka, 1803-1805.* Ed. Derek G. Smith. Toronto: McClelland and Stewart, 1974.
Kirk, Ruth. *Wisdom of the Elders.* Vancouver: Douglas and McIntyre, 1986.
Lévi-Strauss, Claude. *The Way of the Masks.* Vancouver: Douglas and McIntrye, 1982.
Mozino, Jose Mariano. *Noticias de Nutka: An Account of Nootka Sound in 1792.* Trans. Iris H. Wilson. Seattle: University of Washington Press, 1970.
Niblack, Albert P. *The Coast Indians of Southern Alaska and Northern British Columbia.* United States National Museum Report, 1888.
Sapir, Edward, and Morris Swadesh. *Nootka Texts.* Philadelphia: University of Pennsylvania Press, 1939.
Sendey, John. *The Nootkan Indian: A Pictorial.* Port Alberni, BC: Alberni Valley Museum, 1977.
Suttles, Wayne. *Coast Salish Essays.* Seattle: University of Washington Press, 1987.
Swanton, J.R. *Contributions to the Ethnology of the Haida.* New York: American Museum of Natural History, 1905.
Swanton, J.R. *Tlingit Myths and Texts.* Washington, DC: Bureau of American Ethnology, 1905.
Underhill, Ruth. *Indians of the Pacific Northwest.* Washington: U.S. Department of the Interior, Bureau of Indian Affairs, 1945.

Northwest Coast Art

Abbott, D.N., ed. *The World Is as Sharp as a Knife: An Anthology in Honour of Wilson Duff.* Victoria: Royal British Columbia Provincial Museum, 1981.
Acheson, S. "Earliest Stone Industries on the North Pacific Coast of North America." *Arctic Anthropology* 29 (1992): 18-27.
Atwood, Margaret, ed. *The New Oxford Book of Canadian Verse.* Toronto: Oxford University Press, 1982.
Barlee, N.L. *Similkameen: The Pictograph Country.* Surrey, BC: Hancock, 1978.
Boas, Franz. *Primitive Art.* New York: Dover, 1955.
Carlson, R., ed. *Indian Art Traditions of the Northwest Coast.* Burnaby, BC: Archaeology Press, Simon Fraser University, 1976.
Clutesi, George. *Potlatch.* Sidney, BC: Gray's, 1969.
Cronon, William. "Telling Tales of Canvas." In *Discovered Lands, Invented Pasts: Transforming Visions of the American West,* ed. Brian W. Dippe. New Haven: Yale University Press, 1992.
Dewdney, S., and K.E. Kidd. *Indian Rock Paintings of the Great Lakes.* Toronto: University of Toronto Press, 1962.
Drury, N. *The Elements of Shamanism.* Longmead, Dorset: Element, 1989.
Duff, W. "The World Is as Sharp as a Knife: Meaning in Northern Northwest Coast Art." In Carlson, *Indian Art Traditions.*
———. *Prehistoric Stone Sculptures of the Fraser River and Gulf of Georgia.*

Anthropology in British Columbia, Memoir No. 3. Victoria: British Columbia Provincial Museum, 1956.

———. "Stone Clubs from the Skeena River Area." In Provincial Museum Annual Report for 1962, Victoria, BC, 1963.

Duff, W., with Bill Holm and Bill Reid. *Arts of the Raven*. Vancouver: Vancouver Art Gallery, 1967.

Durham, Bill. *Indian Canoes of the Northwest Coast*. Seattle: Copper Canoe, 1960.

Gillanders, Carol, ed. *Theme and Image*. Book 1. Toronto: Copp Clark Pitman, 1976.

Goody, J. *The Domestication of the Savage Mind*. Cambridge: Cambridge University Press, 1977.

Grant, C. *Rock Art of the American Indians*. New York: Crowell, 1967.

Harner, Michael J., and A.B. Elsasser. *Art of the Northwest Coast*. Berkeley: Lowie Museum of Anthropology, 1965.

Harper, Russell, ed. *Paul Kane's Frontier*. Toronto: University of Toronto Press, 1971.

Hill, B. *Guide to Indian Rock Carvings of the Pacific Northwest Coast*. Saanichton, BC: Hancock, 1975.

Hill, Beth, and Ray Hill. *Indian Petroglyphs of the Pacific Northwest*. Seattle: University of Washington Press, 1975.

Holm, Bill. *Northwest Coast Indian Art: An Analysis of Form*. Seattle: University of Washington Press, 1967.

Inglis, Joy. *Spirit in the Stone*. Victoria: Horsdal and Schubart, 1998.

Inverarity, R.B. *Art of the Northwest Coast Indians*. Berkeley and Los Angeles: University of California Press, 1950.

Jilek, W.G. *Indian Healing: Shamanic Ceremonialism in the Pacific Northwest Today*. North Vancouver: Hancock, 1982.

Jones, D.G. *Butterfly on Rock*. Toronto: University of Toronto Press, 1976.

Jung, C.G., M.L. von Franz, J.L. Henderson, J. Jacobi, and A. Jaffe. *Man and His Symbols*. New York: Dell, 1964.

Keyser, J.D. *Indian Rock Art of the Columbia Plateau*. Vancouver/Seatte: Douglas and McIntyre/University of Washington Press, 1992.

Kuhn, H. *The Rock Pictures of Europe*. Trans. A.H. Brodrick. Fair Lawn, NJ: Essential, 1956.

Leroi-Gourhan, A. *The Dawn of European Art: An Introduction to Paleolithic Cave Painting*. Cambridge: Cambridge University Press, 1982.

Lundy, D.M. "Petroglyphs of the Middle Fraser River." In *Annual Report of the Okanagan Historical Society*, Vernon, British Columbia, 21-26, 1978.

Martineau, L. *The Rocks Begin to Speak*. Las Vegas: KC, 1973.

McMurdo, A. "Excavation of a Petroglyph Site on Protection Island, British Columbia." In *CRARA '77: Papers from the Fourth Biennial Conference of the Canadian Rock Art Research Associates*. Royal British Columbia Museum, Victoria, British Columbia, Heritage Record, 1979.

Peterson, L.R. "How to Follow the Rock Painting Trail of Jervis Inlet." In *Northwest Passages: A Collection of Northwest Cruising Stories*. Vol. 1. Ed. B. Calhoun. San Francisco: Miller Freeman, 1969.

Ritter, D.W., and E.W. Ritter. "Medicine Men and Spirit Animals in Rock Art of

Western North America." In *Acts of the International Symposium on Rock Art, Hanko, Norway*. Oslo: Universitets-forlaget, 1978.
Steltzer, Ulli. *Indian Artists at Work*. Vancouver/Seattle: Douglas and McIntyre/ University of Washington Press, 1976.
Suttles, Wayne. *Coast Salish Essays*. Seattle: University of Washington Press, 1987.
Swan, Luke, and David W. Ellis. *Teachings of the Tides*. Pentiction, BC: Theytus, 1981.
Wallas, J.J., as told to Pamela Whitaker. *Kwakiutl Legends*. Victoria: Hancock, 1981.
Wingert, Paul S. *American Indian Sculpture: A Study of the Northwest Coast*. New York: Augustin, 1949.
York, Annie, Richard Daly, and Chris Arnett. *They Write Their Dreams on the Rocks Forever: Rock Writings of the Stein River Valley of British Columbia*. Vancouver: Douglas and McIntyre, 1993.

Select Newspaper Articles on Related Subjects

British Colonist: 13, 15, 16, 26, 31 March; 23, 24, 30 April; 1, 12, 28, 29 May; 23, 24 June; 6, 8, 31 July; 17 August, 1869; 24 February, 10 August, 1871.

Daily Colonist: 1 April, 1934; 15 October, 1950, 20 July, 1958; 15 December, 1974; 15 December, 1974.

Islander: 6 December, 1959; 26 September, 1966; 25 October, 1998.

Province: 27 October, 1956; 9 May, 1958.

Victoria Daily Times: 28 August; 5, 18 September, 1926.

Index

A

African Rifles 96
Ahousat 17, 18, 35, 162, 163, 198
Alberni Valley 43
Alcan Highway. *See* See Alaska Highway
Alcott, Louisa May 70
Alert 128, 129, 197
Aleutian Islands 7
American Revolution 7
Amur River 9
Anayitzaschist, John 144, 145, 147, 149, 152, 155, 157, 160, 164, 168, 169, 170
Arnold, Matthew 70
Astoria 38, 39, 85, 86

B

Badger Cove 129
Baffin Bay 25
Ball, Henry Maynard 149
Bamfield 42, 43, 45, 46, 49, 50, 201, 202, 203, 204, 215
Banfield, William 45
Barkley Sound 13, 17, 29, 128, 131, 132, 136, 192, 203, 204
Barkley, William 28
Begbie, Matthew Baillie 59, 64
Bella Bella 15, 61, 86, 109
Bengal Fur Company 29
Bengal Trading Company 28, 29
Bentley, Ted 112
Billy Goat Creek 46, 47
Blanshard, Richard 55, 94
Blenkinsop, George 100
Blow-Hole Beach 13
Boas, Franz 111, 180
Boston 31, 33, 35, 36, 37, 38, 39, 40, 85, 87

Boston Men 31, 33
Boulder Point 14, 158
Brabant, Augustin 163, 171
British Colonist 14, 60, 65, 66, 67, 68, 101, 121, 124, 125, 126, 129, 132, 134, 135, 138, 140, 144, 145, 146, 147, 148, 155, 159, 160, 161, 162, 176
British East India Company 26, 28, 29
Brown, Lundin 60
Bull Harbour 100, 101
Burgess, <First name?> 123, 126, 162, 163, 170, 176, 184, 214
Burnaby, Robert 145, 146
Bute Inlet 62, 63

C

Canton 26, 29, 30, 31, 32, 33, 35, 38, 59
Cape Alava 175
Cape Flattery 14, 49, 78, 147, 162, 176, 196, 205
Cape of Good Hope 26
Captain Cook 20, 25, 26, 188
Cariboo 58, 62, 93, 136
Carleton, Captain 129, 151
Carlson, Roy 112
Cartier, Jacques 142
Cheecheepe 144, 153
Chilcotin 62, 63, 79
Christenson, James 14, 127, 128, 131, 136, 143, 144, 146, 152, 157, 164, 167, 168, 169, 171, 191, 192, 196, 206
Clayoquot Sound 14, 17, 18, 30, 35, 39, 85, 101, 128, 129, 136, 140, 161, 162, 167, 198
Clerke, Charles 22
Coast Mountains 62

Index

Coast Salish 12, 115
Colnet, James 26, 28
Columbia 7, 8, 9, 11, 13, 14, 31, 38, 39, 43, 48, 55, 57, 58, 59, 62, 67, 68, 69, 82, 83, 85, 86, 88, 89, 90, 99, 100, 106, 109, 110, 111, 113, 120, 122, 134, 136, 141, 144, 171, 177, 178, 199
Columbia River 7, 31, 38, 39, 83, 85, 86, 88, 89, 90, 113, 122, 178
Comrie, Peter 138
Confederation 14, 56, 57, 65, 66, 67, 68, 69, 70, 156, 199
Connell, Robert 52, 177, 179
Cook, James 18, 22, 23, 82, 189, 204
Corn Laws 8
Cowichan 61, 101, 115
Cox, John Henry 29
Cutty Sark 71, 119

D

D.H. 179, 180, 184, 189, 196
Darwin, Charles 70, 87
De Cosmos, Amor 66, 67, 70
Degnan Bay 10, 11, 13, 107, 180
Degnan, Frank 12
Della Falls 43
Dixon Entrance 128
Dixon, George 26, 29
Douglas Channel 15
Douglas, James 55, 66, 90, 94, 98, 101, 102
Drinkwater Canyon 43
Drucker, Philip 111
Duff, Wilson 4, 116, 117, 118
Dumbarton 123
Duncan, William 126, 148, 164

E

Easter Island 9
Edwin 179, 195, 196, 197
Efrat, Barbara 18, 23
Emma 129
Englishman River 107, 110
Esperanza Inlet 16
Esquimalt 60, 61, 64, 78, 82, 83, 90, 91, 92, 96, 99, 134, 135, 136, 140, 142, 157, 162, 194
Experiment 26

F

Falkland Islands 39
Felice 30
Flores, Antonio 25
Flying Dutchman 119
Forest King 163
Fort Clatsop 38
Fort George (Astoria) 90
Fort Rupert (Port Hardy) 100
Fort Simpson 86, 127. *See also* See Port Simpson
Fort Taku 86
Fort Vancouver 86, 90
Fort Victoria 55, 78, 89, 90, 91, 102
Fort William 86
Fraser River 58, 59, 62, 67, 93, 96, 98, 107, 120
Fraser, Simon 85
Fuca, Juan de 25

G

Gabriola Island 10, 12, 13, 15, 108, 113
Gellard, John 4, 42, 72, 201
Georgia Strait 62
Gore, John 22

H

Haida 75, 80, 116, 128, 183, 194
Hanna, James 26
HBC *Beaver* 184, 191
Hesquiat Harbour 16, 158, 159, 167
Higgins, David William 180
Highway 37. *See* See Cassiar-Stewart Highway
Hill, Beth 4, 13, 110, 111
Hill, Ray 13
HMS *America* 89
HMS *Beagle* 87
HMS *Blossom* 87
HMS *Clio* 101
HMS *Collingwood* 89
HMS *Cormorant* 89
HMS *Daedalus* 100

HMS *Daphne* 89, 100
HMS *Devastation* 93, 101
HMS *Ganges* 99
HMS *Grampus* 89
HMS *Juno* 89
HMS *Monarch* 101
HMS *Naiad* 92
HMS *Nereus* 92
HMS *Pique* 91
HMS *Plumper* 93
HMS *President* 91
HMS *Pylades* 92
HMS *Rover* 87
HMS *Satellite* 92, 93, 135, 159, 194
HMS *Sparrowhawk* 55, 57, 80, 83, 135, 136, 141, 190
HMS *Sulphur* 87
HMS *Thetis* 93
HMS *Tribune* 98
HMS *Trincomalee* 101
Holden, Beatrice 123, 130, 176, 184
Hornby, Geoffrey Phipps 98, 99
Howe, Joseph 67
Hysietta 144, 147, 153

I
Imperial Eagle 28, 29, 189
Inglis, Joy 112
Iphigenia 30, 32, 190

J
Jack Point 107
Janet Cowan 47, 50
Jewitt, John 37
Johnson Street 59, 62

K
Kanaka Row 59
Kane, Paul 73, 76, 78
Katkeena 144, 145, 148, 150, 152, 153, 154, 155, 157, 160, 161, 163, 164, 168, 169, 170
Kendrick, John 35
Kennedy, Arthur 102
Khabarovsk 9
King George 22, 26, 28, 29, 30, 31, 32
King George's Sound 22, 26, 28, 29, 32

King George's Sound Company 26, 28, 29, 32
King Oscar 127
Kitimat 15
KlacKianish 144, 145
Klanawa River 48
Krilyatii Korolyeva 203
Kulleet Bay 105, 113
Kyuquot Sound 24

L
Lady Rose 43
Lady Washington 31, 32
Ladysmith 105, 113
Lantzville 43
Leather Pass. *See* See Yellowhead Pass
Lok Bay 15, 106
Lundy, Doris 111
Lydia 38

M
Macao 29, 30, 35, 38
Mackay, John 26, 28
Mackenzie, Alexander 85
Makah 24, 78, 206
Maple Bay 110
Maquinna 18, 23, 28, 30, 35, 37
Martinez, Esteban Josef 25
Marx, Karl 70
Mary Celeste 119
Matlahaw Point 4, 149, 158, 173, 196, 213, 214
Mayne Island 61
McClure, Leonard 67
McKenzie, Thomas 119
McLoughlin, John 90
Mead, Ed 111
Meares, John 29, 31, 32, 35, 164, 204
Metlakatla 126, 135, 145, 148
Michigan 45, 46, 72
Michigan Creek 45
Mist, Henry Wentworth 136, 140, 159, 171
Moachat 18, 19, 21, 22, 23, 24, 28, 36, 38, 198
Moai 9
Molly Golver 13

Moore, Brian 47
Moresby, Fairfax 100
Morrison, Neil 126, 170

N
Nanaimo 75, 98, 101, 102, 107, 109, 115, 208, 210
Nass River 83, 86
Nee-ta-kim 144, 147, 150, 151, 152, 154
Needham, Joseph 120, 139, 143, 145, 146, 147, 148, 149, 150, 152, 154, 156, 170
New Archangel 38, 40
New Caledonia 62, 67, 85
New Westminster 56, 57, 58, 62, 63, 75, 93
Newitty 100
Nitinaht 24, 46, 163, 198, 206
Nitinat Narrows 50, 205, 215
Nitinat River 13, 50, 52, 53, 201, 203, 204, 205, 206
Nootka 14, 18, 20, 21, 22, 24, 25, 26, 28, 29, 30, 31, 32, 33, 34, 36, 38, 48, 116, 124, 168, 170, 189, 213
Nootka Sound 14, 20, 21, 25, 26, 28, 30, 31, 32, 34, 36, 38, 48, 124, 170, 189, 213
North-West Territories 69
Nuu-chah-nulth 18, 21, 23, 24, 39, 78, 80, 112, 128, 144, 175

O
Olympic Peninsula 24, 49, 121, 205
Oregon Territory 8, 38, 85, 86, 88
Ozette 107

P
Pachena Point 17, 45, 50, 72, 116
Pacific Rim National Park 17
Peter the Great 24
Peterloo 8
Petropavlosk 91
Pickersgill, Richard 25
Pitseolak, Peter 15
Polk, James 83, 88
Polynesia 9, 87, 103

Port Alberni 43, 202
Port Gamble 14, 121, 123, 124, 126, 170
Port Ludlow 126
Port Renfrew 13, 24, 46, 49
Portlock, Nathaniel 26
Prevost, James 92
Puget Sound 45, 86, 89, 121, 122, 123, 156, 195

Q
Qualicum 43
Queen Charlotte Islands 57, 92
Quesnelmouth. *See* See Quesnel
Quisitis Point 17

R
Reeve, Ted 12
Reid, Bill 118
Return Passage 15, 109
Riel, Louis 69
Rime of the Ancient Mariner 23
Robert Lowe 61
Rockland 58
Royal Navy 8, 17, 26, 29, 34, 55, 61, 64, 80, 81, 82, 83, 85, 86, 87, 88, 89, 90, 92, 96, 98, 99, 100, 101, 102, 126, 127, 135, 136, 140, 161, 171, 199, 212
Roys, <First name?> 129

S
San Juan Islands 83, 96
San Lorenzo Formation 177
Santiago 21, 25
Sea Otter 29, 30
Seekooseelak (Cape Dorset) 15
Seghers, Charles John 157, 163
Seward, William Henry 65
Seymour, Frederick 55, 57, 89, 102, 125
Seymour, George 89
Sierra Club 13, 214
Silva Bay 12
Skidegate 57
Songhees 59, 61, 63, 132
Sproat Lake 106

Stein Valley 200
Stikine River 86, 87, 94
Strait of Anian 25
Strait of Georgia 10, 12
Strait of Juan de Fuca 14, 24, 47, 49, 89, 93, 122, 158, 162, 175, 192, 196
Surprise 14, 124, 128, 130
Swanton, John 111, 113
Sydney Inlet 16

T

Thermopylae 119
Thompson, David 85
Thompson, John 37, 38
Thorn, Jonathan 39
Tipping, William 29
Tonquin 39, 85
Treaty of Tordesillas 25
Trevick, John 123
Tsimshian 116, 127, 193
Tynemouth 60

U

Ucluelet 128, 153
Unalaska 25
USS *Columbus* 89
USS *Massachusetts* 98

V

Valencia, SS 47
Vancouver, George 33
Victoria 4, 5, 8, 10, 14, 18, 41, 46, 52, 55, 56, 57, 58, 59, 60, 61, 62, 63, 64, 65, 66, 67, 68, 69, 70, 71, 75, 80, 89, 91, 92, 93, 94, 96, 99, 100, 110, 117, 120, 123, 124, 126, 127, 128, 129, 130, 131, 132, 134, 140, 141, 143, 144, 145, 146, 149, 152, 153, 155, 157, 159, 161, 162, 163, 165, 169, 170, 171, 177, 179, 194, 195, 197, 206, 207, 210
Victoria Daily Times 18, 52, 177, 179
Victoria Pioneer Rifle Corps 96

W

Waddington, Alfred 62
War of 1812 40, 85, 86
Washington Treaty 96
Webster, Peter 23, 36
Weekly Chronicle 61, 67
WeenenanaKince 144, 152, 153
West Coast Trail 16, 42, 43, 45, 46, 49, 201, 208, 214, 215
Whitehead, Robert 71
Whyac 46, 52, 205, 206
Whyac Point 205
Wickanninish (chief, Clayoquot Sound) 17, 18, 30, 35
Williams, Ray 18
Wood, Mr. 147, 149, 151, 156
Wreck Bay 17

Y

Yates Street 62, 64
Yuquot 18, 22, 23, 28, 36

Photo Credits

BCARS E-03412 (p. 10), I-33907 (p. 11), #28220 (p. 21), A-2694 (p. 27), D-8316 (p. 27), C-6352 (p. 27), D-8321 (p. 27), #3591 (p. 30), A-7638, (p. 37), F-03806 (p. 46), D-01609 (p. 48), F-07811 (p. 51, b), #77729 (p. 53), A-01230 (p. 56, l), A-08341 (p. 56, r), PDP00263 (p. 56, b), A-01885 (p. 62), F-00157, (p. 65), C-06116 (p. 66), A-02655 (p. 68), A-03021 (p. 69), f-08553 (p. 70), I-30804 (p. 71), PDP02949 (p. 82), F-00338, (p. 84, t), A-05958 (p. 84, b), B-00822 (p. 91), #569 (p. 93), PDP00076 (p. 95, t), PDP05357 (p. 95, b), PDP02616 (p. 96), F-08522 (p. 102), F-04608 (p. 103), I-21971 (p. 106), H-04857 (p. 108), PDP00864 (p. 117), F-09992 (p. 120), #27760 (p. 124), F-09934 (p. 137), F-09729 (p. 143, l), G-06180 (p. 143, r), F-07698 (p. 144), F-09934 (p. 145), H-05538 (p. 164, t), A-02020 (p. 164, b), A-01432 (p. 166, l), A-00011 (p. 187), 20642 (p. 211), E-00392 (p. 212).

John Gellard: (p. 12), (p. 20, t) (p. 42, b), (p. 47), (p. 49), (p. 51, l), (p. 51, r), (p. 73, l), (p. 73, r), (p. 73, b), (p. 107), (p. 114), (p. 139), (p. 151), (p. 174, t), (p. 174, b), (p. 181, t), (p. 181, b), (p. 183), (p. 185), (p. 186), (p. 188), (p. 194), (p. 195), (p. 196), (p. 197), (p. 202), (p. 204), (p. 206), (p. 209), and cover photos.

Heritage House Archives: (p. 20, b), (p. 21, b), (p. 32), (p. 63), (p. 77, t), (p. 77, b), (p. 94), map (p. 97).

BC Provincial Museum: PN 4648 (p. 39).

Peter Johnson, (p. 211)

Royal BC Museum: PN 14000 (p. 79, t), PN 4192 (p. 79, b).

Victoria Daily Times: (p. 178).

People From Our Side, by Peter Pilseolok and Dorothy Eber, Hurtig Publishers, Edmonton 1975, (p. 16);West Baffin Eskimo Co-operative Ltd., Cape Dorset, Nunavut *Airplanes in the Settlemnt* by Pudlo Pudlat: National Gallery (709.7101, p. 97r), (p. 17).

E.W. Wright, ed., *Lewis and Dryden's Marine History of the Pacific Northwest*, Seattle: Superior, 1967 (p. 133).

D.W. Higgins, *The Mystic Spring*, Toronto: Briggs, 1904 (p. 166).

The Author

Born in the English Midlands, Peter Johnson now teaches English in a secondary school in Vancouver. He has bicycled through most parts of Canada, canoed the Canadian Shield country of Ontario, and hiked in the Rockies and Coast Mountains. He has directed a documentary film on the Icelanders of Lake Winnipeg, has taught Canadian History and English in various parts of Canada, and holds graduate degrees from the University of Manitoba and the University of British Columbia.

Peter has sailed the west coast for fifteen years and currently, as part of his regular class program, runs an annual end-of-term sailing, painting, and drawing venture in the Gulf Islands for 25 of his senior students. He has a strong interest in Aboriginal pre-history and has examined petroglyph sites throughout Canada and New Mexico.